The
Bodhidharma
Anthology

A

B O O K

The Philip E. Lilienthal imprint honors special books
in commemoration of a man whose work
at the University of California Press from 1954 to 1979
was marked by dedication to young authors
and to high standards in the field of Asian Studies.
Friends, family, authors, and foundations
have together endowed the Lilienthal Fund,
which enables the Press to publish under this imprint
selected books in a way that reflects the taste and judgment
of a great and beloved editor.

The
Bodhidharma
Anthology

··

The Earliest Records of Zen

Jeffrey L. Broughton

UNIVERSITY OF CALIFORNIA PRESS

Berkeley / *Los Angeles* / *London*

The publisher gratefully acknowledges
the generous contribution to this book
provided by the Philip E. Lilienthal Asian Studies Endowment,
which is supported by a major gift
from Sally Lilienthal.

University of California Press
Berkeley and Los Angeles, California

University of California Press, Ltd.
London, England

© 1999 by
The Regents of the University of California

Library of Congress Cataloging-in-Publication Data

Bodhidharma, 6th cent.
  [Selections. English. 1999]
  The Bodhidharma anthology : the earliest records of Zen /
Jeffrey L. Broughton.
    p. cm.
  Includes bibliographical references and index.
  ISBN 978-0-520-21972-4
  1. Zen Buddhism—Early works to 1800. I. Broughton,
  Jeffrey L., 1944– . II. Title.
BQ9299.B623E5· 1999
294.3'927—dc21   98-18245

Printed in the United States of America

13 12 11 10 09
10 9 8 7 6

The paper used in this publication meets the minimum
requirements of ANSI/ NISO Z39.48-1992 (R 1997)
(Permanence of Paper). ♾

To Patricia

Contents

....

Acknowledgments

I am deeply indebted to the late Professor Philip B. Yampolsky for having introduced me to the study of early Ch'an texts. I am grateful for his kind and gentle guidance and for his suggestion of Tsung-mi's *Ch'an Preface* as a dissertation subject. The National Endowment for the Humanities gave me a Translation Grant in the early 1980s that allowed me to spend two years in Kyoto, during which I began a project to translate the key texts of early Ch'an. I thank NEH. I would like to thank Professor Ueyama Daishun for introducing me to Tibetan Ch'an texts and Tun-huang manuscript studies during that two-year period. I am grateful to the "First Seat" at Shōfuku-ji in Hakata (Fukuoka) in the late 1980s for allowing me a glimpse of a Zen monk. The Press's two readers, Professors Carl Bielefeldt and Lewis Lancaster, wrote insightful reports on the manuscript that made a number of valuable suggestions, and I am grateful. I thank Professor F. Stanley Jones for reading the manuscript and offering judicious comments. Lastly, I thank Michael Murry for all his assistance.

Abbreviations and Conventions

BGMS	*Bsam gtan mig sgron*, by Gnubs-chen Sangs-rgyas-ye-shes
Ch.	Chinese
DG	Yanagida Seizan, trans., *Daruma no goroku*
HKSC	*Hsü kao-seng chuan* (T no. 2060)
KB	Yanagida Seizan, ed., *Kōrai-bon*
MBT	Giuseppe Tucci, *Minor Buddhist Texts Part II*
NSC	Tanaka Ryōshō, "Ninyū shigyōron chōkansu (gi) kenkyū oboegaki"
Peking	Peking collection of Tun-huang manuscripts
Pelliot	Pelliot collection of Tun-huang manuscripts
SC	*Sŏnmun ch'waryo* (in KB)
Stein	Stein collection of Tun-huang manuscripts
T	*Taishō shinshū daizōkyō*
TCL	*Tsung-ching lu* (T no. 2016)
Tib.	Tibetan
TZBK	Tanaka Ryōshō, *Tonkō zenshū bunken no kenkyū*
VN	*Vimalakīrti-nirdeśa* (T no. 475)
ZZ	*Dai-Nihon zokuzōkyō*

Citations from the Stein, Pelliot, and Peking collections are in the following form: Stein Ch. 1880; Pelliot Ch. 3018, Pelliot Tib. 116; Peking *su* 99; and so forth.

Citations from T are in the following form: volume:page, column, (and if necessary) line. Thus, T 50:569b20 indicates volume 50, page 569, column b, line 20. In citations in the form "T no. *x*," *x* indicates T document number.

Citations from ZZ are in the following form: series (1, 2, and 2B), case, volume:page, column. For example, ZZ 1, 14, 3:277a.

The following transliteration systems have been used: Wade-Giles for Chinese; Hepburn for Japanese; and T. V. Wylie for Tibetan.

Sanskrit Buddhist terms that appear in *Webster's Third New International Dictionary* are treated as English words and left unitalicized and without diacritics (except for titles of texts). For a partial list of such terms, see Roger Jackson, "Terms of Sanskrit and Pāli Origin Acceptable as English Words." I have added "madhyamika"/"madhyamaka."

Usage of the readings "Ch'an" (Chinese) and "Zen" (Japanese) for the logograph that was picked originally as a Chinese transliteration of a Middle Indic form of Sanskrit *dhyāna* (meditation) is not entirely consistent. Though both appear in *Webster's Third New International Dictionary*, the latter is far more familiar to English-speaking audiences. I have used "Zen" where the broadest possible recognition is desirable, as in the title of this volume, in the introduction, and in the footnotes to the translation. I have also used it in cases where the subject is Japanese scholarship, the Japanese Zen school, or the whole of the East Asian tradition of this school as it is known in the West. In more technical contexts, such as the commentaries on the translation, the appendices, and the endnotes, I have employed "Ch'an."

I

....

Introduction

Countless portraits by East Asian artists have attempted to
catch the essence of the enigmatic Buddhist master known by the name
Bodhidharma or Bodhidharmatāra, the "founder" of Zen. He is usually
represented as an Indian with a full beard, rings in his ears, dressed in a
simple monk's robe; the best portraits catch an elusive glimmer in his
eyes. Many Zen texts describe him as an aristocratic South Indian in an
incarnation series of the bodhisattva Avalokiteśvara. He is said to be the
twenty-eighth patriarch in the transmission of the lamp of enlightenment
down from Śākyamuni Buddha and the six Buddhas preceding him.

A Japanese scholar some time ago wrote of two approaches to this
Bodhidharma: the approach of Zen monks enduring the rigors of the
training hall; and that of modern scholarship.[1] Needless to say, these
approaches have little in common. The practicing monks try to grasp the
meaning of the patriarch through Zen meditation—that is, by a constant
practice of "gazing at" or "holding up" the topics, usually a word or
phrase, of certain cases (kōan), dialogues or stories associated with him.
This is the form of meditation known as "gazing-at-the-topic Zen," the
mainstay of all Korean Sŏn (Zen) and important as well in Japanese Zen.
As the classic theoretician of the practice of gazing at the topic states, in
this method the trainee is not to employ discriminative understanding,
doctrinal understanding, thinking or calculation, intuition, verbal strategy, absolute nonchalance, engagement, analysis of the words, or anything else; one should simply "twenty-four hours a day and in all four
postures constantly raise up the topic and constantly be aware of it."[2]

(Bodhidharma Studies)

The topic is no more than a tool that can be used to burn up all defilements and views, the things that bind the trainee to the suffering cycle of rebirth, much as a candle flame melts snowflakes. There is no absolute truth in the case and topic, and there certainly is nothing of the scholarly impulse, nothing historical.

Scholars, focused on what "really" happened, have tried to clarify the historical figure Bodhidharma by stripping away the legendary accretions. They have pored over all the sources, Buddhist as well as non-Buddhist, and peeled away the layers of the Bodhidharma onion. More recently, a scholar has brought literary theory into play in an attempt to present Bodhidharma as a literary paradigm.[3] At this point it is useful to make a distinction between the traditional or in-house story, Zen's own history of its origins and development, and the work of modern historians. Some would argue that it is quite impossible for modern scholars of Zen to evade the traditional story and "stand in immediate temporal relation with the sources" in telling the biography of Bodhidharma or that of any other early Zen figure.[4] Their case is quite convincing.

So let us begin with the traditional story. Here is the gist of the traditional story of Bodhidharma found in the tenth-century transmission record entitled *Record of the Patriarchal Hall (Tsu-t'ang chi)*.[5] Prajñātāra, the twenty-seventh patriarch, is an East Indian of the priestly class, a Brahman, who ventures to South India and acquires as a disciple the third son of a great South Indian king. (The third son's name is Bodhitāra, which Prajñātāra eventually changes to Bodhidharma and which in some sources becomes Bodhidharmatāra or Dharmatāra. That his father was a king implies that he was of the warrior, and not the priestly, class, which echoes Śākyamuni Buddha's origins.) At a banquet given by the king, Prajñātāra is the only master who does not read the scriptural sutras; he represents a transmission of Buddhist truth outside the Buddhist scriptures. He transmits the "storehouse of the true Dharma eye" to his successor Bodhidharma and dies in 457 C.E. Prajñātāra's final injunction is for Bodhidharma to go to China sixty-seven years thence.

The disciple's journey is long and presumably hazardous, taking three years. In 527 he lands in the area of present-day Canton in South China. Within days he makes his way to the court of the Liang Dynasty in the city of Nanking, where he has several memorable exchanges with Emperor Wu, perhaps one of the most fervent patrons of Buddhism in all of Chinese history. The emperor asks about the highest meaning of noble truth (*ārya-satya*), and the Indian answers: "There is no noble [truth]." The emperor, perhaps growing a bit frustrated, asks: "Who is standing before me?" The Indian answers: "I do not know." The emperor then asks how much karmic merit he has accumulated from ordaining Buddhist monks, building monasteries, having sutras copied, and commissioning artisans to create Buddha images. The Indian answers: "No merit."

After a few weeks at court Bodhidharma realizes that this encounter with the Chinese emperor is not going well; in Buddhist terms, it is karmically unfavorable. The Indian master then proceeds northward. He crosses the Yangtze River and makes his way to the state of Wei in the North, the Chinese heartland. (Many paintings in East Asia show him crossing the Yangtze on a reed.) Meanwhile Emperor Wu seems to have realized that he has lost a golden opportunity. A mysterious monk, answering the emperor's query about the departed master, states that he is actually the bodhisattva Avalokiteśvara, transmitter of the seal of Buddha Mind.

Bodhidharma's journey brings him to the area of the eastern capital Lo-yang and the nearby sacred mountain Mount Sung. He spends nine years on the western peak of Mount Sung, which is the site of the famous Shao-lin Monastery. (This western peak is known as "Few Caves" or "Small Caves.") A fortyish Chinese monk by the name of Shen-kuang, who is well versed in classical Chinese literature, soon encounters the Indian. Whenever Shen-kuang asks a question of the master, he receives only silence. In order to show his sincerity in seeking the teaching of Buddhism, Shen-kuang stands in the deep nocturnal snow. Bodhidharma's response to this gesture is to ask the Chinese monk why he is standing in the snow and to inform him that he is pursuing Dharma in a petty frame of mind. Shen-kuang thereupon takes a dagger, cuts off his left arm, and politely lays it before the patriarch. The Indian master accepts this demonstration of sincerity and renames his Chinese disciple Hui-k'o, a name meaning something like "his wisdom will do."

There are several dialogues between the two. For example, Hui-k'o asks for his mind to be quieted. Bodhidharma orders Hui-k'o to bring mind to him, but when Hui-k'o says he cannot apprehend it, Bodhidharma states that quieting of mind is over. At these words Hui-k'o has a great awakening. Hui-k'o asks the master if his teaching encompasses any written documents. Bodhidharma replies that his teaching is a mind-to-mind transmission and does not rely on the written word.

Bodhidharma announces that three have apprehended his teaching. He employs a body metaphor to indicate their levels of apprehension. Hui-k'o has gotten the marrow of the bones; the obscure Tao-yü, the Zen version of an independent or solitary Buddha, one who achieves enlightenment but chooses not to teach and retreats into silence, has gotten the bone; and the nun named Dharani (Magic Formula or Incantation) has gotten the flesh. (This metaphor of body parts makes Hui-k'o the straight or direct successor and the other two collateral.) The Indian patriarch also announces to Hui-k'o that he is transmitting to him the robe that has been handed down from patriarch to patriarch since Śākyamuni Buddha as an external sign of the internal Dharma seal.

At the age of 150 Bodhidharma dies and is buried on Mount Hsiung-erh to the west of Lo-yang. Three years later, a Chinese diplomatic official, the Wei commissioner Sung Yün, returning from a mission to the West, meets Bodhidharma in the Pamirs Mountains; Bodhidharma is on his way back to the West. The Indian, with a single shoe in hand, predicts to Sung Yün that his sovereign has died—a prediction that is duly confirmed upon the commissioner's return to China. Bodhidharma's stupa, or reliquary mound, is subsequently opened, and indeed the contents consist of a single shoe. He came to China, left a trace, and went back to the West. Emperor Wu, who missed the point when he had the chance, composed a funeral inscription.

Let us turn to the literature associated with the name Bodhidharma. Of the ten texts we now have attributed to Bodhidharma or claiming to present his teaching, the one generally held to contain material that is authentic in some sense is the *Bodhidharma Anthology*, which itself is composed of seven texts. Over time I have come to consider it crucial to emphasize the individuality of the texts of this anthology rather than to fall into thinking of the anthology as one piece:

1. *Biography*: a preface containing a brief biography of the "Dharma Master," Bodhidharma, who is presented as the third son of a South Indian king who ventures to North China and teaches "quieting mind" or "wall-examining."

2. *Two Entrances*: an exposition of his teaching of entrance by principle and entrance by practice. The former involves awakening to the realiza-

tion that all sentient beings are identical to the True Nature, although the True Nature is not revealed because of an unreal covering of adventitious dust; if one abides in "wall-examining" without dabbling in the scriptures, one will "tally with principle." Wall-examining is not explained. Entering by practice includes four practices: having patience in the face of suffering in the present, because one knows it is due to the ripening of bad intentional actions in the past; being aware that, if good things come to one in the present, the conditions for such things will eventually run out and the things themselves will disappear; seeking for nothing; and being in accord with intrinsic purity.

3. *First Letter:* a letter in which an anonymous author describes how he spent years in fruitless study of the scriptures until he came to realize the pearl of the mind through practice; the appended verses are a friendly admonition to those in the same situation.

4. *Second Letter:* a letter in which an anonymous author argues that delusion and awakening are but one thing, and that some unnamed people are igniting disputations by erecting names, terms, and principles.

5. *Record I:* lecture materials and anonymous dialogues, which contain a substantial number of colloquial elements (in contrast to the first four parts above, which are all cast in a literary, and not a spoken, style); contains one saying attributed to Bodhidharma.

6. *Record II:* named and anonymous dialogues, many of which are attributed to an otherwise unknown master named Yüan and to Hui-k'o, who serves as Bodhidharma's successor in the traditional story; contains even more colloquial elements.

7. *Record III:* named sayings, including sayings attributed to Bodhidharma, Hui-k'o, and Yüan; contains fewer colloquial usages.

The *Bodhidharma Anthology* as a continuum was discovered only in the early part of this century, and it is fair to describe it as one of the most important finds among the Tun-huang manuscripts, a small portion of which constitute the "Dead Sea Scrolls" of Zen (see appendix A). In the early summer of 1935 the Japanese Zen layman Suzuki Daisetsu, also known as D. T. Suzuki, arrived in Peiping, present-day Beijing, in order to seek out Zen texts in the collection of Tun-huang manuscripts housed in the National Library. Tens of thousands of manuscripts had been discovered in a hidden chamber in the Tun-huang cave complex in Northwest China in the early years of the twentieth century and were subsequently carried off to various libraries and museums in Europe and

East Asia. Having perused a catalogue of the Chinese collection and having noted some intriguing Zen-related entries, Suzuki was able to find and reproduce a number of Zen texts, including an anthology that came to be called the *Long Scroll of the Treatise on the Two Entrances and Four Practices* (*Ninyū shigyōron chōkansu*); he subsequently published the reproductions in Japan.[6] The *Long Scroll* is the work I have dubbed the *Bodhidharma Anthology*.

The *Biography, Two Entrances, First Letter, Second Letter,* and even *Record I* of the *Bodhidharma Anthology* were at least known of when Suzuki discovered the *Long Scroll* manuscript, but the dialogues and sayings following *Record I,* which Suzuki called *Miscellaneous Record II* (*Zatsuroku dai-ni*), were unknown at the time, in spite of the fact that brief quotations from these dialogues and sayings were buried in a famous traditional Zen collection transmitted in East Asia. I have given Suzuki's two *Miscellaneous Records* the titles *Record I, Record II,* and *Record III.* (Subsequent manuscript discoveries have considerably extended his *Miscellaneous Record II,* and I have divided it into two parts.) Unfortunately, for the next half century or so virtually no one paid any attention to the highly colloquial *Miscellaneous Record II,* a treasure store of dialogues and sayings of proto-Zen. One of the most important Zen texts found among the Tun-huang manuscripts was totally ignored.

It is the colloquial element in these dialogues and sayings—the fact that they are closer to the spoken words of teaching masters, less reworked into the literary language—that should have caught our attention. Use of the colloquial is at the heart of the Zen tradition and its literature; of the Buddhist traditions of China, Zen is distinguished by its preference for Chinese literary genres, most notably the colloquial record of the sayings and dialogues of the master (*yü-lu*) on the model of the Confucian *Analects.* An eminent scholar of Chinese literature has described the *Analects* as "a collection of fragmentary dialogues and sayings, couched in what appears to be the conversational style of the period, simple in diction and forceful in expression."[7] We can trace the precursors of Zen's adoption of this quintessential Chinese literary genre directly back to *Record II* and *Record III.*[8]

A propensity for choosing vernaculars, spoken languages of localities, to express Buddhist religious teachings is nothing new, for it can be traced back to the Buddha himself. Various early Buddhist texts record a story in which disciples born to the educated elite, the priestly class, make a case to the Buddha that the exalted message is being mispronounced and bastardized by various disciples reciting the message in their own vernaculars.[9] Their suggestion is to recast the teachings in a form of Sanskrit, the language of the learned and priestly class.

The Buddha emphatically rejects this idea, stating that the teachings should be taught in the spoken language of the locality. He stresses that the fine niceties of cultured language are irrelevant; only accurate transmission of the content is important. Thus, the Records of the Bodhidharma Anthology, the earliest Zen books of recorded sayings we have, constitute nothing new in the sweep of Buddhist history. They and the later vast recorded-sayings literature of Zen are perfectly congruent with the thrust of the early Buddhist tradition.

For decades discussion of the Long Scroll or Bodhidharma Anthology, both Japanese and Western, has concentrated on the second section, the Two Entrances, and has come to the consensus that only this text can be attributed to Bodhidharma.[10] Eminent monks of medieval China and modern scholars from around the world have produced many exegeses of the two entrances and the baffling term "wall-examining" (pi-kuan) mentioned in the Biography and Two Entrances; in the traditional story Bodhidharma is usually said to have practiced wall-examining for nine years.[11] Though much exegetical ingenuity has gone into this project, the exclusive focus on the two entrances has obscured the importance of the Records. In fact, the Records have been so eclipsed that they pass unnoticed in most treatments of early Zen.

A purpose of this book is to give the Records, particularly Record II and Record III, their due as the real beginnings of Zen literature, the true ancestors of the Zen genre known as recorded sayings. Any reader—student or practitioner—who has thrilled to the power of the most famous of all Zen recorded-sayings books, the Record of Lin-chi (Lin-chi lu), will recognize the ancestral genius of portions of the Records. Let us now turn to a complete translation of the Bodhidharma Anthology, which is followed by commentary on all seven of its texts.[12]

2

···

Translation of the Seven Texts of the *Bodhidharma Anthology*

Text no. 1: *Biography*

1. The **Dharma** Master was a South Indian of the Western Region. He was the third son of a great Indian king. His divine insight was clear; whatever he heard, he understood. His ambition lay in the Mahayana path, and so he put aside his white layman's robe for the black robe of a monk. He merged with the sagely lineage and made it flourish. His dark mind was empty and quiescent. He comprehended the events of the world. He understood both Buddhist and non-Buddhist teachings. His virtue surpassed that of the leaders of the age.

Lamenting the decline of the true teaching in the outlands, he subsequently crossed distant mountains and seas, traveling about propagating the teaching in **Han and Wei**. Of scholars who had extinguished

Dharma: The word *dharma* has a range of meanings in Buddhist texts. Two of the most important are the teaching of the Buddhas (Law; Doctrine; Dharma; sometimes referring to the sutras that set forth the Dharma), and the fundamental elements of existence (dharmas). There are a number of lists of dharmas, one of the most influential being a list of seventy-five that is divided into conditioned and unconditioned dharmas. The seventy-two conditioned dharmas run from sense organs and respective sense objects (the eye and its object forms, etc.) to mentals (sensation; faith; stupidity; shamelessness; anger; regret; etc.) to nonmentals (acquisition; the no-thought attainment; impermanence; language phrases; etc.). The three unconditioned dharmas include space and nirvana. Though Bodhidharma is here referred to as the Dharma Master, a Dharma master is a specialist in the teachings, as opposed to a dhyana master, a specialist in meditation.
Han and Wei: refers to North China.

mind, there were none who did not come to have faith in him, but those who clung to characteristics and preserved views came to ridicule him. At the time his only disciples were Tao-yü and Hui-k'o. These two monks, even though **born later**, showed a superior aspiration for the lofty and distant. Fortunately they met the Dharma Master and served him for several years. They reverently requested him to inform them; they readily perceived the master's intention. The Dharma Master was moved by their pure sincerity and instructed them in the true path: **thus** quieting mind; thus giving rise to practice; thus according with things; and thus [implementing provisional teaching] **devices**. This is the quieting of mind of the Mahayana Dharma. Make no mistake about it. Thus quieting mind is wall-examining. Thus giving rise to practice is the four practices. Thus according with things is protection against derision. Thus [implementing] devices is to implement devices without attachment. This brief preface draws upon the meaning in the following text.

Text no. 2: *Two Entrances*

2. Now, in entering the path there are many roads. To summarize them, they reduce to two types. The first is entrance by principle and the second entrance by practice. Entering by principle means that one awakens to the thesis by means of the teachings, and one deeply believes that all living beings, common and sagely, are identical to the True Nature; that it is merely because of the unreal covering of adventitious dust that the True Nature is not revealed. If one rejects the false and reverts to the real and in a coagulated state abides in wall-examining, then self and other, common man and sage, are identical; firmly abiding without shifting, in no way following after the written teachings—this is mysteriously tallying with principle. It is nondiscriminative, quiescent, and inactive; we call it entrance by principle.[1]

born later: This is an allusion to *Analects*, Tzu-han: "Those born later should be feared, for how do we know that those to come will be as good as those of the present?"

thus: The significance of the phrase *ju-shih* is unclear. It occurs in the opening line of all sutras ("Thus by me it was heard" or "Thus by me it was heard upon an occasion"), indicating faith that what follows is truly Buddha word.

devices: refers to teaching Dharma by way of devices, means, or expedients (*upāya*), taking into account the varying aptitudes of the audience.

Entering by practice means the four practices, for all other practices are included within these. What are the four? The first is the practice of requiting injury; the second is the practice of following conditions; the third is the practice of having nothing to be sought; and the fourth is the practice of according with Dharma.[2]

What is the practice of requiting injury? If the practitioner who is cultivating the path encounters suffering, he thinks to himself: I, from the past, across innumerable eons, have become estranged from the root and followed after the branches, have flowed along in various existences, producing a great deal of ill will and hatred, antagonizing and harming others endlessly. Though there is no transgression on my part in the present, this suffering is the ripening of bad karma-fruits of the faults of my past lives. It is something that neither the gods nor men have put upon me. With satisfaction I will bear and accept it, with absolutely no ill will or complaining. The sutra says: "When you meet suffering, do not be sad. Why? Because you comprehend the underlying reason behind it."[3] When this thought arises, one is yoked with principle. Taking ill will as an opportunity, one advances on the path, and therefore it is called the practice of requiting injury.

As to the second, the practice of following conditions, sentient beings lack a self and are all whirled around by conditions and karma; suffering and joy are to be equally accepted, for both arise from conditions. If I encounter excellent karmic recompense, such as honor and so forth, it is in response to causes in my past lives. Even if I should encounter such recompense in the present, the necessary conditions for it will exhaust themselves, and it will again cease to exist. What is there to be joyful about in its existence? Gain and loss follow conditions. Mind has neither increase nor decrease. Unmoved by the **winds of joy**, one is mysteriously in accordance with the path. Therefore, it is called the practice of following conditions.

As to the third, the practice of having nothing to be sought, worldly people are in a perpetual state of delusion; everywhere they are covetous and attached, and this is called seeking. The person of insight awakens to reality: Principle is the obverse of the conventional; quiet mind and

winds of joy: may refer to the last of the eight winds: profit; weakness; slander; glory; praise; criticism; suffering; and joy.

practice no-action; forms follow the turnings of fate; the ten thousand existences are thus void; wish for nothing. **Merit and Darkness** always follow each other.[4] A long time dwelling in the **three realms** is like living in a burning house.[5] Having a body is all suffering; who can attain peace? If one comprehends this locus, then in his various existences he will stop thoughts and have no seeking. The sutra says: "Seeking is all suffering; seeking nothing is joy."[6] We clearly know that seeking nothing truly is practice of the path.

As to the fourth, the practice of according with Dharma, the principle of intrinsic purity is viewed as Dharma. According to this principle, all characteristics are void, without defilement and without attachment, without this and that. The sutra says: "In Dharma there are no sentient beings, since it is free of the impurities of sentient beings. In Dharma there is no self, because it is free of the impurities of self."[7] The one of insight who is able to believe in and understand this principle should practice according to Dharma. The Dharma substance has no stinginess; in terms of your life and property, practice giving, your mind free of parsimony. You will comprehend the **three voidnesses**, solicit nothing, and be attached to nothing. Merely for the sake of eliminating impurity embrace and transform sentient beings and yet do not grasp characteristics. This is self-benefit, but, in addition, it can benefit others; it also can

Merit and Darkness: They are sister goddesses. The beautiful Merit enters a house and announces to the owner that she has the power to bestow all sorts of valuable things. The happy owner makes offerings to her and then sees the ugly and unkempt Darkness outside his gate. Darkness announces that her visit to a house brings its complete loss of wealth. The owner threatens her with a knife in order to make her leave. Darkness tells him that he is very stupid, that the one in the house is her sister, and that they always come and go together. To drive away one is to drive away the other. The owner says he has no need of either and they may leave. When they do so, he is very happy.

three realms: Every world of the Buddhist cosmos has a Mount Sumeru at its center and is divided into three planes of sentient existence. The realm of desire has six desire heavens with six classes of gods above, in the middle the human world of four great continents, and below the eight great hells. Above this is the realm of form, in which all objects are pure form (shape and color). It is divided into four dhyanas, which are in turn divided into a total of seventeen heavens. On top is the formless realm, in which nothing material exists. It is divided into four stages. A being ascends to a higher level either through dhyana or by being reborn there due to good intentional actions in this and past lives.

three voidnesses: either voidness, marklessness, and wishlessness, which are called the three gates of liberation, or the voidness of recipient, giver, and gift.

ornament the path of enlightenment. When you give in this spirit, the **other five perfections** follow suit. In order to eliminate false thought one practices the six perfections, and yet there is nothing that is practiced. This is the practice of according with Dharma.

Text no. 3: *First Letter*

3. I have always admired the former wise ones. I have broadly cultivated all the practices. I have always esteemed the **Pure Lands** of the Buddhas and looked up to the teachings that have come down to us as a thirsty man longs for water. Those who have been able to meet Śākyamuni Buddha and realize the great path are in the millions; those who have obtained the **four fruits** are numberless. I really thought that the heavenly mansions were another country and the hells another place, that if one were to attain the path and get the fruit, one's bodily form would change. I unrolled sutra scrolls to seek blessings; through pure practice I [tried to produce karmic] causes. In confusion I went around in circles, chasing my mind and creating karma; thus I passed many years without the leisure to take a rest. Then for the first time I dwelled upright in dark quiescence and settled external objects in the kingdom of mind. However, I had been cultivating false thought for such a long time that my feelings led me to continue to see characteristics. I came to the point where I wanted to probe the difficulties inherent in these illusionary transformations. In the end I clearly apprehended the Dharma Nature and engaged in a coarse practice of **Thusness**. For the first time I realized that within the square inch of my own mind there is nothing that does not exist. The bright pearl comprehends clearly and darkly penetrates the deep tendency of things. From the Buddhas above to the wriggling insects below there is nothing that is not another name for false thought. They are the calculations of thought. And so I have

---

other five perfections: In addition to giving, the supreme virtues of Buddhas that are cultivated by bodhisattvas include: morality; forbearance; striving; dhyana; and insight.

Pure Lands: a Buddha field or world in which a particular Buddha operates.

four fruits: stream enterer (beginner); once returner (will be reborn one more time); never returner (now in last rebirth); and arhat (has achieved nirvana).

Thusness: Thusness (tathata) means true essence, actuality, truth, things as they are. It is a synonym for the truth of the highest meaning.

given written expression to my dark musings. Moreover, I will reveal the *Verses on Devices for Entering the Path* [*Ju-tao fang-pien chi*], to be used as an admonition to those who have the conditions for the same type of awakening. If you have time, unroll and read it:

> Through cross-legged sitting dhyana, in the end you will necessarily see the Original Nature.
> Inevitably you will fuse and purify mind.
> If for a split second [thought] arises, [you will be in the conditioned realm of] arising and extinguishing.
> In the midst [of birth and death], to remember thoughts is [like a Buddhist aspirant] engaging in an **improper means of livelihood**.

> You may search for Dharma and surmise various things, but your karma will not be changed.
> Given revolving and increasing defilement, mind finds it difficult to reach the ultimate.
> The wise one, upon suddenly hearing the **eight characters**,[8] awakens to principle.
> He realizes for the first time that his **six years** of ascetic activity were in vain.

> All over the world, everywhere, are the people of the Evil One
> Who clamor in vain and engage in meaningless arguments.
> Making false explanations, they teach sentient beings.
> Talking about remedies, they cure not one disease.

improper means of livelihood: wrong way of getting a living; for a monk, there are five. Right livelihood is the fifth aspect of the noble eightfold path.

eight characters: The Buddha in a previous birth is practicing asceticism under a bodhisattva named Snow Mountain Youth. The god Indra in the form of a terrifying spirit descends to the mountains and chants the first half of a verse of the Buddhas of the past, which is eight characters in length: "All dharmas are impermanent and are arising-extinguishing dharmas." The ascetic bodhisattva asks about the half verse, and the spirit replies that he is starving and thirsty. The ascetic states that he will become the spirit's disciple if only the spirit will speak the remainder of the verse. Because of hunger the cannibalistic spirit is unable to speak it. The ascetic tells him that once the verse is recited, he will give up his body for food. The spirit finally recites the second half: "Arising-extinguishing having extinguished, quiescence is joyful." The ascetic deeply ponders the meaning and writes this verse everywhere—on rocks, on walls, and so forth. It is called the Snow Mountains verse.

six years: After leaving home, on the bank of the Nairañjanā River Gautama engaged in ascetic activities for six years. Daily he ate one piece of grain or rice. Eventually he came to think that this was not the path and rejected asceticism. He then went to the enlightenment tree, a type of fig known as the pipal (*Ficus religiosa*), and sat beneath it on a seat of grass known as the "thunderbolt seat."

Things have always been in a state of quiescence and there has never existed a
perceiving subject.
How could there be good and evil, false and correct?
Even arising is no-arising; even extinguishing is no-extinguishing.
Moving is no-moving; concentration is no-concentration.

Text no. 4: *Second Letter*

4. Shadows arise from bodily forms; echoes follow upon
voices. Some play with their shadows to the point of tiring their bodies,
not realizing that their bodies are the shadows. Some raise their voices to
stop the echoes, not realizing that the voice is the source of the echo.
Searching for nirvana by eliminating the defilements is like searching for
the shadow by getting rid of the body. Seeking for Buddhahood by
rejecting sentient beings is like seeking for the echo by silencing the
voice. Therefore, we know that delusion and awakening are one road,
that stupidity and wisdom are not different. In a place of namelessness
they mistakenly think of erecting names, and because of these names, is
and is-not are born. In a place without principles they mistakenly think of
creating principles, and because of these principles, disputations flourish
therein. Illusionary transformations are not real, so who is right and who
wrong? Falsity is unreal, so what exists and what does not exist? One
should know that obtaining is having nothing to obtain and losing is
having nothing to lose. Having not yet been able to talk with you, I have
composed these lines, but how can one discuss the dark purport?[9]

Text no. 5: *Record I*

5. Buddhas speak of void dharmas in order to destroy
views, but if you are in turn attached to voidness [as a view], you are one
whom the Buddhas cannot transform.[10] At the point of arising, only
voidness arises.[11] At the point of extinguishing, only voidness extinguishes. In reality there is not one dharma that arises. In reality there is
not one dharma that extinguishes. All dharmas arise due to craving.
Craving has neither inside nor outside, nor does it lie in between. Discrimination is a void dharma, but common men are broiled by it. The
false and the correct have neither inner nor outer, nor do they lie in the

various directions. Discrimination is a void dharma, but common men are broiled by it. All dharmas are like this.

6. The **Dharma Body** is formless.[12] Therefore, one sees it by no-seeing. Dharma is soundless. Therefore, one hears it by no-hearing. Insight does not have knowing. Therefore, one knows by no-knowing. If one takes seeing as seeing, then there is something that is not seen. If one takes no-seeing as seeing, then there is nothing that is not seen. If one takes knowing as knowing, then there is something that is not known. If one takes no-knowing as knowing, then there is nothing that is not known. [Insight] is incapable of knowing itself, and so it is not something that has knowing, and yet, because it knows vis-à-vis things, it is not something that lacks knowing. If one takes apprehending as apprehending, there is something that is not apprehended. If one takes no-apprehending as apprehending, then there is nothing that is not apprehended. If one takes is as is, there will be something that is not. If one takes having-no-is as is, there will be nothing that is not. One gate of insight enters one hundred thousand gates of insight. One sees a pillar and makes the interpretation pillar. This is to see the pillar characteristic and make the interpretation pillar. Observe that mind is the pillar dharma and no pillar characteristic exists. Therefore, when one sees a pillar, it is the apprehension of a pillar dharma. The seeing of all forms is like this.

7. Someone says: "All dharmas are nonexistent." Objection: "Do you see existence? Whether there is no-existence in existence or existence in no-existence, there is still your existing." Someone says: "All dharmas are nonarising." Objection: "Do you see arising? Whether there is no-arising in arising or arising in no-arising, there is still your arising." Also: "I see that all is no-mind." Objection: "Do you see mind? Whether there is no-mind in mind or mind in no-mind, there is **still your mind**."[13]

Dharma Body: The Dharma Body (dharmakaya) is the spiritual body, as contrasted with the form body of a Buddha; it is also the highest of the three bodies of a Buddha, the others being the Enjoyment Body and the Magical-Creation Body.

still your mind: This section is terse and difficult. We can turn to the Tibetan translation for a gloss: "Also a person says: 'Dharmas are not existence.' Explanation: 'Do you see nonexistence? If in existence it becomes nonexistence, in nonexistence it becomes existence, and so the very same is your existing.' A person says: 'I see that dharmas of self are nonarising.' Explanation: 'Do you see nonarising? If in arising it becomes [non]arising, in nonarising it becomes arising, and so the very same is your

8. **Tripiṭaka Dharma Master**[14] says: "When one does not understand, the person pursues dharmas; when one understands, dharmas
pursue the person. When one understands, consciousness draws in
forms; when one is deluded, forms draw in consciousness. The nonproduction of consciousness due to forms is called not seeing forms."[15]
Whether there is no-seeking in seeking or seeking in no-seeking, there
is still your seeking. Whether there is no-taking in taking or taking in
no-taking, there is still your taking. When mind is in need of something,
we call it the realm of desire. When mind is not mind of itself but is
produced due to forms, we call it the realm of form. When forms are not
forms of themselves but are forms because of mind, the fact that mind
and forms are formless is called the formless realm.

9. Question: "What is called Buddha Mind?" Answer: "Mind's having
no mark of variation is called Thusness. Mind's unchangeableness is
called the Dharma Nature. Mind's not being connected to anything is
called liberation. The mind nature's unimpededness is called enlightenment. The mind nature's quiescence is called nirvana."

10. Question: "What is called **Tathagata?**" Answer: "To understand
Thusness and respond to beings is called Tathagata." Question: "What is
called Buddha?" Answer: "To awaken according to Dharma, to awaken
to the fact that there is nothing to be awakened to, is called Buddha."
Question: "What is called Dharma?" Answer: "Mind does not arise in
accordance with Dharma, and mind does not extinguish in accordance
with Dharma. This is called Dharma." Question: "What is called
community?" Answer: "Coming together according to Dharma is called
community."

11. Question: "What is called the voidness samadhi?" Answer:
"Gazing at dharmas and abiding in voidness is called the voidness
samadhi." Question: "What is called abiding in Dharma?" Answer:

---

arising.' Also: 'I see that dharmas of self are no-mind.' Explanation: 'Do you see no-
mind? If in mind it becomes nonexistence [of mind], in no-mind it becomes existence
[of mind], and so the very same is your mind.'" The same pattern occurs in the next
section.

Tripiṭaka Dharma Master: Bodhidharma.

Tathagata: There are two interpretations: the Thus-come One or the Thus-gone
One (the one who has gone in the way of earlier Buddhas). The Chinese took the
former, the Tibetans the latter.

"Neither abiding in abiding nor abiding in nonabiding, but abiding according to Dharma—this is called abiding in Dharma."

12. Question: "What about the phrase 'is male but not male, is female but not female?'" Answer: "When we analyze on the basis of Dharma, the characteristics maleness and femaleness cannot be apprehended.[16] Should you ask how that can be known, it is because forms are not characterized by maleness or femaleness. If forms were characterized by maleness, all the grasses and trees would be male, or they would all be female. Deluded people do not understand and through false thought see maleness or femaleness, but this is an illusionary maleness and an illusionary femaleness, ultimately without reality. The *Sūtra of the Inactivity of All Dharmas* [*Chu-fa wu-hsing ching*] says: 'If you come to know that all dharmas are like an illusion, you will quickly become the foremost of persons.'"[17]

13. Question: "When one realizes nirvana while **retaining the body** and obtains the fruit of arhat, is it awakening or not?" Answer: "It is a dream realization." Question: "When one practices the six perfections, fills up the **ten stages** and the ten thousand practices, awakens to the nonarising and nonextinguishing of all dharmas, remains neither awakened nor knowing, has neither mind nor understanding, is it awakening or not?" Answer: "That is also a dream." Question: "The **ten powers** and the **four fearlessnesses**, the **eighteen special dharmas**, the path culminating in perfect awakening under the enlightenment tree, the

retaining the body: the nirvana that is obtained in this life. It is said to be with remainder because the physical body still remains. Refers to the Hinayana nirvana.

ten stages: Within the fifty-two stages of bodhisattvahood, the forty-first to fiftieth are referred to as the ten stages: (1) the joyous; (2) the free-from-defilement; (3) the illuminating; (4) the flaming wisdom; (5) the invincible; (6) the become-manifest; (7) the far going; (8) the immovable; (9) the good wisdom; and (10) the Dharma cloud.

ten powers, four fearlessnesses, eighteen special dharmas: The ten powers are the ten knowledge powers special to a Buddha. They run from the power to discriminate that which is consistent with reason from that which is not to the power of knowing the destruction of the outflows, the evil influences that bind one to the rebirth process. The four fearlessnesses or four types of self-confidence of a Buddha in speaking Dharma run from the self-confidence coming from his awareness that he is a perfectly enlightened one to the self-confidence coming from being aware that he has informed the disciples about the path of liberation. The eighteen special dharmas that a Buddha alone possesses run from faultlessness concerning bodily karma to knowledge of all matters pertaining to the present. This triple formula is the definition of a Buddha. Thus, this section works systematically through the hearers or disciples, the bodhisattva, a Buddha, and all the Buddhas.

capability of crossing over sentient beings even to the point of entrance into nirvana—how could these not be awakening?" Answer: "They are also a dream." Question: "All the Buddhas of the three times of past, present, and future in sameness teaching sentient beings, those who obtain the path being as numberless as the grains of sand of the Ganges —could this not be awakening?" Answer: "That is also a dream. It is merely that whatever involves mental discrimination, calculation, and [the realm of objects] manifested by one's own mind[18] is a dream. When awakened, there is no dreaming. When dreaming, there is no awakening. These are false conceptualizations of thought, mind, and the consciousnesses. They are no more than insights in a dream. There is neither an awakener nor something to awaken to. If one awakens according to Dharma, when one truly awakens there is no self-awakening at all. Ultimately no awakening exists. The perfect awakening of all the Buddhas of the three times is but a conceptual discrimination of sentient beings. Because of this I call it a dream. If the consciousnesses and thought are calmed, so that there is not a single pulse of thought, it is to be called perfect awakening. Similarly, whatever there is of thought and the consciousnesses that has not been calmed is a dream."

14. Question: "In cultivating the path and cutting off delusion, what mental attitude is employed?" Answer: "Use the mental attitude of devices." Question: "What is the mental attitude of devices?" Answer: "When one examines delusion and realizes that from the outset delusion has no place to arise from, and by this device is able to cut off doubt and delusion, we call it mental attitude." Question: "What delusion does the mind that is in accordance with Dharma cut off?" Answer: "Delusions of interpretations concerning common men, heretics, hearers, **solitary Buddhas**, bodhisattvas, and so forth."

15. Question: "What are the **two truths**?" Answer: "It is like the simmering of heated air.[19] Deluded people see the air waving due to the

---

solitary Buddhas: A hearer is a disciple of a Buddha. In Mahayana texts, followers of the Hinayana are referred to as hearers. A solitary Buddha is a Buddha for himself alone. He is one who has won enlightenment but lives in solitude and does not reveal his knowledge to the world.

two truths: The worldly truth refers to the fact that, though all dharmas are devoid of essence, because of the topsy-turviness of the world, empty dharmas are produced and in the world these are taken as real. However, sages know the nature of this error and so know that all dharmas are void and nonarising.

heat and understand it as water, but it is really not water. It is the simmering of heated air. The meaning of the two truths is also like this. Common men see the truth of the highest meaning as the worldly truth. Sages see the worldly truth as the truth of the highest meaning. Therefore, the sutra says: 'When the Buddhas speak Dharma, they always rely upon the two truths.'[20] The truth of the highest meaning is the worldly truth, and the worldly truth is the truth of the highest meaning.[21] The truth of the highest meaning is voidness. If you see characteristics of existence, then you must tidy up! If there is self or mind or arising or extinguishing, then further tidy up!" Question: "How does one tidy up?" Answer: "If you rely upon Dharma to gaze, then you will lose ways of looking at things and not see one thing. Therefore, the *Classic of the Old One* [*Lao Ching*] says: 'Established virtue is like laziness.'"[22] (These words draw us into emptiness.)

16. Question: "What kind of mind is called craving?" Answer: "The mind of the common man." Question: "What kind of mind is that which is nonarising?" Answer: "The mind of the hearer." Question: "What kind of mind is that which understands the essencelessness of dharmas?" Answer: "It is the mind of the solitary Buddha." Question: "What kind of mind is that which engenders neither understanding nor delusion?" Answer: "The mind of the bodhisattva." Question: "What kind of mind is that which is not awakened and does not know?" **No answer**.[23] The reason there is no answer is that Dharma cannot answer. Because Dharma is no-mind, and an answer is having mind. Dharma is speechless,[24] and an answer is having speech. Dharma is without interpretation, and an answer is interpretation. Dharma is without knowledge, and an answer is having knowledge. Dharma is without this and that,[25] and an answer is having this and that. Such minds and words are no more than calculations. Because mind is not a form, it is not connected to forms, and yet mind is not formless and is not connected to formlessness. The mind's not being connected to anything is liberation. If one breaks the prohibitive precepts, he will turn apprehensive. However, if he knows that his mind of anxiety cannot be apprehended, then he will even attain liberation. He will also know that rebirth in a heaven cannot be apprehended.[26] Even though he knows voidness, voidness cannot be appre-

no answer: the silence of Vimalakīrti.

hended. Even though he knows that nothing can be apprehended, no-apprehension cannot be apprehended.[27]

17. If mind has something to value, it will surely have something to despise. If mind has something that it affirms, it must have something that it negates. If mind takes one thing to be good, then all other things are nongood. If mind has affection for one person, then all other persons become people whom one has a grudge against.[28] Mind does not abide in forms, nor does it abide in formlessness. It does not abide in abiding, nor does it abide in no-abiding. If mind has abiding, it will not avoid being roped in. If mind has a place where it functions, then it is bondage. If mind values dharmas, dharmas will keep you back. If mind honors one dharma, mind necessarily will have something that it considers inferior. When you try to grasp the meaning of the sutras and treatises, you should not value understanding. If there are places that you understand, then your mind has something to be connected to. If mind has something to be connected to, then it is bondage. The sutra says: "It is not through inferior, middle, or superior dharmas that one attains nirvana."[29] Even though mind has entered delusion, you must not produce a thought of delusionlessness. When mind arises, rely on Dharma to gaze at the place it arises from. If mind discriminates, rely on Dharma to gaze at the place of discrimination. Whether greed, anger, or stupidity, rely on Dharma to gaze at the place they arise from. Not seeking the place they arise from is cultivating the path. If there is arising of mind, then investigate and, relying on Dharma, tidy up!

18. Question: "In cultivating and attaining the path, are some slow and some quick?" Answer: "They are separated by millions of eons.[30] In the case of those for whom mind is [the path], it is quick. For those practitioners who produce the thought of enlightenment and practice, it is slow. People of sharp abilities know that mind is the path. People of dull abilities seek everywhere for the path but lack knowledge of its location. Moreover, they do not know that mind from the outset is unexcelled, perfect enlightenment." Question: "What about quickly attaining the path?" Answer: "Mind is the substance of the path, and so one quickly attains the path. When the practitioner himself realizes that delusion has arisen, then, relying on Dharma, he gazes and brings about its exhaustion." Question: "How is mind the substance of the path?" Answer: "Mind is [unconscious] like trees or stones. It is as if there were

someone who painted dragons and tigers with his own hand, and yet, upon looking at them, became **frightened**. Deluded people are also like this. The brush of thought and consciousnesses paints **Razor Mountains and Sword Forests**,[31] and yet it is thought and the consciousnesses that fear them. If you are fearless in mind, then false thoughts will be eliminated. The brush of mind and the consciousnesses discriminates and draws forms, sounds, smells, tastes, and touchables, and, upon looking at them in turn, produces greed, anger, and stupidity. Sometimes it is fascinated and sometimes repelled. Due to the discriminations of thought, mind, and the consciousnesses, various sorts of karma are in turn produced. If you can realize that thought and the consciousnesses from the outset have been void-quiescent and also avoid seeing the locus [of the arising of thought and the consciousnesses], then you are cultivating the path. Some, by discriminations of their own mind, draw tigers, wolves, lions, poisonous dragons, evil spirits, the generals of the five paths of rebirth, King Yama, the ox-headed guards of hell, and the Hell of the **Sound of Cold**.[32] These things are discriminated by their own minds, but they are then controlled by these things, and so they undergo various sufferings. Realize that whatever mind discriminates is merely forms. If you awaken to the fact that mind from the outset has been void-quiescent and know that mind is not itself a form, then mind is unconnected. Forms are not forms. They are constructed in the manner of an illusion by your own mind. If you merely realize that they are not real, then you will attain liberation."

frightened: Due to the similarity to section 62, this seems to be a Hui-k'o section.

Razor Mountains and Sword Forests: There are a variety of schemas for the hells. In one there are eight great hells surrounded by sixteen small hells, eight icy cold and eight flaming hot. The fourth of the hot ones is called Sword Forest and the fifth Razor Path. People who injure and kill with knives and swords, chop down someone's trees to repay a grudge, and speak sincerely but secretly betray fall into Sword Forest. When they enter, a wind blows off the sword leaves, which sever their hands, feet, ears, and noses. Vultures and dogs eat their flesh. On the Razor Path the hell beings are forced to walk across a precipice on a narrow path with upright, sharp razors.

Sound of Cold: The generals of the five paths of rebirth, also known as the five heavenly envoys, are the assistants of King Yama, the god of death and judge of the dead, considered in Buddhism a Dharma guardian. He is often sixteen-armed. The demonic hell guards take on the heads of various animals, including oxen, horses, pigs, eagles, vultures, etc. They chew up and pull apart the hell beings with their teeth. The fourth of the eight icy cold hells is the Hell of the Sound of Cold. The hell beings therein tremble from the penetrating cold wind and cannot open their mouths.

19. When at present you rely on the Dharma's three treasures of Buddha, Dharma, and community to carry out the path, you must not have such views as good/bad, like/dislike, cause/effect, is/is-not, holding the precepts/breaking the precepts, and so forth. If you make these sorts of calculations, they are all delusions manifested by your own mind. You will not notice that the realm of objects arises from your own mind. If you hold that no dharmas exist, it is also [a delusion manifested by your own mind]. The perceptions of your own mind are all deluded thoughts that construct is and is-not. If you say that the wisdom of the Buddhas surpasses all, it is also [a delusion manifested by your own mind]. One's own mind in the manner of a sleight of hand constructs both existence and nonexistence and in turn is deluded by them. The sutra says: "If you rely on the Dharma-Body Buddha to cultivate the path, construct neither illusionary sentient beings nor real sentient beings."[33] Therefore, the **Dharma Realm** is sameness, having neither gain nor loss. If you rely on the Dharma-Body Buddha to cultivate the path, do not seek nirvana. Why? Because Dharma is nirvana. How could you use nirvana to seek nirvana? Also, do not seek Dharma. Because mind is the Dharma Realm. How could you use the Dharma Realm to seek the Dharma Realm? If you wish to rectify mind, neither fear dharmas nor seek dharmas. If you use the Dharma-Body Buddha to cultivate the path, your mind will be like stone—dark, unaware, unknowing, undiscerning, nonchalant about everything like a stupid person. Why? Because Dharma lacks awareness and knowing. Because Dharma can give us fearlessness, it is a place of great peace. It is like someone who commits a mortal crime.[34] He surely must be beheaded. But if it happens that his king grants him a pardon, he avoids the anxiety of a death sentence. Sentient beings are also like this. They commit the **ten evils** and the **five transgressions** and must fall into a hell, but the Dharma King grants them a pardon of great quiescence, and so they avoid all their sins. If someone who is a good friend of the king ventures off to another locale, kills youths there, and is grabbed by

---

Dharma Realm: *Dharmadhātu* means the sphere of reality. It is a synonym for the truth of the highest meaning.

ten evils, five transgressions: The ten evils are: killing living things; stealing; illicit conduct in sexual matters; flowery language; abusive language; lying; idle talk; covetousness; anger; and false views. The five transgressions are: killing your father, mother, or an arhat; harming a Buddha's body; and splitting the monastic community.

local people who want to **requite the injury**, this person becomes fearful, for he has no one to rely upon. When he suddenly sees his great king, he obtains liberation. If someone breaks the precepts and commits murder, commits sexual crimes and thievery, and fears falling into a hell, when he sees his own Dharma King, he will then obtain liberation.

20. In the Dharma of cultivating the path, the vital energy of those who obtain their understanding through the medium of the written word is weak. If one obtains his understanding from events, his vital energy will be robust. Those who see Dharma from the medium of events never lose mindfulness anywhere. When those whose understanding is from the medium of the written word encounter events, their eyes are beclouded. To discuss events from the point of view of the sutras and treatises is to be estranged from Dharma. Though one may chat about events and listen concerning events, it is not as potent as personally experiencing events with the body and mind. If someone's [understanding that] events are Dharma is deep, then worldly people will not be able to fathom him. Even if the cultivator of the path time and again has his belongings stolen by thieves, he will not have a mind of attachment and will not even be **vexed**. If he is time and again cursed and slandered by others, he will not be vexed. If one is like this, his mind of the path will gradually strengthen. It will accumulate over years without end, until he spontaneously has no mind toward any disagreeable and agreeable thing. Therefore, he who is not bound up with events can be called the bodhisattva of great power. If one wishes to make the mind of cultivating the path robust, he should send mind outside the boundaries of the norms.

21. Question: "What events are outside the boundaries of the norms?" **Answer**: "The spontaneously peaceful mind does not realize the understanding of the Mahayana or the Hinayana, does not produce the thought of enlightenment, even to the point of not wishing for the omniscience of a Buddha, does not honor the person who is accomplished in samadhi, does not disdain the person who is attached and craving, even to the point of not wishing for Buddha wisdom. If one does not grasp for un-

requite the injury: the first of Bodhidharma's four practices.

vexed: echoes the first two of Bodhidharma's four practices, the practice of requiting injury and that of following conditions.

Answer: Given the similarities between this answer and the Master Yüan sections of *Record II*, particularly section 55, this may be Yüan material.

derstanding and does not seek wisdom, he will desire to avoid the delusions and confusions of the Dharma masters and dhyana masters. If one can preserve mind[35] and erect will, entertain no wish to be a worthy or a sage, not seek liberation, fear neither the cycle of birth and death nor the hells, and with no-mind directly carry out his responsibilities,[36] then for the first time he will bring to perfection a dull mind of norms. If one can see all the transformations of the worthies and sages due to their **supernormal powers** through hundreds of thousands of eons without producing a desirous mind, then this person will desire to avoid the deceptions and delusions of others." Another question: "How does one produce the state of being outside the boundaries of the norms?" Answer: "The Confucian virtues of humaneness, righteousness, ritual, wisdom, and faith are called the mind within the boundaries of the norms. Birth-and-death and nirvana are also called the mind within the boundaries of the norms. If you wish to go outside the boundaries of the norms to the point of jettisoning the terms 'common man' and 'sage,' you must not know through having a method; you must not know through not having a method; you must not know through both having a method and not having a method. That which ordinary knowledge understands[37] is also said to be within the boundaries of the norms. When you do not produce the mind of the common man, the hearer or bodhisattva mind, and do not even produce a Buddha Mind or any mind at all, then for the first time you can be said to have gone outside the boundaries of the norms. If you desire that no mind at all arise, that you do not produce understanding nor give rise to delusion, then for the first time you can be said to have gone outside of everything. When the worldly morons encounter a devilish, cock-and-bull fellow who babbles a demonic line, they come up with a demonic interpretation and use it as a compass. This is beneath comment. How can they perform the function of a great thing?[38] Hearing that a certain person leads a group of millions, their mind is triggered into motion. Gaze well at the dharmas of your

---

supernormal powers: The six supernormal powers or superknowledges are: (1) divine feet, the power to manifest oneself anywhere; (2) divine eyes, the power to know the future of self and others; (3) divine ears, the power to hear sounds that ordinary people cannot hear; (4) other minds, the power of knowing the thoughts of others; (5) past lives, the power of knowing the past births of self and others; and (6) destruction of the outflows, the power to eliminate the defilements.

own mind to determine whether it harbors the spoken and written word or not."

22. Question: "What is the mind of plainness? What is the mind of ingenious artifice?"[39] **Answer**: "Spoken and written words are called ingenious artifice. Forms and formlessness are equal. Walking, standing, sitting, or lying—all behavior and activity are plainness, even to the extent that when one encounters any sorrowful or joyful event, the mind remains immobile. That for the first time can be called the mind of plainness."

23. Question: "What is called correct and what is called false?" Answer: "Having no mental discrimination is called correct, and having the mind interpret dharmas is called false. When you come to the point of being unaware of both false and correct, that for the first time can be called correct. The sutra says: 'Those who abide in the correct path do not discriminate whether it is false or correct.'"[40]

24. Question: "What are sharp abilities and dull abilities?" Answer: "He who, without relying on the teaching of a master, sees Dharma from events is called one of sharp abilities. He who understands from the spoken teachings of a master is called one of dull abilities. In hearing the Dharma through the spoken teachings of a master there are also levels of sharpness and dullness in ability. In hearing the master's words, if one is not attached to existence and yet does not seize nonexistence; if one is not attached to characteristics and yet does not seize characteristicless-ness; if one is not attached to arising and yet does not seize nonarising, he is a person of sharp abilities. To covet understanding and seize meanings—views such as is and is-not—is the interpretation of meanings of the man of dull abilities. When the person of sharp abilities hears of the path, he does not produce the mind of the common man. He does not even produce the mind of the worthy or sage. Common and sagely are both excised. This is the hearing of the path of the man of sharp abilities. He cares not for material and sensual things, even to the point of not caring for a Buddha's enlightenment. If you care for a Buddha's enlightenment, then you will reject disturbance and seize quietude, reject stupidity and seize wisdom, reject the conditioned and seize the uncon-ditioned. You will not be able to cut off duality and be unimpeded. This

Answer: Again due to the similarity to section 55, this may be a Yüan section.

is a man of dull abilities. To do it in that way[41] is to go beyond all common and sagely realms. The man of sharp abilities hears of the path without producing a covetous mind. He does not even produce right mindfulness and right reflection. He hears of the path without producing the mind of the hearer. He does not even produce the bodhisattva mind. The bodhisattva takes the Dharma Realm as his home and the four **immeasurable minds** as the **locus of the precepts**. All behavior, to the end, does not go outside of the Dharma-Realm mind. Why? Because the body is the Dharma Realm. Even if you say and do all sorts of things, do a dance leap[42] or a horse kick, none of them leaves or enters the Dharma Realm. If you take the Dharma Realm to enter the Dharma Realm, then you are a stupid person. Because the bodhisattva clearly sees the Dharma Realm, he is said to have the purity of the Dharma eye. Because he does not see dharmas arising, abiding, or extinguishing, he is said to have the purity of the Dharma eye. As to the sutra's saying that 'without extinguishing stupidity and craving [he gives rise to liberation],'[43] craving from the outset is nonarising, so how could it now be extinguished? The stupid, craving one seeks internally, externally, and in between, but he can neither see nor apprehend [stupidity and craving]. Even when he seeks in the ten directions for them, there is not the slightest characteristic to be apprehended. Hence it is unnecessary to extinguish them in order to seek liberation."

25. Question: "Worldly people apply themselves to various sorts of learning. Why do they fail to obtain the path?" Answer: "Because they see a self, they do not obtain the path.[44] If they were able to avoid seeing a self, then they would obtain the path. Self means ego. The reason why the sage meets suffering without being sad[45] and encounters pleasure without being happy is that he does not see a self. The reason why he has neither suffering nor pleasure is that he has lost self. When you attain to emptiness, even the self is lost, so what further thing can there be that is not lost? In the world how many can there be who have lost self? If you can lose self, everything from the outset will be nonexistent. The self arbitrarily produces calculations, and then one is affected by birth, aging,

---

immeasurable minds, locus of the precepts: The four immeasurable minds are: friendliness; compassion; joy; and equanimity. The locus of the precepts is the platform erected for the carrying out of the ceremony of receiving the precepts.

sickness, death, sadness, commiseration, suffering, defilements, cold, heat, wind, rain, and everything that is not in accord with one's wishes. These are all manifestations of false thought. In the manner of a magician's sleight of hand, departing [to another birth] and staying [in this birth] are not under the control of a self. Why? Arbitrarily [the ego of worldly people] produces resistance and opposition, and they fail to acknowledge that departing and staying [are not under the control of the ego]. The defilements exist because of the grasping of the self, and from this springs departing and staying. If you know that departing and staying are not under the control of the self, then for you 'mine' will be a sleight-of-hand dharma incapable of holding you back.[46] If you do not resist sleight-of-hand dharmas, then, no matter what may come, you will not be hindered. If you are capable of not resisting transformations, then, no matter what may happen, you will have nothing to repent of."

26. Question: "Since all dharmas are void, who cultivates the path?" Answer: "If there were a who, then it would be necessary to cultivate the path. If there were no who, then it would be unnecessary to cultivate the path. The who is ego.[47] If there were no ego, then, no matter what might come, you would not produce is and is-not. Is is the ego's affirming something; the things are not doing the affirming. Is-not is the ego's negating something; the things are not doing the negating. This can be known through such examples as wind, rain, blue, yellow, **red, white, and so forth**. When it wants to, the ego likes something; the things are not doing the liking. Why? This can be known through such examples as the sense organs eye, ear, nose, and tongue, and the sense objects **forms, sounds, and so forth**."

27. Question: "The sutra says: 'Walking on pathlessness, one comprehends the path of the Buddhas.'[48] [What does this mean]?" Answer: "Walking on pathlessness is to reject neither names nor characteristics. For the one who has comprehended, names are nameless and characteristics are characteristicless. It also says: 'One who walks on pathlessness rejects neither covetousness nor craving.'[49] For the one who has comprehended, covetousness is covetousless and craving is cravingless. When

red, white, and so forth: The ego affirms that the flower is blue; the flower is not doing the affirming.

forms, sounds, and so forth: The ego likes certain musical sounds; the sounds are not doing the liking.

walking on pathlessness, suffering is sufferingless and pleasure is pleasureless, and this is called comprehension. To reject neither birth nor death is called comprehension. When walking on pathlessness, birth is birthless, and yet one does not seize birthlessness. Ego is egoless, and yet one does not seize egolessness. This is called comprehending the path of the Buddhas. If you can attain to the realization that negation is negationless, and yet not seize negationlessness, then it is called comprehending the path of the Buddhas. In summary, mind is no-mind, and this is called comprehending the mind path."

28. Question: "What is comprehending all dharmas?" Answer: "When in the midst of things you do not give rise to views, it is called comprehension. Comprehension means not engendering thought in relation to things, not engendering covetousness for things, and not engendering defilements in connection with things. When forms are formless, it is called comprehending forms. When existence is existenceless, it is called comprehending existence. When birth is birthless, it is called comprehending birth. When Dharma is Dharmaless, it is called comprehending Dharma. No matter what he meets, he directly comprehends. This person's wisdom eye is open. No matter what may come, he is incapable of seeing differences or sameness in characteristics. This is called comprehension."

29. Question: "The sutra says: 'The outsiders take joy in the various views; the bodhisattva is immobile in the midst of the various views. The **Heavenly Evil One** takes joy in birth-and-death; the bodhisattva does not reject birth-and-death.'"[50] Answer: "Because false views are the same as correct views, the bodhisattva is immobile.[51] That the outsiders take joy in the various views means that they view existence [as existence] and view nonexistence [as nonexistence]. Existence does not partake of existence, and nonexistence does not partake of nonexistence. This is called immobility. Immobility means not being apart from the correct and not being apart from the false. Just at the time of correct understanding, there is no false and correct, and it is unnecessary to reject the false to seek the correct. Existence does not partake of existence [and in that light the

Heavenly Evil One: refers to the Māra King who abides in the sixth heaven at the top of the realm of desire. The gods in this slot take joy in freely utilizing the objects of desire that other gods create. The Heavenly Evil One, one of the four or five Māras, creates obstacles when someone is trying to perform a good action.

bodhisattva] in a state of immobility sees existence. Nonexistence does not partake of nonexistence [and in that light the bodhisattva] sees nonexistence. Because he relies on Dharma to gaze at the lack of difference between the false and the correct, [the bodhisattva] is said to be immobile. Also, because it is unnecessary for him to reject the false to enter the correct, he is said to be immobile in the midst of the various views. The sutra says: 'By false characteristics enter the correct Dharma.'[52] It also says: 'Do not reject the **eight falsities** to enter the **eight liberations**.'[53] Because birth-and-death is the same as nirvana, he does not reject [birth-and-death]. Birth is birthless. Death is deathless. He does not depend upon rejecting birth in order to enter birthlessness and upon rejecting death in order to enter deathlessness. Because everything is quiescent, it is nirvana. The sutra says: 'All sentient beings from the outset have been quiescent. They are not extinguished again.'[54] It also says: 'All dharmas are nirvana.'[55] It is unnecessary to reject birth-and-death for it to begin to be nirvana,[56] just as it is unnecessary that a person reject a chunk of ice for it to begin to be water. They have the same essence. Because birth-and-death and nirvana are also in essence the same, it is unnecessary to reject [birth-and-death]. Therefore, the bodhisattva does not reject birth-and-death. As to the bodhisattva's being fixed to immobility, being fixed to the unfixed is called fixedness.[57] Because the outsiders take pleasure in the various views, the bodhisattva teaches that views are viewless and that one does not toil over getting rid of views, only afterward to have viewlessness. That the Heavenly Evil One takes pleasure in birth-and-death and the bodhisattva does not reject it means that [the bodhisattva] wishes to make [sentient beings] awaken to the fact that birth is birthless and that one does not have to wait for the rejection of birth in order to enter birthlessness. It is unnecessary to reject water to find wetness, to reject fire to get heat. Water is wetness, and fire is heat. Birth-and-death is nirvana. Therefore, the bodhisattva does not reject birth-and-death to enter nirvana, because birth-and-death is identical to nirvana.[58] The

---

eight falsities, eight liberations: The eight falsities are the opposites of the noble eightfold path. The eight liberations in one formula are: the first dhyana; the second dhyana; the fourth dhyana; the four formless concentrations (the four stages of the formless realm: limitlessness of space; limitlessness of consciousness; nothingness; and neither perception nor nonperception); and the extinction attainment. These lead to the nirvana of the arhat.

hearer cuts off birth-and-death and enters nirvana. The bodhisattva experientially comes to know that in essence they are sameness, and so he can by means of great compassion identify with beings and take on the function [of transforming sentient beings]. 'Birth' and 'death' are different terms with one meaning. 'Immobility' and 'nirvana' likewise are different terms with one meaning."

30. Question: "Is the great path **near or far**?" Answer: "It is like [a mirage arising from] the simmering of heated air. It is neither near nor far. An image of a face in a mirror is also neither near nor far. The needles and flowers that [a person who has ingested the hallucinogenic plant] **henbane** [discerns] in the sky are also neither near nor far. If you say that they are near, how is it that, when he seeks for them in the ten directions, he cannot apprehend them? If you say they are far, how is it that they pass clearly before his eyes? The treatise says: 'Near and yet you cannot see them. This is the nature of the ten thousand things.'[59] If you see the nature of things, it is called attaining the path. Seeing the mind of things is [seeing that] the nature of things is not characterized by thingness, that things are thingless. This is called seeing the nature of things. As is said, all things that have the characteristic of shape are things. To see the nature of things truly without error is called seeing the reality [of the highest meaning]. It is also called seeing Dharma. 'Near and yet you cannot see them' refers to dharma characteristics. The wise one trusts to things and does not trust to self,[60] and so he has no grasping and rejecting; he also has no opposing and agreeing. The stupid one trusts to self and does not trust to things, and so he has grasping and rejecting and has opposing and agreeing. If you can empty the mind, be unhurried and loose, and completely lose the world, then you are one who trusts to things and follows the times. Trusting to things and following the times is easy, but opposing, resisting, and transforming things is difficult. When

near or far: The Confucians Mencius and Hsün Tzu both said that the Tao is near. *Mencius,* Li-lou shang: "The Tao lies near but people seek it in distant places." *Hsün Tzu,* Hsiu-shen: "Even though the Tao is near, if one does not practice it, one does not attain it."

henbane: Henbane (*Hyoscyamus niger* var. *chinensis*) is a poisonous plant that grows in the wild. It is about fourteen to twenty-eight inches in height, with elongated leaves and flowers of a light purple color. The root was used for pharmacological purposes. Because the ingestion of the fruit made one "mad and loose" it was called *lang-tang.*

things desire to come, trust them; do not go against them. If they desire to depart, let them go; do not pursue them. What has been done—pass it by and do not regret it. Events that have not yet arrived—let them go and do not think about them. This is the person who is walking the path. If you can trust to things, then put them in the charge of the world. Gain and loss do not arise from the ego. If you trust to things and do not resist, relax and do not oppose them, where and when will you not roam in the remote?"[61]

31. Question:[62] "How is it that the great path is said to be very easy to come to know and easy to walk on, but no one in the world is capable of knowing it and walking it?[63] Please explain this." Answer: "What you say is correct. When one is eminent, at rest, loose, trusting, not doing one thing, he is said to be walking the path. Not seeing one thing is called seeing the path. Not knowing one thing is called cultivating the path. Not practicing one thing is called practicing the path. It is said to be easy to come to know and easy to walk."

32. Question: "The *Classic of the Old One* [*Lao-ching*] says: 'Be as careful at the end as at the beginning and there will be no failures.'[64] What about this?" Answer: "This refers to the fact that, when the person who has faith in the teachings just one time makes up his mind to achieve enlightenment, he never retreats or loses sight of it from the past up to now. Making up one's mind for the first time constitutes now. Looking at old times from the point of view of now constitutes the past. Looking at the first step toward enlightenment from the point of view of the past constitutes now. One whose mental focus on the path runs continuously from beginning to end is called one with faith in the Dharma of the Buddhas. That past and now are unchanging[65] is called **fruit** [of actuality]. That the unreal deceives is called **flower** [of illusion]."

33. Question: "What is the bodhisattva practice?" Answer: "It is not the practice of the worthies and sages. It is not the practice of the common man. It is the practice of the bodhisattva.[66] If one is training to be a bodhisattva, one neither seizes worldly dharmas nor rejects worldly dharmas. If you can enter the path with thought and the consciousnesses

---

fruit, flower: The word for fruit, *shih*, also means actuality. *Flower* suggests the flower in the sky, a stock simile for an illusion or sleight of hand. Thus, these lines can be read as simultaneously contrasting kernel/external ornament and actuality/unreal illusion.

[as they are], there will be no common men or hearers capable of taking your measure. As is said, every locus of events, every locus of forms, and every locus of evil karma is used by the bodhisattva, and all are made into Buddha events. They are all made into nirvana. They are all the great path. Every locus is without locus. This is the locus of Dharma. This is the locus of the path. The bodhisattva examines the fact that every locus is the locus of Dharma. The bodhisattva does not reject any locus, does not seize any locus, does not select any locus, and makes all of them into Buddha events. Birth-and-death is made into a Buddha event, and delusion is made into a Buddha event." Question: "All dharmas are without dharma. How is it that they are made into Buddha events?" Answer:[67] "The locus of making [every locus into a Buddha event] is not a locus of making. There are no dharmas of making, and so in all places, good or otherwise, [the bodhisattvas] see the Buddhas."

34. Question: "What is 'seeing the Buddhas?'" Answer: "To see no characteristic of greed in greed is to see the greed dharma. To see no characteristic of suffering in suffering is to see the suffering dharma. To see no characteristic of dream in dream is to see the dream dharma. This is called 'in every locus seeing the Buddhas.' If you see characteristics, then in every locus you will see demons."[68]

35. Question: "Where is the essence of the Dharma Realm?" Answer: "Every locus is the locus of the Dharma Realm." Question: "Within the essence of the Dharma Realm are there such things as holding the precepts or breaking the precepts?" Answer: "Within the essence of the Dharma Realm there exists neither the common nor the sagely. Heavenly mansions and hells also do not exist. Is and is-not, suffering and joy, and so forth are constant like space."

36. Question: "Where is the locus of enlightenment?" Answer: "The locus you are walking on is the locus of enlightenment. The locus you are lying on is the locus of enlightenment. The locus you are sitting on is the locus of enlightenment. The locus you are standing on is the locus of enlightenment. Wherever you lift your feet or put them down is the locus of enlightenment."[69]

37. Question: "Please explain the realm of the all the Buddhas." Answer: "Dharmas neither exist nor inexist. Not seizing the understanding that they neither exist nor inexist is called the realm of the Buddhas. If mind is [unconscious] like trees or stones, it cannot know by a wisdom

of existence, nor can it know by a wisdom of nonexistence. Buddha Mind cannot be known from the point of view of existence. The Dharma Body cannot be seen through imagery. That which ordinary knowledge understands[70] is the discrimination of false thought. Though you make various interpretations, they are all the calculations of your own mind, false thoughts of your own mind. The insight of all the Buddhas cannot be shown to people through speech,[71] nor can it be hidden away, nor can you plumb it by means of dhyana. Cutting off understanding and cutting off knowing are called the realm of all the Buddhas. That which cannot be measured is called Buddha Mind. If you can have faith that Buddha Mind is like this, then you will extinguish the defilements, which are as innumerable as the grains of sand of the Ganges. If you can preserve such a mind[72] and be mindful that Buddha insight is like this, your mental focus on the path will grow stronger day by day."

38. Question: "Why is it said that the sun of Tathagata insight sinks beneath the land of existence?"[73] Answer: "If you see the nonexistent as existent, the sun of insight sinks beneath the land of existence. This is also the case if you see characteristiclessness as one more characteristic."

39. Question: "What is called characterized by immobility?" Answer: "When you do not apprehend existence, there is no existence to be moved by. When you do not apprehend nonexistence, there is no non-existence to be moved by. When mind is no-mind, there is no mind to be moved by. When characteristics are characteristicless, there are no characteristics to be moved by. Therefore, we say characterized by im-mobility. If there is one who comes to this sort of realization, he is said to have deluded himself. The above is not yet understanding. When you understand, there are no dharmas to be understood."

40. Question: "In what appears before us one sees that there is arising and extinguishing. Why is it said that there is no arising and extinguish-ing?" Answer: "That which arises from conditions is not said to have arisen, precisely because it arose from conditions. That which extin-guishes due to conditions is incapable of extinguishing on its own, pre-cisely because it extinguishes due to conditions." Question: "Why is it that that which arises from conditions is not said to have arisen?" Answer: "It arises from conditions. It does not arise from another, nor does it arise from itself; it does not arise from both [another and itself], nor does it arise without a cause.[74] There are no dharmas that arise.

There is nothing that arises. There is no locus of arising. Therefore, we come to know nonarising. That which you see as arising and extinguishing is illusionary arising, not real arising, and illusionary extinguishing, not real extinguishing."

41. Question: "Why does the common man fall into **evil rebirths?**"[75] Answer: "Because he has an ego, is stupid, and therefore says: 'I drink wine.' The wise one says: 'When you have no wine, why don't you drink winelessness?' Even if [the stupid person] were to say 'I do drink winelessness,' the wise one would say:[76] 'Where is your I?' The stupid person also says: 'I commit a sin.' The wise one says: 'What sort of thing is your sin?' All of this is conditioned arising, lacking an essence.[77] When it arises, you already know there is no ego, so who commits the sin and who receives punishment? The sutra says: 'Common men insist on discriminating: "I crave; I am angry." Such ignorant people will then fall into the three evil rebirths.'[78] The sutra says: 'Sin is intrinsically neither internal nor external, nor is it between the two.'[79] This illustrates that sin is unlocalized. The unlocalized is the locus of quiescence. When human beings fall into a hell, from mind they calculate an ego. They remember and discriminate, saying: 'I commit evils, and I receive punishments. I do good deeds, and I receive rewards.' This is the evil karma. From the outset no such things have existed, but they arbitrarily remember and discriminate, saying that they exist. This is the evil karma."

42. Question: "Who can cross over the ego to nirvana?" Answer: "Dharma can cross over the ego. How can this be known? By seizing characteristics, one falls into a hell. By examining Dharma, one is liberated. If you see characteristics, remember, and discriminate, then you will suffer from a scalding cauldron, a blazing furnace, the ox-headed [guards of hell], the Hell of the **Sound of Cold**, and so forth. You will see manifested before you the characteristics of birth-and-death. If you see that the Dharma-Realm nature is the nirvana nature and you are without memory and discrimination, then it is the substance of the Dharma Realm."

43. Question: "What is the substance of the Dharma Realm like?" Answer: "The mind substance is the substance of the Dharma Realm.

evil rebirths: rebirth as an animal, hungry ghost, or hell being—the three lowest of the paths of rebirth.
Sound of Cold: See the footnotes to section 18.

This Dharma is insubstantive. It is without boundaries, as expansive as space, invisible. This is called the substance of the Dharma Realm."

44. Question: "What is knowing Dharma like?" Answer: "Dharma is called no-awakening and no-knowing. One whose mind is without awakening and without knowing is a person who knows Dharma. Dharma is called not knowing and not seeing. If mind does not know and does not see, this is called seeing Dharma. Not knowing any dharma is called knowing Dharma. Not apprehending any dharma is called apprehending Dharma. Not seeing any dharma is called seeing Dharma. Not discriminating any dharma is called discriminating Dharma."

45. Question: "Dharma is said to be no-seeing. What is unimpeded knowing and seeing?" Answer: "Not knowing is unimpeded knowing. Not seeing is unimpeded seeing." Question: "Dharma is said to be no-awakening. 'Buddha' means 'awakened one.' Why is this?" Answer: "Dharma is said to be no-awakening, and 'Buddha' means 'awakened one.' No-awakening is awakening, and awakening in a state of identity with Dharma is Buddha awakening. If you are diligent in the practice of gazing at the characteristics of mind, you will see dharma characteristics. If you are diligent in the practice of gazing at the locus of mind, [then you will realize that] it is the locus of quiescence, that it is the locus of nonarising, the locus of liberation, the locus of voidness, the locus of enlightenment. The mind locus is unlocalized. It is the locus of the Dharma Realm, the locus of the seat of enlightenment, the locus of the Dharma gate, the locus of wisdom, the locus of dhyana unimpeded. A person who has this sort of understanding is a person who has fallen into a pit or slipped **into a ditch**."

46. Question: "The six perfections can produce omniscience. [What about this]?" Answer: "The perfections have neither self nor other, so who receives and who obtains? The fruits of the common karma of the **sentient-being class**[80] are indistinguishable from the marks of [a Tathagata's **field of**] **merit**.[81] The sutra says: '[If the giver with an equal

into a ditch: suggests that such a person is a living corpse.

sentient-being class: When the common karma of all sentient beings increases, the world comes into being. When common karma is exhausted, the world is destroyed.

field of merit: Buddhas, solitary Buddhas, and arhats are all merit fields, because their defilements are exhausted without residue. The idea is that the karmic world is no different from Buddhahood.

mind gives to] the Invincible Tathagata and the lowest beggar in the assembly, it is equal to great compassion and is complete Dharma giving.'[82]
This is called the perfection of giving. There are neither events nor
causes. There is no taking joy or growing weary. The substance is
Thusness. Since ultimately there is no is-not, who seeks is? If is and is-not
do not arise, then the precept body will be pure and so will be called the
perfection of morality. The mind has no internal or external. What do
this and that have to rely on? The nature of sound lacks anything to be
defiled. It is sameness,[83] like space. This is called the perfection of forbearance. Divorced from the measurings of the various organs of perception, ultimately [the mind substance] opens up, but it does not abide
in characteristics. This is called the perfection of striving. The three times
[of past, present, and future] have no characteristics. Not for a moment is
there a locus to abide in. One dwells in neither events nor Dharma. Quiet
and disturbance are intrinsically Thusness. This is called the perfection of
dhyana. Nirvana and Thusness are in essence invisible. When you do not
engage in **futile discourse**, are divorced from thought, mind, and the
consciousnesses, and do not abide in devices, it is called Thusness. There
is nothing to be used. You use, and yet it is not using. The sutra says:
'Teaching devices with insight is release.'[84] Therefore, this is called the
perfection of insight."

47. Question: "What is called the mind[85] of liberation?" Answer:
"Because mind is formless, it is not connected to forms, and yet mind is
not formless and is not connected to formlessness. Although mind illuminates forms, it is not connected to forms. Although mind illuminates
formlessness, it is not connected to formlessness. Mind is not something
that can be seen through the form characteristic. Although mind is
formless, its formlessness is not a mere absence. Mind is formless,[86] and
yet mind is not the same as the emptiness of the sky. The bodhisattva
clearly illuminates the void and the nonvoid. Even though the Hinayana
illuminates the void, it does not illuminate the nonvoid. Even though the
hearer apprehends the void, he does not apprehend the nonvoid."

48. Question: "Why is it said that all dharmas are neither existent
nor nonexistent?" Answer: "The mind substance is without substance. It
is the Dharma substance. Mind is formless, and so it is not existent. It

---

futile discourse: This includes speech, signs, concepts, and discrimination.

functions ceaselessly, and so it is not nonexistent. Also, because it functions yet is constantly void, it is not existent. Because it is void and yet constantly functioning, it is not nonexistent. Also, because it lacks an essence, it is not existent. Because it arises due to conditions, it is not nonexistent. The common man abides in existence. The Hinayana abides in nonexistence. The bodhisattva abides in neither existence nor nonexistence. [However, this schema] is a false thought calculated by your own mind. Forms are formless and are not defiled by formness. Formlessness is formless and is not defiled by formlessness. Also, not seeing seeing and not seeing no-seeing is called seeing Dharma. Not knowing knowing and not knowing no-knowing is called knowing Dharma. An understanding such as this is also called false thought. Mind is no-mind. Because mind is no-mind, it is called Dharma mind. Today's practitioners understand this as the destruction of all delusions. Mind is like space, indestructible, and therefore it is called the thunderbolt mind. Mind does not abide in abiding, nor does it abide in nonabiding, and therefore it is called the mind of insight. The mind nature is broad and great. Its operation is directionless. Therefore, we call it the Mahayana mind. The mind substance is penetrating, without obstacles, unimpeded, and therefore it is called the enlightenment mind. Mind has no boundaries. It is unlocalized. Because mind is without characteristics, it does not have limits. Because it functions ceaselessly, it is not borderless. It does not have limits nor is it limitless, and therefore it is called the mind of the **Reality Limit**. Mind has neither variation nor variationlessness, and so mind is substanceless. It is variationless, and yet it is not substanceless. It is not variationless. It has neither variation nor variationlessness. Therefore, it is called the mind of Thusness. Mind's lack of transformation is called variation. Its transformation according to things is called variationlessness. And so it is also called the mind of True Thusness. Mind is neither internal, nor external, nor in between. It does not lie in any of the directions. Mind's having no locus to abide in is the locus wherein Dharma abides, the locus wherein the Dharma Realm abides, and it is also called the Dharma-Realm mind. The mind nature is neither existent nor nonexistent. Past and present do not change. Therefore, we call it the mind of the Dharma

---

Reality Limit: Reality Limit (*bhūta-koṭi*) is a synonym for the truth of the highest meaning.

Nature. Mind has neither arising nor extinguishing, and therefore it is called the nirvana mind. If you make these sorts of interpretations, [you are under the sway of] the **perversion of false thought**. You do not understand the realm of objects manifested by your own mind. Such is called the mind of [undulating] waves."[87]

49. Question: "How is [the realm of objects] manifested by one's own mind?" Answer: "If you see that all dharmas exist, that existence is not existent in and of itself. The calculations of your own mind have created that existence. If you see that all dharmas do not exist, that nonexistence is not nonexistent in and of itself. The calculations of your own mind have created that nonexistence. This extends to all dharmas. In all cases the calculations of one's own mind create existence, and the calculations create nonexistence. What is greed like that you create the greed interpretation? Because in all these cases one's own mind has produced views, one's own mind has calculated about the unlocalized. This is called false thought. If you yourself say that you are beyond the calculated views of those who follow non-Buddhist paths, it is also false thought. If you engage in talk about no-thought and nondiscrimination, it is also false thought. When walking, Dharma is walking. It is not the ego walking. It is not the ego not walking. When sitting, Dharma is sitting. It is not the ego sitting. It is not the ego not sitting. Entertaining these sorts of interpretations is also false thought."

Text no. 6: *Record II*

50. Dharma Master Yüan[88] says: "When you are on the verge of seizing a lofty sense of willpower, bondage and **habit energy**[89] will surely melt away." Question: "What is meant by bondage proper,

---

perversion of false thought: Given the statement of reversal at the end of this section, wherein it is asserted that those who concoct these sorts of interpretations are under the sway of false thought, it is possible that the doctrinal formulations here are intentionally convoluted. This brings to mind the garbled statement of the *Chuang Tzu*, Ch'i-wu lun, where Chuang Tzu makes fun of those immersed in metaphysics by parodying their style.

habit energy: Even after production of the defilements of greed, hostility, and stupidity has been stopped, the habit energy of the defilements persists as lingering traces. Yüan seems to be saying that, if you have élan, the initial bondage and its residual habit energy will be cut off. Sections 50–56 are Yüan sections, as is section 90 of *Record III*.

and what is meant by residual habit energy?" Answer: "Arising and extinguishing are bondage proper, and nonarising and nonextinguishing are the residual habit energy of a **stupid person**. Do not allow them."

51. Question: "Does one **rely on Dharma** or does one rely on people?"[90] Answer: "When in accordance with my understanding, you rely on neither people nor Dharma. If you rely on Dharma and do not rely on people, it is still one way of viewing things. If you rely on people and do not rely on Dharma, it is the same." Further: "If you have bodily energy, you will avoid the deceptive delusions of people and Dharma, and your spirit will be all right.[91] Why? Because when you esteem knowledge, you are deceived by men and Dharma. If you value one person as correct, then you will not avoid the deceptive confusions of this person, and this is true even to the point where, if you say that a Buddha is the supreme person, you will not avoid deception. Why? Because you are deluded about the realm of objects. Because, by relying on this person, your mind of faith becomes heavy." Further: "Stupid people say that a Buddha is supreme among men. They say that nirvana is supreme among dharmas. Thus they are deluded and confused by men and dharmas. If you say that it matters not whether one knows or does not know the **Dharma Nature** and the Reality Limit and you say that the self-nature neither arises nor extinguishes, then you are deceiving and deluding yourself."

52. Dharma Master Chih saw Dharma Master Yüan on the street of butchers and asked: "Do you see the butchers **slaughtering the sheep**?"[92] Dharma master Yüan said: "My eyes are not blind. How could I not see them?" Dharma Master Chih said: "Master Yüan, you are saying you see it!" Master Yüan said: "You're seeing it on top of seeing it!"

---

stupid person: One possible interpretation is the following: Ordinary people see things as arising and extinguishing. They are under the sway of the defilements themselves. Some within the Buddhist fold speak of things as neither arising nor extinguishing. They remain under the sway of the lingering traces or vestiges of the defilements.

rely on Dharma: There is an early tradition of reliance on the Dharma.

Dharma Nature: Dharma Nature (*dharmatā*) means the natural condition of dharmas.

slaughtering the sheep: The Vinaya or disciplinary code prohibits monks from witnessing such things. The butchering of sheep is listed as the first of twelve wicked things. Monks should not go the house of a thief, the house of a low-caste person, the house of a butcher, the house of a prostitute, or a wine house.

53. Master Chih again asked: "If you hold a view with characteristics, it is the view of a common man. If you hold a view of voidness of essence, it is the view of the **two vehicles**. If you hold a view of neither existence nor nonexistence, it is the view of a solitary Buddha. If you hold a view of pity and sympathy, it is the view of **compassion with love**.[93] If you use mind to view, then it is the view of the followers of the non-Buddhist paths. If you make use of the consciousnesses to view, it is the view of the Heavenly Evil One. If you do not see forms and form-lessness, you will no longer have views. How should one view in order to be free of all these errors?" Master Yüan said: "I have nothing what-soever to do with these sorts of views at all, and that is what is properly called taking a view. Because you create various false thoughts such as these, you are deluding and confusing yourself."

54. A certain person asked Master Yüan: "Why do you not teach me the Dharma?" Answer: "If I were to set up a Dharma to teach you, it would not be leading you. If I were to set up a Dharma, it would be deceiving you; it would be failing you. If I had a Dharma, how could I explain it to someone else?[94] How could I speak of it to you? It comes down to this: If there are terms and written words, all of it will deceive you. How could I tell you even a mustard seed's worth of the meaning of the great path? If I could speak of it, what purpose would that serve?" When asked again, [Master Yüan] **did not reply**. Later, another question: "How does one quiet mind?" Answer: "You must not engender a mental focus on the great path. In my opinion mind in and of itself cannot be known. It is mysterious and not something to be concerned about."

55. Another question: "What is the path?" Answer: "When you desire to produce the thought of moving toward the path, crafty ingenuity will arise, and you will fall into having mind. If you desire to give rise to the path, ingenious artifice will arise. If you have devices in your mind, crafty artifice will always arise." Another question: "What is crafty artifice?" Answer: "If you use intellectual understanding to seek a name, a hundred

---

two vehicles: refers to the vehicle of the hearers or disciples and the vehicle of the solitary Buddha.

compassion with love: Erroneously thinking that sentient beings exist, one engenders love attachments in the mind, and due to these, compassion is produced. This compassion with a loving view should be rejected.

did not reply: again the silence of Vimalakīrti.

ingenious schemes arise. If you desire to cut off crafty artifice, don't produce the thought of enlightenment and don't use knowledge of the sutras and treatises. If you can accomplish this, then for the first time you will have bodily energy. If you have spirit, do not esteem understanding, do not seek Dharma, and do not love knowledge, then you will find a little quietude." Further: "If you do not seek wonderful understanding, do not serve as a teacher for people, and also do not take Dharma as your teacher, you will walk alone spontaneously." Further: "If you do not give rise to a demon mind, I can lead you."

56. Question: "What is a demon mind?" Answer: "**Closing the eyes** [in the cross-legged sitting posture] and entering samadhi." Question: "[What if] I gather the mind into dhyana so that it does not move?" Answer: "This is bondage samadhi.[95] It is useless. This holds even for the four dhyanas, each of which is merely one stage of quiescence from which you will return to **disturbance again**. They are not to be valued. These are created dharmas, dharmas that will be destroyed again, not ultimate Dharma. If you can understand that intrinsically there is neither quiescence nor disturbance, then you will be able to exist of yourself. The one who is not drawn into quiescence and disturbance is the man of spirit." Further: "If one is capable of not seizing on interpretations, not creating the mind of delusion, and not esteeming profound knowledge, then he will be a peaceful person. If there is one dharma to be esteemed or valued, this dharma will be the one most capable of binding and killing you, and you will fall into having mind. This is an unreliable state of affairs. There are innumerable common men throughout the world who are bound by terminology and the written word."

closing the eyes: Zen manuals on cross-legged sitting urge keeping the eyes slightly open. Those who do cross-legged sitting with the eyes closed are said to be in the hungry ghost cave of Black Mountain. Black Mountain is the abode of the singers and musicians of the gods (kinnara), who have a bird's figure for the lower part of the body.

disturbance again: Before the enlightenment, Gautama practiced under two sages, Ārāḍa and Udraka. Under the former, Gautama ascended through the four dhyanas and reached the third of the four stages in the formless realm, the stage of nothingness. He concluded that this was not the ultimate path, that it is a produced dharma, that eventually the practitioner will return to bondage. Under Udraka, Gautama reached the fourth stage in the formless realm, the stage of neither perception nor nonperception, but again found that the practitioner will return to bondage. This is an old theme.

57. A certain person asked **Master K'o**: "How can one become a sage?" Answer: "All common men and sages are created by the calculations of false thought." Another question: "Since they are false thought, how does one cultivate the path?" Answer: "What sort of thing is the path, that you want to cultivate it? Dharmas are not characterized as high or low; dharmas are not characterized as going or coming."⁹⁶

58. Another question: "Teach me, your disciple, to quiet mind." Answer: "Bring your mind here and I will quiet it for you." Also: "Just quiet my mind for me!" Answer: "This is like asking a craftsman to cut out a garment. When the craftsman obtains your silk, then he can for the first time set his cutting tool to work. At the outset, without having seen the silk, how could he have cut out the pattern from space for you? Since you are unable to present your mind to me, I don't⁹⁷ know what mind I shall quiet for you. I certainly am unable to quiet space!"

59. Also: "**Administer confession** to me, your disciple." Answer: "Bring your sins here, and I will administer confession to you." Also: "Sins lack any characteristic of form that can be apprehended. I [don't]⁹⁸ know what to bring!" Answer: "My administration of confession to you is over. Go to your quarters." Comment: If there is a sin, one must confess, but since he did not see any sins, it was unnecessary for him to confess. Also: "Teach me to cut off the defilements." Answer: "In what location are the defilements that you want to cut off?" Also: "In fact, I don't know their location." Answer: "If you don't know their location, they are like space. You [don't] know what they are like and yet you desire to cut off space."⁹⁹ Also: "The sutra says: 'Cut off every evil, cultivate every good, and you will be able to become a Buddha.'"¹⁰⁰ Answer: "These are false thoughts manifested by your own mind."

60. Another question: "All the Buddhas of the ten directions have cut off the defilements and completed the path of the Buddhas." [Answer:] "You recklessly make such a calculation without any fixed frame of reference." Another question: "How do Buddhas cross over sentient beings to nirvana?" Answer: "When the image in a mirror crosses over sentient beings, Buddhas will cross over sentient beings."

Master K'o: Sections 57–62 are Hui-k'o sections.

administer confession: Requests for absolution were a regular part of the Buddhist calendar. The monks assembled every two weeks and carried out a ceremony. Following a reading of sections of the disciplinary code, each monk said whether there were any transgressions on his part. He then received a judgment.

61. Another question: "I fear the hells, undergo confession, and culti-vate the path." Answer: "Where is the I located? And what is this I like?" Further: "I don't know its location." Answer: "You don't even know the location of this I, so who falls into a hell? Since you do not know what it is like, this is a case of false thought's calculating existence. There are hells precisely because false thoughts calculate existence."

62. Another question: "This path is completely created by false thought. What is creation by false thought?" Answer: "The Dharma has no big or small, form or characteristics, high or low.[101] It is as if within your residence there were a great stone in the foreground of the gar-den.[102] Should you fall asleep on it or sit on it, you would be neither alarmed nor fearful. Suddenly you get the idea to create an image. You hire someone to paint a Buddha image on it. When your mind creates the interpretation Buddha, then you fear committing a sin and no longer dare to sit on top of it. It is the original stone, but this Buddha inter-pretation was created by your mind. What is mind like? It is always your mind-consciousness brush painting and creating these interpretations. You yourself bring on the anxiety. You yourself bring on the fear. In reality within the stone there is neither sin nor merit. Your mind itself creates these interpretations. It is as if someone were to paint the forms of **yaksas**, ghosts, dragons, and tigers. He himself paints them, but when he looks at them in turn, he himself gets fearful. In the paint ultimately there is no locus to be feared. It is always your mind-consciousness brush discriminating and creating these interpretations. How could there be one thing? It is always your false thought creating these interpretations."

63. Question: "How many types of Buddha discourse on the Dharma are there?" Answer: "The *Laṅkā Sūtra* has four types of Buddha dis-course.[103] As is said, the Dharma Buddha's discourse consists of the Dharma of comprehending[104] that substance is empty; the **Outpouring Buddha** discourses on the Dharma of the unreality of false thought; the Knowledge Buddha discourses on the Dharma of awakening to detach-ment; and the Magical-Creation Buddha discourses on the Dharma of the six perfections."

---

yaksas: misshapen dwarfs. They are part of the retinue of Vaiśravaṇa, guardian of the northern direction. They devour evil people but not good ones. Common attrib-utes are the citron, the snake-killing mongoose, and the protuberant belly.

Outpouring Buddha: The Outpouring (*niṣyanda*) Buddha corresponds to the Enjoyment Body (sambhoga-kaya).

64. A certain person asked Dhyana Master Leng:[105] "When mind takes past and future events as objective supports, then it will be bound. How can this be stopped?" Answer: "If objective supports arise, know that they are characterized by extinction, and ultimately they will not be produced again. Why? Because mind lacks any essence. Therefore, the sutra says: 'All dharmas are natureless.'[106] Therefore, when one thought [seems to be] produced, it [actually] neither arises nor extinguishes. Why? When mind arises, it does not come from the east, nor does it come from the south, the west, or the north. From the outset it has no locus to come from, and so it is nonarising. If you know it is nonarising, then it is nonextinguishing."

65. Another question: "If you bind mind to bring karma into being, how can it be cut off?" Answer: "Since there is no mind, it is unnecessary to cut it off. This mind has neither a locus of arising nor a locus of extinguishing, because false thought gives rise to dharmas. The sutra says: 'The sins of karmic obstacles do not come from the south, the west, or the north, or from the four corners, or from above or below. They all arise due to perverted views.'[107] There is no need to doubt this. The bodhisattva, examining the Dharma of all the Buddhas of the past, seeks [the sins of karmic obstacles] in the ten directions but cannot apprehend any of them."[108]

66. A certain person asked Dhyana Master Hsien:[109] "What is medicine?" Answer: "All of the Mahayana is words for counteracting disease. If you can have a mind that engenders no disease, what need is there for medicine to counteract disease? As medicine to counteract existence, [the Mahayana] speaks the medicine of voidness and nonexistence. To counteract the existence of an ego, it speaks the medicine of egolessness. To counteract arising and extinguishing, it speaks of nonarising and nonextinguishing. To counteract stinginess, it speaks of giving. To counteract stupidity, it speaks of insight. Down to: To counteract views, it speaks of correct views. To counteract delusions, it speaks of understanding. These are all words to counteract disease. If there is no disease, what need is there for these medicines?"

67. A certain person asked Dhyana Master Hsüan:[110] "What is the substance of the path?" Answer: "Mind is the substance of the path. This is a substantive substancelessness. It is the inconceivable Dharma, neither existent nor nonexistent. Why? Mind is natureless, and so it does not

exist. It arises from conditions, and so it does not inexist. Mind does not have the characteristic of form, and so it is not existent. It functions ceaselessly, and so it is not inexistent."

Text no. 7: Record III

68. **Dhyana Master Yüan**[111] says: "If you know that all dharmas are ultimately void, then knower and known are also void; the knowing of the knower is also void; and the dharmas that are known are also void. Therefore: 'Dharmas and knowing are both void; this is called the voidness of voidness.'[112] Therefore, the *Buddha Store Sūtra* [*Fo-tsang ching*] says: 'The Buddhas of the past preached that all dharmas are ultimately void. The Buddhas of the future will preach that all dharmas are ultimately void.'"[113]

69. Dharma Master Tsang[114] says: "The one for whom in all dharmas there is nothing to be apprehended is called the person who is cultivating the path. Why? As one whose eyes see every form, his eyes do not apprehend any form. As one whose ears hear every sound, his ears do not apprehend any sound. The realms that his mind takes as objective supports are all like this. Therefore, the sutra says: 'Mind has nothing to apprehend, and the Buddha gives a **prediction [of Buddhahood]**.'[115] The sutra says: 'No dharma can be apprehended, and even nonapprehension cannot be apprehended.'"[116]

70. Dhyana Master Hsien[117] says: "The locus that the eyes see is the Reality Limit. All dharmas are the Reality Limit. What beyond that are you searching for?"

71. Dhyana Master An[118] says: "Direct mind is the path.[119] Why? The person who has long walked the path has direct mindfulness and direct functioning, is not examining voidness any further, and is not looking for devices. The sutra says: 'Direct seeing does not look; direct hearing does not listen; direct mindfulness does not think; direct perception does not activate; and direct speech does not annoy.'"[120]

72. Dhyana Master Lien[121] says: "The Dharma Nature is insubstantive. Directly function and do not doubt. The sutra says: 'All dharmas

Dhyana Master Yüan: This is not the Yüan so prominent in *Record II*.

prediction of Buddhahood: A Buddha gives assurances to his disciples that in the future they will become Buddhas.

from the outset are nonexistent.'[122] The sutra says: 'Because from the outset there is no mind, there is the mind of Thusness; because of the mind of Thusness, from the outset there is no [mind].'[123] The sutra says: 'If all dharmas had always been existent and now for the first time were nonexistent, every one of the Buddhas would have committed a sinful error.'"[124]

73. Dhyana Master Hung[125] says: "All behavior and activity are Thusness. Seeing forms and hearing sounds are also Thusness. In fact, all dharmas are Thusness. Why? Because there is no transformation or variation. When eyes see forms, eyes have no locus of variation. This is Thusness of mind. If you understand the Thusness of all dharmas, then you are a Tathagata. The sutra says: 'Sentient beings are Thusness. Worthies and sages are also Thusness. All dharmas are also Thusness.'"[126]

74. Dhyana Master Chüeh[127] says: "If you awaken to the realization that mind has nothing to be connected to, you have apprehended footprints on the path. Why? Eyes see every form,[128] but eyes are not connected to any form. Eyes[129] are intrinsically liberated. Ears hear every sound, but ears are not connected[130] to any sound. In fact, mind passes through every dharma,[131] but mind is not connected to any dharma. It is intrinsically liberated. The sutra says: 'It is because all dharmas are unconnected to one another.'"[132]

75. Dhyana Master Fan[133] says: "If you come to know that all dharmas are one Dharma, then you will obtain liberation. The eye as an organ is a dharma. Its object forms are also a dharma. Dharmas do not associate with dharmas to create bondage. The ear as an organ is a dharma. Its object sounds are also a dharma. Dharmas do not associate with dharmas to create liberation. Mind is a dharma. Objects of mind are dharmas. Dharmas do not associate with dharmas to create sin, nor do dharmas associate with dharmas to create merit. They are intrinsically liberated. The sutra says: 'One does not see dharmas reassociating with dharmas to create bondage, nor does one see dharmas reassociating with dharmas to create liberation.'"[134]

76. **Master Tao-chih**[135] says: "All dharmas are unimpeded. Why? All dharmas are undefined and so unimpeded."

Master Tao-chih: presumably the Chih who is an associate of Yüan in sections 52–53 of *Record II*.

77. The nun Yüan-chi[136] says: "All dharmas are nonreacting.[137] They are intrinsically liberated. Why? When the eye sees forms, there are none that it does not see. Even when the mind consciousness knows, there is nothing that it does not know and nothing that it knows. At the time of delusion there is no understanding; at the time of understanding there is no delusion. During a dream there is no awakening; at the time of awakening there is no dream. Therefore, the sutra says: 'The great assembly, having seen Akṣobhya Buddha, **no longer saw that Buddha.** Ānanda! No dharma associates with the eye and ear organs to create a reaction. Why? Dharmas do not see dharmas. Dharmas do not know dharmas.'[138] Also, the sutra says: 'The nonproduction of consciousness due to forms is called not seeing forms.'"[139]

78. Dhyana Master Chien[140] says: "In enlightenment there is neither purity nor impurity. Darkness does not exist in mind. Mind does not know dharmas. Though you say that dharmas bind the ego, the substance of all dharmas has neither bondage nor liberation. If sentient beings were to come to know this on their own, then it would be nirvana even when their feelings are in motion.[141] When they do not understand this, it is not nirvana whether their feelings are in motion or not. When you do not yet know, in your own mind you falsely calculate movement and quiescence. When you understand, self does not exist any longer, and so who can calculate movement and quiescence? When you do not understand, you say that dharmas cannot be understood at all. When you understand, there is no dharma to be understood. When you do not understand, you are deluded. When you understand, there is nothing for delusion to be deluded about, nothing for understanding to understand. That there is nothing for delusion to be deluded about is called great understanding."

79. Dhyana Master Yin[142] says: "Scholars say that the **six consciousnesses** are false thought and refer to them as perpetrators of the deeds of the Evil One."

---

no longer saw that Buddha: The Buddha through his magical power manifests Akṣobhya to the assembly, and Akṣobhya preaches Dharma. The Buddha then withdraws his magical transformation, the assembly no longer sees Akṣobhya, and the Buddha announces to Ānanda that all dharmas are like this. Akṣobhya Buddha is the present Buddha of the eastern quadrant. Ānanda, a Śākyan, is a well-known disciple of Śākyamuni and is called servant of the Buddha.

six consciousnesses: They are the eye, ear, nose, tongue, body, and mind consciousnesses.

80. **Tripiṭaka Dharma Master**[143] says: "When the unreal [seems to] arise, there is [in reality] no arising. This is the Dharma of the Buddhist fold. From forgetting grasping and rejecting down to the point of Thusness and sameness and entrance into the bodhisattva mind, it is all identical to the Dharma Nature. However, the deluded person says that the six consciousnesses create the defilements." Tripiṭaka Dharma Master asks: "What do your six consciousnesses rely upon to arise?" The deluded one answers: "They arise from void illusion." Tripiṭaka Dharma Master says: "In empty illusion there are no dharmas. How are the defilements created?" [The deluded one] answers: "Although all dharmas are void, when conditions assemble, [dharmas come into] existence. The one who knows this attains sagehood, but the one who is deluded about it is an idiot. Because he is idiotic, he undergoes suffering. How can you discuss a nihilistic [voidness] that eliminates all dharmas?" Tripiṭaka Dharma Master answers: "You exert effort to get to the Buddha stage, and yet you say that the six consciousnesses are characterized by the defilements. If through effort you were to arrive at the Buddha stage, the six consciousnesses would be the locus wherein you would attain the path. The sutra says: 'Without entering the great sea of the defilements you will not get the priceless pearl.'[144] Furthermore: 'The class of sentient beings is the Buddha lands of the bodhisattvas.'[145] These sutra passages verify that these six consciousnesses are the locus of the ultimate fruit, but the deluded all day long create deluded interpretations and fail to recognize that delusion is delusionless. Speaking from the point of view of the truth of the path, there is neither understanding nor delusion. What is there to be distressed about?"

81. Dhyana Master Jen's[146] idea: "If you know the principle of mind for yourself, there will be neither depth nor shallowness. Movement and quiescence will merge into the path. You will see no place of gain or loss. And yet the deluded ones remain deluded about voidness and deluded about existence. They mistakenly produce tainted views. They employ mind to get rid of mind, saying that there are defilements to be cut off. Such people are forever sinking in the sea of suffering and constantly undergoing birth and death."

Tripiṭaka Dharma Master: refers to Bodhidharma. This title also appears in the next section.

82. **Dhyana Master K'o**[147] says: "Because common men lack under-standing, they say that the past differs from the present and say that the present differs from the past.[148] Furthermore, they say that, apart from the **four elements**, there is in addition the Dharma Body. When you understand, the **five aggregates** right now are the perfect, pure nirvana, and this body and mind are endowed with the ten thousand practices. Truly, this is proclaimed as the great thesis. If you have such an under-standing, you see the bright, pure pearl in the sea of defilements, and you are capable of illuminating the darkness of all sentient beings in radiance."

83. Dhyana Master Liang[149] says: "When you clarify the truth of all dharmas, in reality there is neither identity nor difference. Speaking in esoteric and exoteric terms, there are the two modes of rolling up and stretching out. In the case of the rolling-up mode, without seeing the arising of mind and without examining understanding or practice, trust to the feelings in your actions and intrinsically dwell in the Dharma of the Buddhas. In the case of the stretching-out mode, mind stretches out to connect to the other. It is manipulated by name and profit, drawn in by cause and effect, bound by is and is-not, and unable to exist in and of itself. This is called the stretching-out mode."

84. Master T'an[150] says: "'All dharmas' refers to the five aggregates. They are intrinsically pure from the outset. Therefore, the Buddha says that the mundane is the supramundane.[151] Because sentient beings are deluded about the mundane, they say they are dwelling in the mundane. When you understand, the mundane and the supramundane do have void names, but in reality there is no mundane or supramundane to be apprehended. One who has such an understanding is a person who knows the meaning of the five aggregates."

85. Master Hui-yao[152] says: "If you clearly understand that thought and the consciousnesses, intrinsically, in their very substance, are reality, then, of the loci of the objective supports of mind, there will be none that will not be Buddha dharmas, Buddha vehicles, nirvana. Mind reflects on

Dhyana Master K'o: presumably Hui-k'o.

four elements: refers to the four elements from which all things are made: earth (solidity); water (wetness); fire (heat); and wind (movement).

five aggregates: These are the constituents of the person: form; feeling; mental images, or the symbolizing function; will, or latent mental tendencies inherited from the past and past lives; and consciousness, or the differentiating function.

the ten thousand objects.[153] In the Indic language it is called 'Buddha.' In Chinese it is called 'Awakened One.' The awakened one is mind; his could hardly be an unawakened mind. Mind vis-à-vis awakening is analogous to the distinct terms 'eye' and 'vision.' When sentient beings do not understand this, they say that mind is not Buddha, and they employ mind to pursue mind. If they understand, mind is Buddha, and Buddha is mind. Therefore, I say that the intrinsically pure mind of sentient beings from the outset has lacked[154] the defilements. If mind were not Buddha, then you wouldn't know anything else outside of mind to call 'Buddha.'"

86. Dhyana Master Chih[155] says: "The two gates common and sagely have been as they are from without beginning. The common is the cause of the sagely. The sagely is the effect of the common. The effects of past actions are an errorless response. If virtue[156] arises from the sage's knowing, evil arises from the idiot's delusion. The perfected texts of the sutras and treatises are not something that those of inferior temperament can discuss. The sutra says: 'Though there is neither the self nor the person, virtue and evil are **not thrown out**.'[157] It is said: 'Those who maintain the **five precepts** obtain a human body. Those who maintain the **ten virtues** are assured of rebirth in a heaven. Those who uphold the **250 precepts**, examine voidness, and cultivate the path will attain the fruit of the arhat.'[158] If one commits a great many wrongs, commits errors and ultimate evils, and is covetous, hostile, and indulgent, he will obtain only the three evil rebirths. This will be his end. Thus, the principles [of cause and effect] are free of any discrepancies, just as a sound and its echo are in accordance, or the real thing and its reflection are as they should be."

---

not thrown out: From here onward, whenever lacunae have been tentatively reconstructed from the Tibetan translation, the reconstructions are given in italics.

five precepts: The five precepts for a layperson are: do not kill living things; do not steal; do not engage in illicit sexual conduct, particularly adultery; do not lie; and do not take intoxicants. The first is considered the most important.

ten virtues: The ten virtues refer to not committing the ten evils. The first three have to do with the body: no killing living things; no stealing; and no illicit sexual conduct. The next four are related to speech: no speaking flowery language; no using abusive language; no lying; and no idle talk. The last three are related to mind: no covetousness; no thought of doing harm; and no false views.

250 precepts: Refers to the full precepts to be observed by a monk. Depending on the disciplinary text, the number varies somewhat.

87. Dhyana Master Chih[159] says: "All dharmas are Buddha *dharmas;*[160] *that is the so-called* Dharma eye. All behavior and activities are enlightenment. Following mind, you will go straight to the path of the Buddhas. Do not be alarmed. Do not be *frightened.*[161] All *loci are equal.* If one's own mind . . . **then it is incorrect.**[162] If you can quiet mind, then everywhere you will dwell loftily, immobile, and this is also. . . ."[163]

88. Dhyana Master Wen[164] says: "Because of the existence of the **truth of suffering**, it is not voidness. Because of the nonexistence inherent in the truth [that all dharmas] are devoid [of essence], it is not existence. Because the two truths are dual, it is not oneness. The sage illumines nonduality *in voidness.*"

89. Dhyana Master . . .[165] says: "All the sutras and treatises delude people into seeing sin in the locus of sinlessness. For the one of understanding, the locus of sin is *sinless.*"

90. **Dhyana Master Yüan**[166] says: "All the sutras and treatises are dharmas that produce mind. If you produce a mental focus on the path, then ingenious artifice will give rise to knowledge and a complement of events. If mind is not produced, what need is there for cross-legged sitting dhyana? If ingenious artifice does not arise, why toil over right mindfulness? If you do not raise the thought of enlightenment and do *not* seek insight and understanding, then you will exhaust both phenomena and principle."

91. Dhyana Master Lang[167] says: "If mind arises, then gaze and make it . . . attachment and not see forms. When delusion arises, you see forms and make the forms interpretation. Mind is[168] a created dharma. Dharmas gaze at. . . . It is said: 'All dharmas are the calculations of false thought.'[169] Their creation lacks reality. . . . Whatever is [seen is all a manifestation of one's own] mind. What sort of thing is the path, that

---

then it is incorrect: From here onward ellipsis points indicate lacunae that could not be reconstructed from the Tibetan.

truth of suffering: Refers to the first of the four noble truths: suffering; cause of suffering; cessation of suffering; and path leading to the cessation of suffering.

in voidness: Because of its terseness this saying is difficult. The Tibetan translation may be helpful as a gloss: "Dhyana Master Wen says: 'Because the conventional reality exists, it is not voidness. Because the fruit of the arhat is nonexistent, it is not existence. Because the two truths are dual, it is not oneness. When the sage sees, he sees nonduality in voidness.'"

Dhyana Master Yüan: This is the Yüan of *Record II.*

you want to cultivate it? What sort of things are the defilements, that you want to cut [them off]? *Mind is the self-nature of the path. Body is the vessel of the path.* The **good friend**[170] *appears due to conditions. If mind is pure, objects are also pure. When there is neither grasping nor rejecting of the two extremes, you will be gazing at the eighteen elements."*

good friend: said of one, not as a rule a Buddha, who helps in spiritual progress.

two extremes, eighteen elements: The two extremes are it-is-ness and it-is-not-ness. The eighteen elements are the six sense organs (eye; ear; nose; tongue; body; and mind), the six objects (forms; sounds; smells; tastes; touchables; and dharmas), and the corresponding six consciousnesses.

3

....

Commentary on the *Biography,*
Two Entrances, and *Two Letters*

Biography

The biography of the Dharma Master, Bodhidharma, and
explication of his two entrances of principle and practice were compiled
by T'an-lin, an erudite Sanskritist active in the first half of the sixth
century in North China.[1] His scholarly credentials eventually led to his
demotion within the Ch'an genealogy. T'an-lin has traditionally been
considered a disciple of Bodhidharma, but it is more likely that he was a
student of Hui-k'o, who in turn was a student of Bodhidharma.[2]

The *Biography* is exceedingly simple. T'an-lin gives us but four points:
the Dharma Master was the third son of a great South Indian king; he
"crossed distant mountains and seas" to propagate Buddhism in North
China; some ridiculed him; he acquired two younger Chinese disciples
who served him for several years. As many have pointed out, the
"mountains and seas" here need not refer to and probably do not refer to
an ocean voyage from South India to South China, the route always
found in the traditional story, but rather to the tortuous journey around
the Tarim Basin of Central Asia—the Silk Road.

Standard versions of the traditional story place Bodhidharma's arrival
in the Lo-yang area in 527.[3] A guide to Lo-yang's magnificent Buddhist
heritage entitled *Record of the Buddhist Monasteries of Lo-yang* (*Lo-yang
chia-lan chi*), a reliable non-Buddhist source, mentions a Bodhidharma in
Lo-yang at about this time. There is one difference from the traditional

53

story. The guide's Bodhidharma is an Iranian, not an Indian. There is, however, nothing implausible about an early sixth-century Iranian Buddhist master who made his way to North China via the fabled Silk Road. This scenario is, in fact, more likely than a South Indian master who made his way by the sea route.

In the early sixth century Lo-yang, east of the great bend in the Yellow River, was an international Buddhist city, the eastern terminus of the Silk Road. It was the capital of the Northern Wei Dynasty (386–532), a non-Chinese conquering people originally from the steppe. Lo-yang was in continuous contact with the cultural products of the Western Region: unusual goods of all kinds, military technology, art, Buddhism. The city overflowed with Buddhist temples and monasteries, over a thousand of them. There were many exotic Buddhist masters from the Western Region.

But by 547 the Northern Wei had fallen, and Lo-yang's walls lay in ruins, its palaces, temples, and monasteries burned down. It was then that Yang Hsüan-chih, who held a number of modest official posts, revisited the city and compiled the *Record of the Buddhist Monasteries of Lo-yang* in order to show the former preeminent glory of the capital's Buddhist establishments. He was not really interested in the masters and teachings of Buddhism, only in fabulous sites and entertaining stories. He had no ax to grind when describing Buddhist masters.

Of course, Yang may have been referring to another Bodhidharma. His record mentions a Bodhidharma twice in passing. This minor player's role is merely to illustrate that even a Westerner could be astonished by the imposing stupas and monasteries of metropolitan Lo-yang. Yang's Bodhidharma did contribute one element to the Bodhidharma story that stuck—the age of 150:

> Yung-ning Monastery was erected by Empress Dowager Ling of the Hu family in Hsi-p'ing 1 [516]. . . . At that time there was a monk of the Western Region named Bodhidharma, a Persian Central Asian. He traveled from the wild borderlands to China. Seeing the golden disks [on the pole on top of Yung-ning's stupa] reflecting in the sun, the rays of light illuminating the surface of the clouds, the jewel-bells on the stupa blowing in the wind, the echoes reverberating beyond the heavens, he sang its praises. He exclaimed: "Truly this is the work of spirits." He said: "I am 150 years old, and I have passed through numerous countries. There is

virtually no country I have not visited. But even in India there is nothing comparable to the pure beauty of this monastery. Even the distant Buddha realms lack this." He chanted homage and placed his palms together in salutation for days on end. . . . Hsiu-fan Monastery had a statue of a fierce thunderbolt bearer guarding the gate. Pigeons and doves would neither fly through the gate nor roost upon it. Bodhidharma said: "That catches its true character!"[4]

Yung-ning Monastery within Lo-yang, the nine-storied stupa of which so impressed the Iranian Bodhidharma, was a key center of translation activity in the midst of a thriving Northern Wei Buddhism. Erected in 516, Yung-ning did not last long. It suffered a series of natural and military disasters after 526, leading to its final destruction a few years later.[5] Since the Iranian traveler saw this structure at the height of its glory, he would have been in Lo-yang between 516 and 526.

Just about a century after the compilation of the *Record of the Buddhist Monasteries of Lo-yang* and T'an-lin's *Biography* and *Two Entrances* we come to the next milestone in the recording of the Bodhidharma story, a biographical entry for a Bodhidharma in Tao-hsüan's *Continued Biographies of Eminent Monks* (*Hsü kao-seng chuan*), the first redaction of which was completed in 645. This monumental work attempts a comprehensive biographical coverage of the Buddhist world in China for the century and a half from the beginning of the Liang Dynasty to the early T'ang Dynasty. Tao-hsüan divides his hundreds of principal biographical entries into ten categories: translators, exegetes, meditation practitioners, specialists in the monastic disciplinary code, protectors of the Dharma, thaumaturges, martyrs, reciters, doers of good works, and miscellaneous figures. We, of course, are concerned with the section on meditation practitioners.

The *Continued Biographies of Eminent Monks* contains not only a Bodhidharma entry, but an entry on the Dharma Master's disciple Hui-k'o.[6] In addition, in his general comments at the end of his section on meditation practitioners, Tao-hsüan ventures a critique of Bodhidharma's style of meditation. The Bodhidharma entry is nothing more than a very slightly reworked version of T'an-lin's *Biography* and *Two Entrances*.[7] The only real addition is the mention of the age of 150, which Tao-hsüan clearly picked up from the *Record of the Buddhist Monasteries of Lo-yang*. Tao-hsüan provides T'an-lin's third son of an Indian king with a Brahman or priestly lineage and has the disciples Hui-k'o and Tao-yü serving for four or five years rather than T'an-lin's several years.

One other change, however, catches the attention. Tao-hsüan ignores T'an-lin's ambiguous statement about how Bodhidharma made his way to China, which simply implies that he undertook a long voyage, and substitutes a specific itinerary: a sea voyage to South China and a subsequent trek across the Yangtze River to the North. Since the Bodhidharma of the *Continued Biographies of Eminent Monks* is said to have put ashore on the south coast of China within the borders of the Sung Dynasty, we might deduce that he must have arrived by 479, the year in which the Sung fell.[8]

At the very end of the entry Tao-hsüan remarks that "a scroll recording his oral injunctions is in circulation." This seems to refer to the *Biography* and *Two Entrances*, though it could also refer to one or more of the *Records*.[9] But why did Tao-hsüan not quote from the *Records* in his Bodhidharma entry and especially in his Hui-k'o entry? Either the *Records* were not available to him or he chose to ignore them. In either case, we seem to have a foreshadowing of the *Records'* fall into obscurity in the Ch'an tradition.

There are two layers in the *Continued Biographies of Eminent Monks:* those entries that were in existence by 645, when Tao-hsüan completed his first draft; and the approximately 150 new biographies and supplements to existing biographies compiled in the period between 645 and the compiler's death in 667.[10] During the last decades of his life Tao-hsüan encountered new sources of information and so continuously made additions and supplements to his original draft. He was a scholar's scholar—never content to say the work was finished. Everything suggests that the Bodhidharma entry, the first third of the Hui-k'o entry, and the critique all belong to the 645 layer and that the final two-thirds of the Hui-k'o entry belongs to the 645–67 layer.

The modern Chinese scholar Hu Shih had a wide knowledge of Chinese historiography and applied it astutely to the study of early Ch'an sources. He pointed out the fissure in the Hui-k'o entry of the *Continued Biographies of Eminent Monks*, the demarcation between the original layer and the supplementary layer. It is a typical ending for a biographical entry, which runs: "In the end his undertaking came to a close without producing any illustrious successors."[11] In 645 this was the end of the entry. However, the Hui-k'o entry does not end with that line but abruptly launches into a disjointed account of various successors, at least some of whom were presumably illustrious. Hu further pointed out that the latter two-thirds of the entry is riddled by the scars of erasures and additions by caret. One can almost see the editor, Tao-hsüan or an assistant, shifting chunks of material here and there.

Hu's observations allow us to say with some confidence that the latter portion of the entry (hereafter referred to as Hui-k'o B, as opposed to Hui-k'o A) was one of the 645–67 supplements to existing biographies. Sometime during those two decades Tao-hsüan came upon new information about Hui-k'o and became convinced that Hui-k'o's undertaking had not ended and that he had indeed left behind successors. Though Hui-k'o B was not compiled that many years after Hui-k'o A, Hui-k'o B embodies a different perspective, one that belongs not to the time of its subject and Bodhidharma nor to the early seventh century but to the two decades between 645 and 667. Within that narrow time frame Tao-hsüan came to see the Bodhidharma circle in a different light. He must have encountered materials that shaped his new perspective. This shift, which has so much to do with how we understand the first two sections of the *Bodhidharma Anthology*, deserves scrutiny.

HUI-K'O A

Hui-k'o A reads as follows:

Śākya Seng-k'o, also known as Hui-k'o, family name Chi, was a man of Hu-lao [Honan]. In external learning he looked into the classics and histories; in Buddhist learning he penetrated the texts of the canon. In the end, thinking of the capital of the path, he silently scrutinized the fashions of the times. In solitude he accumulated great illumination, and his intellectual awakening far surpassed that of the crowd. Still, perfecting the path is not something done anew by each practitioner, and people valued having a transmission from a master. In unison the prestigious ones criticized him: "His path is merely one of expedience and lacks a real strategy. He seems to possess understanding, but it is not lofty. Who could possibly moor himself to the essence of his teaching?"

When he reached forty years of age, he encountered the Indian monk Bodhidharma, who was traveling about propagating the teaching in the area of Mount Sung and Lo-yang. Hui-k'o came to cherish him as a treasure, realizing that Bodhidharma embodied the path. In a single glance Bodhidharma was pleased with him, and he came to serve Bodhidharma as his master. To the end of the master's life he received the purport of the teachings. He trained for six years, making a subtle investigation of the one vehicle. Principle and phenomena fused; suffering and joy became unobstructed. His understanding was not of the provisional sort, for his wisdom emerged from a divine mind. Hui-k'o treated sensory objects in the manner of a potter, grinding up the duality of purity and defilement, shaping it as if it were clay, and coming to a realization. The resilient strength of his pottery was due to his power and dynamism, not to the qualities of the mound of clay.

Bodhidharma died at Lo River Beach. Hui-k'o concealed the body [or buried the body without the proper ceremonies] on a bank of the river, but Bodhidharma had enjoyed a fine reputation in the past, and so a proclamation was transmitted throughout the imperial domain. This brought monks and laypeople to come and politely ask if they could follow the master's model. Hui-k'o then unleashed his astounding discourse and presented his mind essence: "Though you may be able to spread the verbal formulation of Bodhidharma's teaching throughout the world, the intention behind it will not be established. Abstruse books are but a look from afar. You have not even begun to experience it in your minds!"

Later, at the beginning of the T'ien-p'ing era [534–37], he went north to Yeh, the new capital of the Eastern Wei, and opened many secret parks. Those stagnated on the written word were wrangling about is and is-not. At the time there was a Dhyana master Tao-heng who had undergone training in meditation. Within the royal lineage in Yeh his followers numbered a thousand. Upon coming into contact with Hui-k'o's Dharma discourse, his feeling was that it in fact conveyed nothing, and he called it the talk of the Evil One. He then dispatched one of his clever followers to terminate Hui-k'o's school. The follower arrived and heard Hui-k'o's Dharma, and in his mind he was very much inclined to submit. His sadness moved him to overflowing thoughts, and he had no intention of returning to report to Tao-heng. Tao-heng summoned him once more, but he still ignored the order. Of the many envoys who followed one after the other, none returned. On another day the clever follower encountered Tao-heng, and Tao-heng said: "Why was it necessary to dispatch those envoys?" Answer: "My vision is intrinsically perfect. It became faulty because of you, Master."

Subsequently Tao-heng's deep hostility led him to vilify Hui-k'o. He bribed a common imperial guard to assassinate Hui-k'o for no reason whatsoever. In the beginning Hui-k'o had not a bit of hatred as he approached death. Tao-heng's group rejoiced. Tao-heng subsequently sent' someone to finish the matter, to cut off Hui-k'o's study of frivolities. This vilifier hesitated with sword in hand, for the first time awakening to the Dharma expounded with one sound [which each sentient being understands according to its type]. Joy and fear crisscrossed in his bosom. The depth of the sea and the shallowness of a wet hoofprint in the road coexisted within him. Hui-k'o was relaxed, accepting, and in accord with all that is worldly. At the time he blessed the assassin with pure counsel; with no eye for the future he began humming a tune. With this Tao-heng was cleansed of the malice he harbored, and his crudities were dispelled. The true path is far off and difficult to spot. But block off what is near at hand, and it is easy to unite with it. That is the point of this story.

Subsequently Hui-k'o wandered away from Yeh and Wei and frequently happened upon coldness and warmth. His path, in the final analysis, was obscure and dark. Therefore, in the end his undertaking came to a close without producing any illustrious successors....[12]

This story is in effect a fleshing out of the four practices of Bodhidharma, particularly the first, the practice of retribution for the ill will of previous lives. Whereas T'an-lin's exposition of the four practices dryly recites the practice of retribution for ill will as a doctrinal statement, here we see its concrete expression in the life of a man. In terms of biographical facts, this Hui-k'o entry tells us very little:

a. He was a northerner who studied Buddhism alone.
b. He was forty when he met Bodhidharma.
c. He trained under Bodhidharma for six years.
d. Around 534, at the collapse of the Northern Wei Dynasty, he moved from the Lo-yang area to Yeh (and thus Tao-hsüan's Bodhidharma must have died before 534).
e. In Yeh a rival by the name of Tao-heng launched an assassination attempt.
f. Later he left the Honan/Hopeh area without having established an enduring school.

We probably should not pay too much attention to the age of Hui-k'o, since it is almost certainly an allusion to the line in the *Analects* where Confucius claims to have achieved freedom from doubt at the age of forty.[13] Those details that remain tell us little. There is no way to attach even approximate dates to Hui-k'o's life. The leitmotifs of the entry—criticism, violence, secrecy, and assassination—should be the focus:

a. Hui-k'o encountered criticism from prestigious people early in his career.

b. Lo River Beach, where Bodhidharma died, though Tao-hsüan does not mention it, was an execution grounds.[14]

c. Hui-k'o either concealed his master's body, probably in a cave on the riverbank, or in some way did not perform the proper burial ceremonies, though Tao-hsüan does not give a reason.

d. Hui-k'o established "secret parks" in Yeh.

e. In Yeh there were assassination attempts on Hui-k'o, one with a sword or knife.

f. He showed a lack of ill will toward the assailants, a relaxed acceptance, in the face of death.

g. Hui-k'o seems in the end to have been driven from the Yeh area by the unremitting hostility of his enemies.

This portion, Hui-k'o A, is what Tao-hsüan knew about Hui-k'o before 645, which places the report about a century after Hui-k'o. Hui-k'o A exudes the atmosphere of Hui-k'o's Yeh circle: A learned Chinese intellectual becomes the disciple of a foreign meditation master, encounters criticism, paranoia, and violence, and in the end has no success in establishing an enduring lineage. Also, arguments over is and is-not are a standard theme of the *Records*.

HUI-K'O B

Hui-k'o B is a disjointed hodgepodge. The main thread is one of the translations of the *Laṅkāvatāra Sūtra* into Chinese, the Sung translation, which is not mentioned in Hui-k'o A or the Bodhidharma entry.

Hui-k'o B reads as follows:

There was a Layman Hsiang who hid away in the forests and fields and ate off the trees. At the beginning of the T'ien-pao era [550–59] this master of the flavor of the path sent a letter communicating his goodwill: "Shadows arise from bodily forms; echoes follow upon voices. Some play with their shadows to the point of tiring their bodies, not realizing that their bodies are the shadows. Some raise their voices to stop the echoes, not realizing that their voices are the source of the echoes. Searching for nirvana by eliminating the defilements is like searching for the shadow by getting rid of the body. Searching for Buddhahood by rejecting sentient beings is like seeking for the echo by silencing the voice. Therefore, we know that delusion and awakening are one road, that stupidity and wisdom are not different. In namelessness they create names, and because of these names, is and is-not are born. In principlelessness they create principles, and because of these principles, disputations arise. Illusionary transformations are not real, so who is right and who wrong? Falsity is unreal, so what is void and what exists? One should know that obtaining is having nothing to obtain and losing is having nothing to lose. Having not been able to talk with you, I have related these ideas. I harbor the thought that you will answer them."

Hui-k'o took up his writing brush and stated his ideas:

Your speech on this true Dharma is as it really is,
Ultimately no different from the true, dark principle.
From the outset one is deluded about the pearl of mind and
    considers it a piece of broken pottery,
But suddenly one becomes aware that it is the true pearl.
Nescience and insight are equal, without difference.
You should know that the ten thousand dharmas are all Thusness.
Taking pity on these followers of the two extreme views,
You have composed these lines, taken up the brush, and created this
    letter.
Examining the fact that self and Buddha are without difference,
What further need is there to seek for nirvana without physical
    remainder?

He produced these truthful words without resorting to erasure and rewrites. Eventually someone expanded it, created sectional divisions, and published it as a separate scroll.

At that time there were also Hua-kung, Yen-kung, and Dhyana Master Ho. Each penetrated the covering on the dark mystery. Their oral disclosures were pure and remote. They investigated events and expressed their feelings. I have heard various stories about them, but, though in terms of generations they are not far from us, I have not heard of funerary inscriptions for them. Their subtle words have not been transmitted, so who can write of their pure virtue? It is so deeply painful!

At that time there was Dharma Master T'an-lin. In the capital of Yeh he frequently lectured on the Śrīmālā Sūtra and composed a commentary on it. Each time he lectured, people collected, and he then selected those who were conversant with the triple canon. He got seven hundred people to take part in his lectures. At the time of the Chou suppression of the Dharma [574–77], together with fellow students of K'o, he protected sutras and images from destruction.

In the beginning Dhyana Master Bodhidharma took the four-roll *Laṅkā Sūtra*, handed it over to Hui-k'o, and said: "When I examine the land of China, it is clear that there is only this sutra. If you rely on it to practice, you will be able to cross over the world."

Hui-k'o specialized in handing over the dark principle as stated above. He encountered scoundrels who cut off his arm. He took Dharma to manage mind so that he was not aware of the pain. He burned the wound with fire, and when the bleeding abated, he bandaged it with silk. He then went on his begging rounds as before, informing no one. Later T'an-lin also had his arm cut off by scoundrels. He cried out throughout the night. Hui-k'o applied bandages to his arm, begged food and offered it to T'an-lin. T'an-lin thought it strange that Hui-k'o did not have full use of his hand and so became angry with him. Hui-k'o said: "The pastries are in front of you. Why don't you wrap them up yourself?" T'an-lin said: "I don't have an arm! You didn't know this, K'o?" Hui-k'o said : "I too lack an arm. How could you become angry with me?" And thus they questioned each other and realized that there was karmic merit in their situation. Therefore, the world speaks of "Armless Lin."

Each time Hui-k'o discoursed on Dharma he would end by saying: "This sutra, after four generations, will degenerate into mere doctrinal terminology. How sad!"

There was a Dhyana Master Na whose conventional name was Ma. For twenty-one years he had dwelled in Tung-hai, the coastal area south of the Yangtze River, and lectured on the classical texts *Ritual* and *Changes*. He traveled about training and visited four hundred locales. While going south he arrived at Hsiang-chou near the capital Yeh and encountered Hui-k'o's discourse on Dharma. Then with ten scholars he left home and took ordination. East of Hsiang-chou students set up a farewell banquet of vegetarian dishes, and the sound of their crying moved the town. Since he had left worldly life, Na no longer took up the writing brush and conventional books. He wore but one robe and had but one begging bowl. His idea of permissible practice was one meal per day, and he underwent ascetic practices. And so, wherever he ventured, he never visited towns or residences.

There was a Hui-man, a man of Ying-yang [Honan], family name Chang. For some time he had dwelled at the Lung-hua Monastery in

Hsiang-chou. He happened upon Na's Dharma discourse and took ordination. He applied himself exclusively to nonattachment. He had a single robe and took a meal a day, and he kept only two needles. In winter he begged for supplementary clothing, and in the summer he discarded it and barely covered his nakedness. He himself related that he had never experienced fear. There were no fleas or lice on his body, and his sleep was free of dreams. He never stayed overnight twice in the same place. When he arrived at a monastery, he chopped firewood and made sandals. He always attended to his begging rounds.

In Chen-kuan 16 [642] at the side of South Hui-shan Monastery on Mount Sung outside Lo-yang he was staying within a cemetery of cedar trees, and it happened that a snowstorm reached three feet. In the morning he entered the monastery and saw Dharma Master T'an-k'uang, who was amazed that he had emerged from that. Hui-man said: "Does a Dharma friend come?" T'an-k'uang sent someone to investigate the place where Hui-man was sitting in the snow. It was five feet deep on all sides, and in places there were unfathomable snowdrifts. Some of the monks who heard of this made a lot of inquiries and went into hiding. Hui-man then took up his robe and bowl and traveled about the villages, but no one could convince him to stay the night. Whether acting or apart, he was solitary, empty, and quiet. When someone invited him to stay over for a night or attend a vegetarian banquet, he would announce: "In all the world there is no one to receive your invitation."

Therefore, each time Hui-man spoke Dharma, he said: "The Buddhas speak of mind in order to enable us to realize that mental conceptualization is unreal. Now you are re-adding mental conceptualization. It is in deep contradiction to the Buddhas' intention, and to add discussion to it is to pervert the great principle."

Therefore, the Masters Na and Hui-man always handed over the four-roll *Laṅkā Sūtra* and took it as the essence of mind. Whether preaching or practicing, they did not fail to hand it down. Later, in Lo-yang, without illness, Hui-man died in cross-legged sitting posture. He was about seventy. These followers Na and Hui-man are both in the lineage of Hui-k'o, and so they shall be entered into the genealogical sequence of another entry.[15]

How different from the atmosphere of Hui-k'o A is this Hui-k'o B! Here we are in a world of the sacramental transmission of the four-roll *Laṅkāvatāra Sūtra*, miraculous feats, and asceticism. Bodhidharma transmits the *Laṅkāvatāra* to Hui-k'o, and the Masters Na and Hui-man also practice a sacramental transmission of that sutra. Hui-k'o is imperturbable despite the amputation of an arm, cauterizes and bandages the wound, and goes about his normal begging rounds. Hui-man never experiences fear, sleeps without dreaming, and does cross-legged sitting in a cemetery all night long in snow over his head. The reclusive Hui-man's possessions amount to two needles, and the extra robe he begs for winter is discarded in the summer.

Where did all of this thaumaturgic material come from? There is an entry for a Fa-ch'ung in the wonder-workers section of the *Continued Biographies of Eminent Monks*. Like Hui-k'o B it belongs to the second layer. Hui-k'o B and this Fa-ch'ung entry show a strong affinity in their fabric. They are cross-referenced. The Fa-ch'ung entry refers to a separate Hui-k'o entry. Hui-k'o B mentions at the end a genealogical list of Hui-k'o's successors "in another entry," and such a list does occur in the Fa-ch'ung. For Tao-hsüan they were linked; he probably worked them up at approximately the same time, the last few years of his life. It is likely that at least the mystery-sutra theme of Hui-k'o B—that is, the information concerning the transmission of the four-roll *Laṅkāvatāra Sūtra*—and quite possibly a good deal more of Hui-k'o B were related to Tao-hsüan by Fa-ch'ung or someone in his Laṅkā group.[16]

Fa-ch'ung was born in the extreme Northwest about 586–88, a decade or so after the Bodhidharma circle fled from Yeh, and was active in the North from about the 630s through the 650s. What was Fa-ch'ung's relationship to Hui-k'o? The passage in the Fa-ch'ung entry that describes that relationship is ambiguous in the extreme and susceptible to widely divergent readings:

> Fa-ch'ung considered the *Laṅkāvatāra Sūtra* a mysterious text that had been sunk in obscurity for a long time. He was always seeking out people associated with the *Laṅkāvatāra* and making inquiries. He feared neither the level places nor the dangerous passes. He met Master Hui-k'o's later descendants, among whom there was a thriving practice of this sutra. Fa-ch'ung then followed their master to train but frequently attacked the important points in that master's approach to the *Laṅkāvatāra*. That master then gave up his group and entrusted the work of spreading the *Laṅkāvatāra* teaching to Fa-ch'ung. He then lectured on the *Laṅkāvatāra* thirty consecutive times.
>
> He also met someone who had personally received a transmission [of the *Laṅkāvatāra*] from Master Hui-k'o. Fa-ch'ung lectured on it one hundred more times in accordance with the South India one-vehicle thesis.

This sutra was translated into Chinese by Tripiṭaka Guṇabhadra of the Sung period and copied down by Dharma Master Hui-kuan. Its wording and principles harmonize; its practice and substance are connected. Its sole focus is meditation on a type of insight that does not lie in the spoken word. Later Dhyana Master Bodhidharma transmitted it to the South and the North. Forgetting words, forgetting thoughts, nonapprehension, and correct examining are the thesis. Later this was practiced on the Central Plain of the North. Dhyana Master Hui-k'o was the first to apprehend the key point of this teaching. Many of the literati of the Wei region could not sink their teeth into it, but those who received this thesis and got the idea attained awakening immediately. Because that generation is becoming ever more distant from us, later trainees have been led into error. A separate biographical entry for Hui-k'o gives a summary of the particulars.

I will now relate what the Master [Fa-ch'ung] acknowledged as the succession. There is evidence for every detail of what I have learned. After Dhyana Master Bodhidharma there were the two Hui-k'o and Hui-yü [i.e., Tao-yü]. Master Hui-yü received awakening in his mind but never spoke of it.

After Dhyana Master Hui-k'o:

Dhyana Master Ts'an
Dhyana Master Hui
Dhyana Master Sheng
Old Master Na
Dhyana Master Tuan
Tripiṭaka Master Ch'ang
Dharma Master Chen
Dharma Master Yü

The above all spoke of the dark principle but did not produce written records. . . .[17]

Fa-ch'ung is associated with the sacramental transmission of a mystery sutra, the four-roll Guṇabhadra rendering of the *Laṅkāvatāra*, the voidness teachings of Śūnyavāda or Madhyamaka, and asceticism. A close reading of the above passage leaves one with the feeling that Fa-ch'ung was really not a part of the Hui-k'o legacy but learned something of it and felt it compatible with his understanding of the *Laṅkāvatāra Sūtra*, perhaps so compatible that he or his followers presented him to Tao-hsüan, the collector of biographical lore, as an integral part of a Bodhidharma tradition.

BODHIDHARMA'S AND SENG-CH'OU'S MEDITATION STYLES

Tao-hsüan appended a short essay to his section on meditation practitioners. This piece is an overview of the meditation traditions of sixth- and seventh-century China and contains a brief comparison of the meditation styles of Bodhidharma and Seng-ch'ou (480–560), who has his own entry in the meditators section.[18] Why Tao-hsüan chose these two masters in order to summarize Buddhist meditation between the Liang Dynasty and his own time is not clear:

> At the time there was Bodhidharma. His divine transforming of beings rested in the truth. He carried out instruction in the Yangtze River and Lo-yang regions. The results of his Mahayana wall-examining were of the highest. Students of that generation who committed themselves to him and looked up to him were like the crowds of the marketplace. However, his discourse was difficult to comprehend. There were few disciplined and clever enough. When we examine what he was driving at, the ambition to expel or negate was present. When we examine the sayings he left behind, we find that the poles sin and merit are both rejected. In short, the real and the conventional are a pair of wings; voidness and existence are two wheels on one axle. His teaching is not to be trapped in the mesh of Indra's net, nor can it be sucked in by any view tainted with craving. His dhyana tallied with this nonduality and so transcended verbalization. Thus, when we examine the two theses of Seng-ch'ou and Bodhidharma, we can ride them like two ruts in a road.
>
> Seng-ch'ou embraced the fourfold meditation of the foundations of mindfulness. He was a model of purity worthy of veneration. Bodhidharma took as his Dharma the teaching of emptiness. Its mysterious purport is profound. Seng-ch'ou was a model to be venerated, and so human feelings were easily manifested by his disciples. Bodhidharma's purport was profound, and so coming to an intellectual grasp of his principle was difficult. Therefore, people got the fish trap [rather than catching the fish and forgetting the trap].[19]

Tao-hsüan seems to think of "wall-examining" (pi-kuan) as the core of Bodhidharma's meditation style. This term appears at the end of the Biography and in the following Two Entrances. In the former we find the line: "Thus quieting mind [ju-shih an-hsin] is wall-examining." In the latter we find the description: "If one rejects the false and reverts to the real and in a coagulated state abides in wall-examining [ning-chu pi-kuan], then self and other, common man and sage, are identical; firmly abiding without shifting, in no way following after the written teachings—this is mysteriously tallying with principle."

The elusive term *wall-examining* has been the subject of countless exegeses, from the most imaginative and metaphorical to the suggestion that it refers to the simple physical act of facing a wall in cross-legged sitting posture. Tibetan Ch'an, a new and exciting subfield of early Ch'an studies, offers us one more. Various Ch'an texts were translated into Tibetan, one of the most important being the *Bodhidharma Anthology*, which in Tibetan is usually referred to as the *Great Chinese Injunctions* (*Rgya lung chen po*). The recently discovered ninth-century Tibetan treatise *Dhyāna of the Enlightened Eye* (*Bsam gtan mig sgron*) contains translations of some of the *Two Entrances*, some material from *Record I*, and the whole of *Record III*.[20] Early on the *Dhyāna of the Enlightened Eye* gives summaries of four teachings known in early Tibet: the gradualist gate; the all-at-once gate (Chinese Ch'an); Mahāyoga; and Atiyoga (Rdzogs-chen).

The summary of Ch'an ends with a series of quotations from Ch'an masters, the first of whom is Bodhidharmatāra, the version of the name that is encountered in Tibetan sources: "From the sayings of the Great Master Bodhidharmātara [Bo-dhe-dar-mo-ta-ra]: 'If one reverts to the real, rejects discrimination, and abides in brightness, then there is neither self nor other. The common man and sage are equal. If without shifting you abide in firmness, after that you will not follow after the written teachings. This is the quiet of the principle of the real. It is nondiscriminative, quiescent, and inactive. It is entrance into principle.'"[21] A Tibetan Tunhuang manuscript gives a virtually identical rendering.[22] This understanding of wall-examining must have been widespread in early Tibet.

The Tibetan closely follows T'an-lin's Chinese with one exception, the line "in a coagulated state *abides in wall-examining*" (*ning chu pi-kuan*), for which the Tibetan reads: "rejects discrimination and *abides in brightness*" (*rtogs pa spangs te | lham mer gnas na*). This is a curious and consistent divergence. Why not a literal rendering, since the Tibetan translations of Chinese Ch'an materials are as a rule quite literal? We have the gloss of a Tibetan commentator.

The subsequent summaries of Mahāyoga and Atiyoga give us the context of this gloss, since both of these tantric teachings center on luminosity (*gsal ba*). Of the Mahāyoga thesis it is said: "All dharmas are a self-knowing brightness wherein the two truths do not exist. It is not made by a maker. The universal bright light and the infinity of gnosis are nondual."[23] Of the Atiyoga thesis it is said: "What is there to cultivate in the bright, bright [*lhan ne lhang nge = lham me lham me*] primordial light that is self-knowing, does not split, does not move, is undefiled, and does not abide?" The translator most certainly did not see wall-examining as a practice of sitting cross-legged facing a wall—an interpretation that often appears in later Ch'an texts. He saw it not as a physical posture but as an analogue of tantric teachings on all-at-once perfection.

Two Entrances

T'an-lin, or Armless Lin as he is known in Hui-k'o B of the *Continued Biographies of Eminent Monks*, not only was a member of the Bodhidharma circle, but also had an illustrious reputation as one deeply involved in the translation of Indian Buddhist books into Chinese. He knew Sanskrit to some degree, perhaps quite well. Though we possess no biography for this scholar monk, translation records and prefaces, a genre that provides us with a wealth of detail concerning the history of Buddhist translation in China, tell us that he took part in many translation projects at the great monasteries of the Eastern Wei capital Yeh during the late 530s and early 540s.[24]

In these vast translation projects of the Yeh monasteries T'an-lin's role was invariably to copy out a draft translation as one or another Indian master was expounding the text.[25] The title Tripiṭaka Dharma Master, which occurs repeatedly in those entries of the translation records and prefaces concerned with T'an-lin, is honorific. It implies that the Indians across from T'an-lin were versed not just in one section of the Buddhist canon but in all three of its divisions. T'an-lin, quite naturally, refers to Bodhidharma as the Dharma Master, and the *Records* sometimes refer to him as Tripiṭaka Dharma Master.

Lin's fame arose from his deep knowledge of the *Śrīmālā Sūtra*, a sutra centering on the royal laywoman Śrīmālā. As Hui-k'o B tells us, Lin lectured on the *Śrīmālā* and wrote a commentary on it, a commentary that exerted enormous influence on the study of the *Śrīmālā* in China but has not come down to us. Fortunately, the *Precious Cave of Śrīmālā* (*Shengman pao-k'u*), a commentary executed by the well-known Madhyamika

Chi-tsang in the first decades of the seventh century, quotes Armless Lin's lost commentary repeatedly, particularly in the area of translation terminology.[26] These excerpts sometimes give cumbersome but accurate transliterations for the wording of the Sanskrit original. The key to the *Two Entrances* lies not in Bodhidharma but in the *Śrīmālā* and Armless Lin's commentary on it.

The two entrances are entrance by principle and entrance by practice (*li-ju* and *hsing-ju*). The former refers to awakening to the thesis by means of the teachings (*chieh-chiao wu-tsung*) and coming to a deep belief that all beings are identical to the True Nature (*chen-hsing*), which is merely covered by adventitious dust (*k'o-ch'en*). If one reverts to Reality and in a coagulated state abides in wall-examining (*ning-chu pi-kuan*) and in no way follows after the written teachings (*keng pu-sui yü wen-chiao*), he is tallying with principle. The latter refers to the four practices:

1. the practice of requiting an injury (*pao-yüan hsing*; the practitioner thinks to himself: I, from the past [*wo ts'ung wang-hsi*], across eons have produced much ill will, and thus any suffering I encounter in this rebirth is due to the ripening of the effects of bad intentional actions in past lives and hence is to be patiently accepted without ill will)

2. the practice of following conditions (*sui-yüan hsing*; the practitioner thinks to himself: If I encounter honor and so forth in this rebirth, it is due to intentional actions in past lives and hence the necessary conditions for it will eventually dry up; gain and loss follow conditions)

3. the practice of having nothing to be sought (*wu so-ch'iu hsing*; stop thoughts and have no seeking)

4. the practice of according with Dharma (*ch'eng-fa hsing*); intrinsic purity (*hsing-ching*) is Dharma, which is free of stinginess (*wu-chien*), and so in terms of your life and property (*shen-ming ts'ai*), practice the perfection of giving

The first two practices are explicitly cast in the first-person mode and are essentially vows or aspirations to show patience in the face of both good and bad karmic fruits. The last two inculcate not seeking for anything and in the light of the intrinsic purity of Dharma practicing the perfection of giving. The four practices are what might be called the basic Buddhist ethos, and one is inclined to wonder how they can be squared with the *Continued Biographies of Eminent Monks*'s picture of Bodhidharma's teaching as some sort of mysterious legacy "difficult to comprehend."

A much later Ch'an text, the *Record of the Orthodox Lineage of the Dharma Transmission (Ch'uan-fa cheng-tsung chi)* by Ch'i-sung (1007–72), illustrates the traditional story's marginalizing of the *Two Entrances* by relegating it to the sphere of an expedient teaching:

> The phrase "wall-examining Brahman" has come to be a slogan. How could the theory of the four practices be the ultimate of Bodhidharma's path? Now, of Bodhidharma's followers, the closest was Hui-k'o. The next were Tao-fu [i.e., Seng-fu] and Tao-yü. The words of Hui-k'o's generation, which have been transmitted by Ch'an people from ancient times down to the present, have all been made into books, and these abundantly fill the world, but talk of the four practices never was the general view. It is T'an-lin alone who wrote a preface to the four practices. Those in the Ch'an school, however, have always considered T'an-lin ordinary and unworthy of praise. Even though T'an-lin did in fact receive a transmission from Bodhidharma, in my opinion the patriarchal master at the time accorded with T'an-lin's limited karmic propensities and spoke only in terms of expedient devices.[27]

Let us assume that T'an-lin's karmic predispositions were indeed limited, that he could not, as we say, see the forest for the trees. Where would he have gotten his limited, tunnel-vision framework? The answer, of course, is in his specialization, the *Śrīmālā Sūtra*. Let us begin with a brief description of the contents of the *Śrīmālā*. The sutra opens with King Prasenajit of Kośala and his queen, Mallikā, talking together. They think that if their clever daughter Śrīmālā sees the Buddha, she will quickly understand his Dharma, and so they dispatch a letter to her praising the Buddha. Śrīmālā and her retinue do obeisance to the Buddha, and she receives a prediction of Buddhahood.[28]

In the second section Śrīmālā, having received the prediction from the Buddha, stands respectfully and assumes the ten undertakings. All ten begin with the first-person phrase "World-honored One, I from today [*wo ts'ung chin-jih*] until enlightenment" (which is omitted here):

1. toward the precepts received will not raise a thought of transgression.

2. toward those worthy of respect will not raise a disrespectful thought.

3. toward all sentient beings will not raise a hostile thought.

4. toward another's physical looks and external possessions will not raise an envious thought.

5. toward internal and external dharmas will not raise a thought of stinginess.

6. will not for myself receive animals or property, and whatever I do receive will be for ripening poor, suffering sentient beings.

7. will not for myself practice the four methods of bringing beings to the Buddhist path, and for the sake of all sentient beings will without a thought tainted by affection, without a thought of having had enough, without a thought of hindering, embrace sentient beings.

8. if I see sentient beings who are lonely, gloomy, suffering from illness, undergoing various kinds of difficulties and distress, will never even temporarily forsake them. I will necessarily desire to put them at ease and will be indulgent with them and enable them to drop off all their woes. Only afterward will I leave them.

9. if I see the various evil rules involved in the catching and raising of animals and the breaking of the precepts, will never reject the being doing it. When it is within my power and I see these sentient beings at various places, if I should subdue them, I will subdue them; if I should embrace them, I will embrace them.

10. will embrace the true Dharma and never forget it and lose it.

In the third section, in front of the Buddha Śrīmālā makes three great vows:

1. By this true vow I will soothe immeasurable, limitless sentient beings. By these good karmic roots in all rebirths may I attain true Dharma knowledge.

2. After I attain true Dharma knowledge, with an untiring mind may I speak Dharma for the sake of sentient beings.

3. In embracing the true Dharma may I set aside my life and property to protect the true Dharma.

Most of the remaining twelve sections (4–15) are doctrinal in content. We find a reinterpretation of the four noble truths (suffering; cause of suffering; cessation of suffering; and path thereto) and of the voidness (sunyata) of the *Prajñāpāramitā Sūtras* and the Madhyamaka school (dependent origination = sunyata [all dharmas are devoid of essence, neither existent nor nonexistent] = conventional designation = the middle path). The explanation of the profound meaning of the four noble truths, which is subtle and difficult to know, is in the realm of nonthinking. The four truths explain the profound Tathagatagarbha, meaning both Buddha-in-embryo and Buddha-womb. The Tathagatagarbha is the Buddha realm. The locus of the Tathagatagarbha is where the meaning of the noble truths is explained. The Dharma Body of the Buddhas when not free of the store of defilements is called the Tathagatagarbha. Knowledge of the Tathagatagarbha is the voidness knowledge of the Buddhas. There are two aspects to the Tathagatagarbha voidness knowledge: The Tathagatagarbha is devoid of all stores of defilements; the Tathagatagarbha is not devoid of the inconceivable Buddha dharmas. The rebirth process is grounded in the Tathagatagarbha. The intrinsically pure Tathagatagarbha is merely tainted by the adventitious dust of the defilements. The concluding section of the sutra has the Buddha telling Śrīmālā that in past births she has been in the company of millions of Buddhas capable of discoursing on this teaching.

The parallels between the *Two Entrances* and the *Śrīmālā Sūtra* are very striking. First, compare the overall structure of the two. The four practices, the first two of which are explicitly cast in the first person, function as undertakings or vows indicating a dedication to patience in the face of the good and bad effects of karma, and the True Nature, which merely undergoes the unreal covering of adventitious dust, is but another name for the *Śrīmālā*'s Tathagatagarbha. Though the order is reversed, with the *Two Entrances* presenting the True Nature teaching before the four practices, even some of the vocabulary is identical: "adventitious dust," the first-person pronoun, "intrinsic purity," "stinginess," "life and property." Assuming that T'an-lin used both the structure and some of the vocabulary of the *Śrīmālā* in composing his *Two Entrances*, where did he get the terminological polarity "principle" and "practice"?

He borrowed it from the commentarial tradition of sutra exegesis. Though his commentary on the *Śrīmālā* has not come down to us, we do have three Śrīmālā commentaries of T'an-lin's age and a bit later, and they label the ten undertakings, section 2, "practice" (hsing) and the sections on such doctrinal topics as the noble truths, Tathagatagarbha, Dharma Body, voidness, and intrinsic purity, sections 6–13, "principle" (li).[29] The *Record of the Meanings of the Śrīmālā Sūtra (Sheng-man ching i-chi)* of Hui-yüan (523–92) labels the first five sections the "practice Dharma [*hsing-fa*] of the one vehicle" and sections 6–13 the "principle Dharma [*li-fa*] of the one vehicle." Chi-tsang's (549–623) *Precious Cave of Śrīmālā* observes that the first three sections are "mundane practice" (*shih-chien hsing*) and the fourth, "Embracing the Dharma," is "awakening to principle [*li*]—that is, supramundane practice." K'uei-chi's (632–82) *Notes on the Śrīmālā Sūtra (Sheng-man ching shu-chi)* designates the first four sections as "practice" [*hsing*] and 6–13 as "principle of the teachings" [*chiao-li*]. T'an-lin's lost commentary surely made the same basic distinction. When composing his summary of Bodhidharma's teaching, it would have been the most natural thing for him to fall back on this principle-and-practice polarity.

Let us narrow our focus to look at commentarial traditions on the ten undertakings, the core of the practice portion of the Śrīmālā. Chi-tsang's *Precious Cave of Śrīmālā* lays out the comments of five specialists on the ten undertakings, and some of their observations on the structure of the ten sound as if they could be applied to the four practices.[30] T'an-lin is quoted as referring to the undertakings as vows, saying "this section is the ten great vows and after this there is a separate three vows in one." The second master observes that "the first five are for stopping evil and the second five are for producing good." The third master labels the first undertaking "general" and the remainder "differences." The fourth commentator says: "The first nine are the receiving of the precepts of the worldly teaching; in the last one, one obtains the precept of the True Dharma. Prohibitions concerning events are called receiving the precepts of the worldly teaching. Realizing the real and attaining release from faults is called obtaining the precepts of the True Dharma." The fifth master says: "The first five gather up the rules of the disciplinary code; the next four gather up sentient beings; and the last one gathers up the good Dharma."

This Indian-style commentarial world of fine distinctions and classification schemas is a world that T'an-lin knew very well indeed. Of the four practices, perhaps we could say that the first two, requiting injuries and following conditions, are stopping evil, and the last two, seeking nothing and according with Dharma, are producing good. Or we might come up with the formulation that the first three involve the taking of the precepts of the worldly teaching, and the last is the taking of the precepts of the True Dharma. These suggestions are given merely to show that the four practices are woven of the same kind of fabric as the *Śrīmālā*'s undertakings.

First Letter

The identity of the author of the *First Letter* is unknown. One possibility is Hui-k'o, the educated Chinese layman who comes into contact with the foreign meditation master and in time receives his teaching, and nothing in the letter seems to contradict that. Another possibility is T'an-lin, and to some extent the tone of the letter is perhaps more congruent with the career of Armless Lin, the Sanskrit scholar and exegete who becomes involved with the Bodhidharma circle of wall-examining. The letter portrays a dedicated sutra reader in a state of confusion for years who undergoes some sort of transformation through the attainment of meditative concentration and subsequent awakening:

> I really thought that the heavenly mansions were another country and the hells another place, that if one were to attain the path and get the fruit, one's bodily form would change. I unrolled sutra scrolls to seek blessings; through pure practice I [tried to produce karmic] causes. In confusion I went around in circles, chasing my mind and creating karma; thus I passed many years without the leisure to take a rest. Then for the first time I dwelled upright in dark quiescence and settled external objects in the kingdom of mind.

Does "dwelling upright" (*tuan-chü*) refer to "upright sitting" (*tuan-tso*) —that is, cross-legged sitting? It probably does, but it is best not to put too much weight on that assumption. This letter is in a balanced literary style without the slightest hint of a colloquial element. In that sense its tone is drastically different from the *Records*, and thus, in the history of Ch'an literature, far less interesting. At the end of the letter the author states that he will quote a work called *Verses on Devices for Entering the*

Path (Ju-tao fang-pien chi). There are many problems with both this title and the verses themselves.[31] The opening line does not sound like something from T'an-lin's age: "Through cross-legged sitting dhyana, in the end you will necessarily see the Original Nature." This is one of only two occurrences of the term *cross-legged sitting dhyana (tso-ch'an)* in the entire *Bodhidharma Anthology*.

Second Letter

The *Second Letter* is incorporated into Hui-k'o B of the *Continued Biographies of Eminent Monks*. There the author is identified as a forest recluse by the name of Layman Hsiang, and the letter is intended for Hui-k'o. Hui-k'o B follows this letter with Hui-k'o's answer in verse form, which is missing in the *Bodhidharma Anthology*. Nothing more is known of Layman Hsiang.

An eighth-century author suggests a connection between this letter and the two entrances. The *Jewel King of the Buddha-Mindfulness Samadhi (Nien-fo san-mei pao-wang lun)* of Fei-hsi, who advocated a fusion of Pure Land and Ch'an practice, quotes both this letter and Hui-k'o's answer and then makes the following observation: "These two superior masters relied on Great Master Bodhidharma's practice of according with Dharma to exert effort in principle-examination [*li-kuan*]. Both practiced mindfulness on the Dharma-Body Buddha and the highest meaning of the middle path."[32]

Fei-hsi, of course, is making the fusionist case, to Ch'an people of a much later age, that even the fourth practice and wall-examining of their founder Bodhidharma were forms of Buddha-mindfulness, the Pure Land practice. It is nevertheless interesting to think of wall-examining as a form of Buddha-mindfulness (*buddhānusmṛti*) focused on the truth of the highest meaning. This does not sound all that different from the Tibetan tantric interpretation of wall-examining as abiding in the primordial light.

4

Commentary on the *Records*

Record I

Tun-huang manuscript research has retrieved the long-forgotten *Records*, but the question arises: What happened to them? Even if Tao-hsüan, the compiler of the *Continued Biographies of Eminent Monks*, by ignoring them in his Bodhidharma-related entries set the stage for their drop from sight within the Ch'an tradition, it would seem likely they would have at least partially survived somewhere in the vast corpus of Ch'an literature circulating in the T'ang Dynasty. I think they were circulating and were incorporated into the *Collection of Explanations of the Ch'an Source (Ch'an-yüan chu-ch'üan-chi)* of Kuei-feng Tsung-mi (780–841).

Tsung-mi, who practiced cross-legged sitting in the Ch'an style for a decade and was a recognized Ch'an master, spent many years collecting all the works of Ch'an literature for a gigantic compendium intended to serve as a sourcebook for students and prospective teachers of Ch'an— the *Collection of Explanations of the Ch'an Source*. Unfortunately, this compendium is lost. Tsung-mi's scholarship extended well beyond Ch'an literature; we know of many commentaries, essays, compilations, and so forth, and they encompass all genres of Buddhist literature.[1]

Though Tsung-mi's monumental collection has not come down to us, we do have his lengthy and renowned introduction to it, the *General Preface to the Collection of Explanations of the Ch'an Source (Ch'an-yüan chu-ch'üan-chi tu-hsü)*, and through this preface we can envision the structure of the collection: "The order of the present collection: At the beginning I will record Bodhidharma's one thesis; next will come the miscellaneous writings of the various Ch'an houses; and, lastly, I will reproduce the noble teachings [i.e., canonical teachings] that seal [*yin*] the Ch'an theses. As to the noble teachings being placed last, it is analogous to a worldly legal document in which the clerk's decision is first and the honored official's decision last. (Since I have copied only those passages of the sutras and treatises that strike the mark, they will total a little more than ten rolls.)"[2]

The collection was arranged to show the three corresponding levels of the Ch'an theses and the canonical teachings, devoting about ninety rolls to Ch'an texts and ten rolls to canonical sutra and treatise passages "sealing"—that is, providing legitimizing precedents for—the Ch'an theses. The Ch'an portion of the collection was to be a *Ch'an Piṭaka* (*Ch'an-tsang*), an addition to the Buddhist canon's traditional threefold division into discipline, sutra, and scholasticism. And, in fact, Tsung-mi's vision of the place of Ch'an literature within Buddhist literature as a whole eventually did come to pass.

In terms of structure, contents, theme, and size (on the order of one hundred fascicles), Tsung-mi's lost collection sounds a lot like a collection we do have: the *Record of the [Ten-Thousand-Dharmas] Mirror of the [One-Mind] Thesis* (*Tsung-ching lu*) of Yung-ming Yen-shou (903/4–76).[3] The first half of the first fascicle of the *Record of the Mirror of the Thesis* is devoted to making known the essence of the One-Mind thesis. The material from that point through the ninety-third fascicle is a collection of questions and answers, with an enormous number of quotations. The material from the ninety-fourth to the hundredth consists of quotations "sealing" or "verifying" (*yin-cheng*) the contents. At the beginning of the ninety-fourth fascicle Yen-shou states: "Now I will again for the sake of those whose faith power is not yet deep and whose minute doubts are not yet severed further quote one hundred twenty Mahayana sutras, one hundred twenty books of the sayings of the Ch'an patriarchs (*chu-tsu yü i-pai erh-shih pen*), and sixty collections of the worthies and sages—altogether the subtle words of three hundred books."[4]

Based on the similarities, there is a strong possibility that the *Record of the Mirror of the Thesis* is related to Tsung-mi's collection and preserves some of the materials originally gathered by Tsung-mi in T'ang times.[5] Tsung-mi's materials may have been passed down to Yen-shou in a sort of Ch'an transmission of sacred regalia.[6] Since all three *Records* are quoted at length after Yen-shou mentions that he will proceed to quote from one hundred twenty Ch'an sayings books, it is likely that the *Records* were among these Ch'an books.[7]

The ninety-seventh chapter of the *Record of the Mirror of the Thesis* announces that it will explicate the ideas of the Ch'an patriarchs, but it does not commence with the first patriarch in China. It begins with the seven Buddhas of the past, culminating in Śākyamuni. Only Śākyamuni has a saying, which is addressed to his disciple Mahākāśyapa. Yen-shou then proceeds through the twenty-seven patriarchs of India, giving at least a transmission verse for each. We then arrive at the first patriarch of this land of China, Bodhidharmatāra (Yen-shou uses the form of the name known to the Tibetans). After giving a brief account of the encounter of Bodhidharmatāra with his master Prajñātāra in India, a work attributed to Bodhidharmatāra is extensively quoted:

> The Master composed the *Method for Quieting Mind* [*An-hsin fa-men*], which says: "When one is deluded, the person pursues dharmas; when one understands, dharmas pursue the person. When one understands, consciousness draws in forms; when one is deluded, forms draw in consciousness. It is merely that whatever involves mental discrimination, calculation, and [the realm of objects] manifested by one's mind is a dream. If the consciousnesses and thought are calmed, so that there is not a single pulse of thought, it is to be called correct awakening. Question: 'How is [the realm of objects] manifested by one's own mind?' Answer: 'If you see that all dharmas exist, that existence is not existent in and of itself. The calculations of your own mind have created that existence. If you see that all dharmas do not exist, that nonexistence is not nonexistent in and of itself. The calculations of your own mind have created that nonexistence. This extends to all dharmas. In all cases the calculations of one's own mind create existence, and the calculations of one's own mind create nonexistence.' Also, if someone commits all sorts of crimes, when he sees his own Dharma King, he will then obtain liberation. If one obtains his understanding from events, his vital energy will be robust. Those who see Dharma from the medium of events never lose mindfulness anywhere. The vital energy of those who obtain their understanding through the medium of the written word is weak. Events are Dharma. Even if you do all sorts of things, do a dance leap or a horse kick, none of them leaves or enters the Dharma Realm. If you take the [Dharma] Realm to enter the [Dharma] Realm, then you are a stupid person. All behavior, to the end,

does not go outside of the Dharma-Realm mind. Why? Because mind and body are the Dharma Realm. Question: 'Worldly people apply themselves to various sorts of learning. Why do they fail to obtain the path?' Answer: 'Because they see a self, they do not obtain the path. Self means ego. The reason why the accomplished person meets suffering without being sad and encounters pleasure without being happy is because he does not see self. The reason why he knows neither suffering nor pleasure is that he has lost self. When you attain to emptiness, even the self is lost, so what further thing can there be that is not lost?' Question: 'Since all dharmas are void, who cultivates the path?' Answer: 'If there were a who, then it would be necessary to cultivate the path. If there were no who, then it would be unnecessary to cultivate the path. The who is ego. If there were no ego, then, no matter what might come, you would not produce is and is-not. Is is the ego's affirming something; the things are not doing the affirming. Is-not is the ego's negating something; the things are not doing the negating.' Mind is no-mind, and this is comprehending the path of the Buddhas. When in the midst of things you do not give rise to views, it is called comprehending the path. No matter what he meets, he directly understands its source. This person's eye of wisdom is open. The wise one trusts to things and does not trust to self, and so he has neither grasping nor rejecting, neither opposing nor agreeing. The stupid one trusts to self and does not trust to things, and so he has grasping and rejecting, opposing and agreeing. Not seeing one thing is called seeing the path. Not practicing one thing is called walking on the path. Every locus is without locus. This is the locus of Dharma. The locus of making is not a locus of making. There are no dharmas of making, and this is seeing the Buddhas. If you see characteristics, then in every locus you will see demons. By seizing characteristics one falls into a hell. By examining Dharma one attains liberation. If you see [characteristics], remember, and discriminate, then you will suffer from a scalding cauldron, a blazing furnace, and so forth. You will see manifested before you the characteristics of birth-and-death. If you see that the Dharma-Realm nature is the nirvana nature and you are without memory and discrimination, then it is the Dharma-Realm nature. Mind is formless, and so it is not existent. It functions ceaselessly, and so it is not nonexistent. Also, because it functions yet is constantly void, it is not existent. Because it is void and yet constantly functioning, it is not nonexistent."[8]

This entire section is a string of quotations from *Record I*, which Yen-shou calls Bodhidharmatāra's *Method for Quieting Mind*.[9] That certainly suggests the centrality of *Record I* as a Bodhidharma document in Yen-shou's mind at least. There is no quotation from any other work attributed to Bodhidharma, and by Yen-shou's time there were quite a few such works in circulation. There is no mention of the standard slogans attributed to Bodhidharma, nothing about a "mind-to-mind transmission without reliance on the written word" and so forth. Yen-shou, who was active at the time a new Ch'an literature was just coming into being, for a Bodhidharma quotation looked to materials that in his own day must have been considered archaic.

Record I, the Method for Quieting Mind, consists of forty-five sections. The format is both lecture and dialogue. Some sections are fairly lengthy, some only a few lines. One characteristic separates Record I from the Two Entrances, the First Letter, and the Second Letter. The latter are in literary style, and Record I contains quite a few colloquial elements. Record I shows a negative at the end of the sentence, indicating a question; an indefinite expression; a conditional; adverbs; an auxiliary verb; a noun of joined substantives; the second-person pronoun; and an interrogative pronoun.[10]

These colloquial forms should alert us. They are the beginnings of a tendency that culminates in Sung Dynasty Ch'an literature, the most conspicuous characteristic of which is the use of colloquial language. Of course, in that literature the colloquial once again solidifies into a literary language. In fact, the Japanese have from the beginning acted as if the Ch'an literature of the Sung and Yüan Dynasties is a form of literary Chinese.[11]

Record I takes the first big step toward breaking into the colloquial range of the recorded-sayings (yü-lu) genre of Ch'an literature; Record II is on the verge of breaking into that range. The vibrancy, the resonance with the spoken word, tells us more about original Ch'an than T'an-lin's elegant, balanced Two Entrances. These texts tell us of the deepening Sinification of Buddhism, in the sense of a move toward a spoken Chinese form of expression and away from the venerable, but artificial, style of the translation and commentarial traditions, of which T'an-lin is a pre-eminent representative. In fact, here we find an important phase in the development of vernacular literature in China.

What of the teachings of Record I? They are overwhelmingly of the Śūnyavāda, the school of sunyata or voidness. Two Śūnyavāda texts weave their way through Record I, the Vimalakīrti-nirdeśa, a sutra, and the

Middle Treatise (*Chung-lun*), which consists of Nāgārjuna's *Middle Verses* (*Madhyamaka-kārikā*) and a commentary by the Indian Madhyamika Pingala. Not only are these two texts quoted numerous times; their teachings inform a good deal of *Record I*.

The *Vimalakīrti-nirdeśa* in Kumārajīva's translation is nothing less than a masterpiece, full of wordplay and humor.[12] Vimalakīrti is said to be a householder living in the city of Vaiśālī, a city in the heartland of Buddhism that the Buddha frequented. As a device Vimalakīrti gives out that he is sick. The Buddha asks many of the great disciples and others to go and inquire about Vimalakīrti's illness, but none of them dares to do so. The bodhisattva Mañjuśrī eventually acquiesces and with a great retinue of bodhisattvas and disciples enters Vaiśālī. Seeing that they are coming, Vimalakīrti empties (as in sunyata) his room, places only a bed in it, and lies down as if sick. Mañjuśrī enters and sees that the room is void. Vimalakīrti says: "Welcome, Mañjuśrī! You come without any characteristic of coming. Your are seen without any characteristic of seeing."[13] The episodes that follow give life to the teachings on voidness of the *Prajñāpāramitā Sūtras* and the Madhyamaka school. Śāriputra, first of the ten major disciples and the patron saint of the early Buddhist schools, is made fun of on occasion.

The culmination of the sutra is the section on entering the Dharma gate of nonduality. Vimalakīrti tells the assembly of bodhisattvas that each of them should speak on how the bodhisattva enters the Dharma gate of nonduality. Numerous bodhisattvas do so, ending with Mañjuśrī. This scene echoes through the *Records*. The sutra says: "Mañjuśrī said: 'According to my opinion, in all dharmas there are neither words nor speech, neither showing nor knowing. It is free of all questions and answers. This is the Dharma gate of nonduality.' At that time Mañjuśrī asked Vimalakīrti: 'Each of us has spoken and now you should do so. What is the bodhisattva's entering the Dharma gate of nonduality?' Vimalakīrti was silent, wordless. Mañjuśrī exclaimed: 'Good! Good! Even to there being neither the written nor spoken word—this is truly entrance into the Dharma gate of nonduality.'"[14]

Record I focuses on several themes from the *Vimalakīrti-nirdeśa*:

a. One does not cut off the defilements of greed, hostility, and stupidity to enter nirvana.

    b. Dharma as well as all dharmas do not have speech, showing, knowing.

    c. The essence of anything is neither internal, nor external, nor in the middle.

    d. All dharmas are the site of enlightenment; whatever you are doing is the site of enlightenment.

    e. Bodhisattvas are in the midst of the rebirth process but do not reject it, are in the midst of views but unmoved.

    f. Bodhisattvas show covetousness and craving but remain uncontaminated.

    g. The true path involves discriminating neither false nor true.

    h. Silence, no answer.

Record I opens with a verse from the *Middle Verses* of Nāgārjuna. It is a well-known verse and sets the tone: "Buddhas speak of void dharmas in order to destroy views, but if you are in turn attached to voidness [as a view], you are one whom the Buddhas cannot transform."[15] The *Middle Treatise* commentary on this verse is instructive: "The great sages in order to destroy the sixty-two views of the non-Buddhist schools, ignorance, and such defilements as craving and so forth preach voidness. If someone reifies voidness as a view, he is untransformable. It is analogous to a sick person's need to take medicine to effect a cure. If the medicine itself becomes a pathogen, no cure can be accomplished. If fire emerges from firewood, with water it can be extinguished. If the water catches fire, what can be used to extinguish it? Voidness is like water. It can extinguish the fire of the defilements." The words of *Record I* are simply an antidote to views, ignorance, and the defilements. Voidness itself is void, devoid of essence, own-being, own-nature. If one treats voidness as an essential property and holds that all dharmas possess this essential property, nothing can be done, for he is incurable.

    Record I contains one saying attributed to Bodhidharma (section 8): "Tripiṭaka Dharma Master (*san-tsang fa-shih*) says: 'When one does not understand, the person pursues dharmas (*pu-chieh shih jen chu fa*); when one understands, dharmas pursue the person (*chieh shih fa chu jen*). When one understands, consciousness draws in forms; when one is deluded, forms draw in consciousness.'" Yen-shou's lengthy quotation from the *Method for Quieting Mind* in his *Record of the Mirror of the Thesis* even begins with this saying, and it was incorporated into a number of later Ch'an texts. It has a plausibility as a Bodhidharma utterance lacking in anything found in the *Two Entrances*. One can, for instance, easily imagine the Indic terms: *dharma* and *pudgala* (dharmas and person); and *rūpa* and *vijñāna* (forms and consciousness). The first pair is well known from the formula of the nonself of both dharmas and the person (*dharma-pudgala-nairātmya*). In any case, this saying is likely to garner more votes as an authentic Bodhidharma saying than any phrases in the *Two Entrances*. With it we may be hearing an initial hint of the stress on the self-reliant person in the rhetoric of later Ch'an literature. The unrealized being chases after the void things of the everyday world, but the void things of the world chase after the realized being.

Record II

    Record II truly constitutes the beginnings of the recorded-sayings genre of Ch'an literature. There is a direct line from this work to the vast literature of Ch'an recorded sayings, and neglect of *Record II* has led us to place the beginnings of the recorded-sayings genre much too late in the history of Ch'an literature—usually in the ninth century. *Record II*'s eighteen sections seem to break naturally into three parts. Sections 50–56 center on Master Yüan; sections 57–62 center on Hui-k'o; and sections 63–67 provide miscellaneous dialogues. We could dub *Record II* the *Recorded Sayings of Yüan and Hui-k'o*. The miscellaneous dialogues at the end seem removed from the Yüan and Hui-k'o portions. In any case, attention here will be exclusively on the first two portions.

    Colloquial usage is considerably more intense here than in *Record I*; the second-person colloquial pronoun crops up again and again, giving some of the dialogues a directness and vividness unequaled by the talk or lecture style of *Record I*. Many other colloquial forms appear: an adverb, a passive construction, a form strengthening the negative, interrogative adverbs, a first-person-singular pronoun, an indefinite expression, an intensive, an interrogative pronoun, and a nominal suffix.[16] This colloquial dynamic reaches an apex in one of the Master Yüan sections (54). Some of the sentences in *Record II* are reasonably close to modern Chinese and with a few changes could be read aloud and understood on a street in China today.

Every biographical source up to this point has suggested that after Bodhidharma the most important figure in the proto-Ch'an tradition is his disciple Hui-k'o. This is the case with T'an-lin's treatment of the Dharma Master's career in the *Biography* and with the relevant entries of Tao-hsüan's *Continued Biographies of Eminent Monks*. Nowhere in these two is there any mention of a master by the name of Yüan, variously called Dharma Master and Dhyana Master. Even when we search through the *Continued Biographies of Eminent Monks*, we find no biographical entry for him, nor any mention of his name in another's entry. He is a cipher in the traditional story of Ch'an's origins and likewise in modern scholarship on Ch'an, but he is the outstanding figure in *Record II* and *Record III*, where he rivals Hui-k'o or even the founder Bodhidharma. Yüan is a lost link of early Ch'an, and it is worthwhile to try to bring him back into the picture.

Who is this Yüan? We do not know, and we will never know, but below I will list him as one of Bodhidharma's disciples. We might call him a forgotten Bodhidharma disciple, or at the very least a forgotten member of the Bodhidharma circle. He was probably erased from the genealogical tree in order to clear the way for Hui-k'o as the sole successor, much like Seng-fu. The culprit may have been the historian Tao-hsüan, who seems to be the figure determining much of the ultimate direction of Ch'an genealogical lore. Beyond Yüan's compelling words— and they are, with little doubt, the most compelling in *Record II* and *Record III*—about all that can be said of him is that his name is fascinating.

His name is a Buddhist technical term. The Sanskrit would be *pratyaya* (condition). Related expressions include *idaṃpratyayatā* (this-conditionality) and *pratītya-samutpāda* (dependent origination). Perhaps we could call him "Master Conditioned," his name suggesting the profound teaching of conditionality, which must be seen and understood or one remains in samsara. The name thus merits attention. A later Ch'an text, entitled *On Cutting off Examining* (*Chüeh-kuan lun*), is a dialogue between a disciple named Gate-of-the-Conditioned (Yüan-men) and a master named Entrance-into-Principle (Ju-li). The master's name derives from the entrance by principle of the *Two Entrances*, and Master Entrance-into-Principle is clearly a literary creation standing in for Bodhidharma. The name of the disciple, Gate-of-the-Conditioned, may be a literary representation of Master Yüan.[17]

The opening exchange in *On Cutting off Examining* seems to be a variant on the quieting-mind dialogue of *Record II* (section 58): "Thereupon Master Entrance-into-Principle was silent, wordless. Gate-of-Conditioned suddenly arose and asked Master Entrance-into-Principle: 'What is mind, and what is quieting mind?' Answer: 'You need not set up mind, and you do not need to exert yourself in quieting it. That is called quieting.'"[18] *On Cutting off Examining* may have been compiled by someone familiar with the legacy of Master Yüan, perhaps even someone in a Master Yüan lineage.

The Master Yüan sections of *Record II* are true Ch'an question-and-answer encounters (*wen-ta*) between practitioners. Later Ch'an literature is filled with such encounters, but it is startling to see them in such an early text and in such a developed form. One section of *Record I* (22) is so close in phraseology and tone to section 55 that it should be designated a Master Yüan section as well. This would mean that Master Yüan appears in all three *Records*, suggesting a very high level of importance in the Bodhidharma circle or its aftermath. Master Yüan, not Hui-k'o or Bodhidharma, is the key to the *Records* as a whole.

Yüan (section 50) speaks of escaping karma—the force of the effects of intentional actions in this and past lives that binds one to the wheel of the rebirth process—through a singularity, an act of will: "When you are on the verge of seizing a lofty sense of willpower [*jo yü-ch'ü yüan-i shih*], bondage and habit energy will surely melt away." He is iconoclastic, consistently criticizing reliance on the Dharma, reliance on teachers, reliance on meditative practice, reliance on canonical texts. Faith in Buddhist teachings and teachers, praxis according to the traditional rules, and learning in scripture lead to nothing but self-deception and confusion. From this stance Master Yüan never budges. His relentless boldness prefigures much in the stance of the full-blown Ch'an tradition.[19]

He does speak positively of one thing. He calls it "bodily energy" (*t'i-ch'i*) or "spirit" (*ching-shen*). The first is a general term for physical strength, and the latter is found in classical Taoist texts, the *Chuang Tzu* and the *Lieh Tzu*, where it means the spirit or mind associated with Heaven, and in medical works, where it means vim, vigor, or stamina. This is not the only classical Taoist terminology he employs, for he says that if one evinces even the slightest desire to advance in religious training, "ingenious artifice" (*ch'iao-wei*) gains the upper hand. This term also comes from the *Chuang Tzu*. Energy and spirit are all a practitioner needs (sections 51 and 55–56):

> If you have bodily energy, you will avoid the deceptive delusions of people and Dharma, and your spirit will be all right. Why? Because when you esteem knowledge, you are deceived by men and Dharma. If you value one person as correct, then you will not avoid the deceptive confusions of this person.... If you desire to cut off crafty artifice, don't produce the thought of enlightenment and don't use knowledge of the sutras and treatises. If you can accomplish this, then for the first time you will have bodily energy. If you have spirit, do not esteem understanding, do not seek Dharma, and do not love knowledge, then you will find a little quietude.... If you can understand that intrinsically there is neither quiescence nor disturbance, then you will be able to exist of yourself. The one who is not drawn into quiescence and disturbance is the man of spirit.

Does this make Master Yüan a Taoist rather than a Buddhist? Hardly. He can more convincingly be portrayed as a Chinese who learned from Bodhidharma or the Bodhidharma circle and cast what he learned in Chinese terms or as a Chinese Vimalakīrti, right down to the silence. In the following passage (section 54) we find the same *Vimalakīrti* theme found in *Record I*, that expounding Dharma lacks both expounding and explaining: "A certain person asked Master Yüan: 'Why do you not teach me the Dharma?' Answer: 'If I were to set up a Dharma to teach you, it would not be leading you. If I were to set up a Dharma, it would be deceiving you; it would be failing you. If I had a Dharma, how could I explain it to someone else? How could I speak of it to you? It comes down to this: If there are terms and written words, all of it will deceive you. How could I tell you even a mustard seed's worth of the meaning of the great path? If I could speak of it, what purpose would that serve?' When asked again, [Master Yüan] did not reply."

The jewel of *Record II*—in fact, the jewel in the crown of the *Records* as a whole—is an encounter between Master Yüan and Master Chih in the market street of a town somewhere in North China (section 52): "Dharma Master Chih saw Dharma Master Yüan on the street of butchers and asked: 'Do you see the butchers slaughtering the sheep?' Dharma Master Yüan said: 'My eyes are not blind. How could I not see them?' Dharma Master Chih said: 'Master Yüan, you are saying you see it!' Master Yüan said: 'You're seeing it on top of seeing it!'"

The Buddhist disciplinary code, of course, prohibits monks from even witnessing such things as the grisly scenes found in the stalls of butchers, but more is going on here than a simple violation of the disciplinary code. This is very close to the atmosphere of the later recorded-sayings genre, particularly to those dialogues that involve testing and discriminating levels of understanding or, as it is often phrased, determining guest and host. Master Yüan is presumably hinting that Master Chih has not only viewed the butchering of sheep but has put viewing the violation of the disciplinary code on top of that. He has reified both the scene and the violation, piling view upon view, and it is the destruction of views, among other things, that gains one freedom from the wheel of rebirth in the Buddhist vision. In this encounter clearly Master Yüan is the host, Master Chih the guest. In the very next section, Master Chih asks Yüan how one should view, and Yüan replies that he has nothing to do with any sort of view. This is applied Śūnyavāda, the annihilation of all views and hence the road to liberation.

The next six sections of *Record II* (57–62) seem to be a series of questions asked of Hui-k'o by disciples, though Yen-shou's *Record of the Mirror of the Thesis* attributes the last of these to Master Yüan and by doing so suggests linkage between Yüan and Hui-k'o.[20] *Record II*'s juxtaposition of the two blocks of Yüan and Hui-k'o dialogues itself suggests such a connection. These Hui-k'o sections show much the same characteristics as the previous portion of *Record II*: a strong dose of colloquial language and the influence of the *Vimalakīrti-nirdeśa*. The *Vimalakīrti* theme here is that dharmas cannot be characterized as high or low, going or coming, big or small. Dharmas are *śūnya*: void, zero, neither existent nor nonexistent, the middle way between the extremes of it-is-ness and it-is-not-ness. Extremes of any kind—pleasure/asceticism, eternalism/annihilationism, and so forth—lead to rebirth on the samsaric wheel, but the middle way is the way to freedom from the wheel.

Two of the Hui-k'o sections (58 and 59) allow us to see how some of the *Record II* material was recycled in later Ch'an literature. They are two parallel dialogues in which anonymous disciples ask the master to quiet mind and administer confession. The first runs: " 'Teach me, your disciple, to quiet mind.' Answer: 'Bring your mind here and I will quiet it for you.' Also: 'Just quiet mind for me!' Answer: 'This is like asking a craftsman to cut out a garment. When the craftsman obtains your silk, then he can for the first time set his cutting tool to work. At the outset, without having seen the silk, how could he cut out the pattern from space for you? Since you are unable to present your mind to me, I don't know what mind I shall quiet for you. I certainly am unable to quiet space!'" The second runs: "'Administer confession to me, your disciple.' Answer: 'Bring your sins here, and I will administer confession to you.' Also: 'Sins lack any characteristic of form that can be apprehended. I [don't] know what to bring!' Answer: 'My administration of confession to you is over. Go to your quarters.'"

The first may be two versions of one encounter or two separate encounters, perhaps even one encounter and commentary. The transmission record *Patriarchal Hall Collection*, published in 952, inherits both of these Hui-k'o dialogues. It makes the first an exchange between Bodhidharma and Hui-k'o, at which Hui-k'o has his great awakening, and it turns the second into an exchange between Hui-k'o and the traditional story's "third patriarch," Seng-ts'an.[21] Thus, by the tenth century at least, and probably well before that time, the two dialogues were stripped of their *Record II* context—an interaction between Hui-k'o and anonymous disciples—and provided with a new one: the standard patriarchal transmission for the first three generations, Bodhidharma to Hui-k'o to Seng-ts'an.

Very shortly thereafter we find these two dialogues of *Record II* in the *Recorded Sayings of Ch'an Master Fen-yang Wu-te* (*Fen-yang Wu-te ch'an-shih yü-lu*), which seems to have been first published during the lifetime of Fen-yang (947–1024), who is in the sixth generation of the Lin-chi lineage. The middle fascicle of this recorded-sayings book consists of three case (*kōan*) collections of one hundred cases each. It is a precursor of the case literature, the earliest example we have of that genre.[22] The very first case of the first collection, entitled "Praises of the Ancients" (*sung-ku*), is a fusion of *Record II*'s two dialogues:

> The second patriarch asks Bodhidharma: "Please, Master, quiet my mind." Bodhidharma says: "Bring your mind here and I will quiet it for you." The patriarch says: "I am searching for my mind but, in the end, cannot apprehend it." Bodhidharma says: "My quieting of your mind is over."
>
> Nine years facing a wall waiting for the appropriate encounter
> Standing in snow up to his waist without raising an eyebrow
> Respectfully requesting the Dharma of quieting the mind ground

Searching for mind but not apprehending it—for the first time no
doubts.[23]

Now we have commentary in the form of a four-line verse. The same
case shows up in the thirteenth-century case collection entitled *No-Gate
Checkpoint* (*Wu-men kuan*), and here the commentary on the reworked
proto-Ch'an material is growing closer to the sphere of belles lettres.
Here is the *No-Gate Checkpoint's* version as its forty-first case:

> Bodhidharma is facing a wall. The second patriarch, standing in the snow,
> cuts off his arm and says: "The mind of your disciple is not yet quieted. I
> beg you, Master, to quiet my mind." Bodhidharma says: "Bring your mind
> here and I will quiet it for you." The patriarch says: "I am searching for
> my mind but, in the end, cannot apprehend it." Bodhidharma says: "My
> quieting of your mind is over."
>
> Wu-men says: "The toothless old foreigner sailed thousands of miles
> just to come here. We might say that in spite of a lack of wind, waves
> were stirred. In the end he got one disciple, but that was the cripple
> [armless Hui-k'o]. Ha! Hsieh San-lang didn't even know one character be-
> yond the three of his name."
>
> Verse:
>
> He came from the West and directly pointed to mind.
> Disturbance broke out due to entrusting Dharma to his successor.
> The one who threw the Meditation Hall into confusion
> Was you from the outset![24]

Here we are immediately struck by the humorous prose commentary
added by the compiler of the *No-Gate Checkpoint*, Wu-men Hui-k'ai (1182–
1260). The toothless old foreigner Bodhidharma and his disciple the crip-
ple Hui-k'o are striking images, much more striking than the image of
the tailor cutting a piece of silk in the *Record II* version. Of course, in
some circles such literary tendencies would completely gain the ascendancy and strangle the practical side of such teaching devices as the case
and topic.

Record III

Record III is a collection of sayings, not dialogues.
Eschewing the question-and-answer mold, it consists of sayings of nu-

merous masters, many with the title Dhyana Master. Some sayings seem to be followed by commentary, often including one or more sutra quotations. The one exception to this format is a dialogue between Tripiṭaka Dharma Master, Bodhidharma, and an unnamed scholiast (section 80). Commentary is not marked as such, and it is impossible to be certain where a saying ends and commentary begins. Here the Tibetan translation in the *Dhyāna of the Enlightened Eye* is useful in at least attempting to determine a line between saying and commentary. *Record II* and *Record III* overlap significantly in their selection of masters, and, as mentioned earlier, the division between these two is problematic judging from the manuscripts and should not be overemphasized.

Record III shares with *Record II* three names: Master Yüan; Hui-k'o; and Dharma Master Chih, the associate of Master Yüan who challenges Yüan on the street of the butchers. The other names of *Record III* are unknown, but from information gleaned from biographical entries in the *Continued Biographies of Eminent Monks* we can make guesses about the identity of several of them, and these guesses mesh with the content of the sayings in question. Before proceeding to those guesses, let us draw up a genealogical tree based on the disciples mentioned in Hui-k'o B of the *Continued Biographies of Eminent Monks* and on surmises about Master Yüan's line (see figure 1).

The lineage descending from Dhyana Master Ho is a Three-treatises (San-lun) tradition.[25] The central texts of this wing of the Three-treatises tradition or Chinese Madhyamaka are the *Prajñāpāramitā Sūtras*, the *Vimalakīrti-nirdeśa*, the *Nirvāṇa Sūtra*, the three treatises of Nāgārjuna, of which the core is the *Middle Treatise*, and the gigantic commentary on the *Twenty-Five Thousand Prajñāpāramitā Sūtra* entitled *Great Perfection of Insight Treatise* (*Ta chih-tu lun*) and attributed to Nāgārjuna. These works underlie much of *Record III*. The five names in boldface type in the genealogical tree are possible identifications for the abbreviated names (frequently only half of a monk's name is used in our sources; e.g., Hui-k'o is referred to as K'o and T'an-lin as Lin) of four of the masters of *Record III*. Given that the content of those sayings is in fact Madhyamaka in flavor, *Record III* might be called, at least in its first portion, a repository of the Madhyamaka legacy of Hui-k'o. Let us try to fill in some of the details of that legacy from biographical entries in the *Continued Biographies of Eminent Monks*.

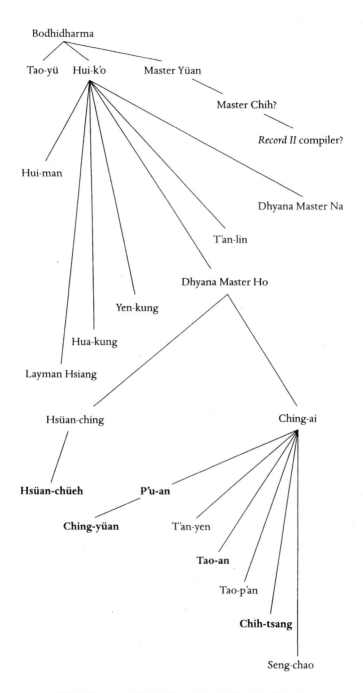

FIGURE I. A BODHIDHARMA LINEAGE CHART

It is probable that the founder, Dhyana Master Ho, was active in North China before 550 and died during the 570s.[26] He was a lecturer, and his specialization was the *Prajñāpāramitā Sūtras* and the *Vimalakīrti-nirdeśa*. Though he engaged in ascetic practices, they were probably not as severe as those of his fellow students under Hui-k'o: Dhyana Master Na, who had one robe and one bowl; and Hui-man, who discarded his extra garments during the summer and barely covered his nakedness. Dhyana Master Ho's disciple Ching-ai (534–78) lectured on the four treatises of Nāgārjuna.[27] At the time of the Chou Dynasty suppression of Buddhism in the 570s, which caused T'an-lin to flee, Ching-ai hid out in the Chung-nan Mountains outside the capital Ch'ang-an with more than thirty of his disciples. His students were associated with Madhyamaka studies, dhyana, and ascetic practices. Thus we seem to have a fusion of Bodhidharma's wall-examining and Madhyamaka.

P'u-an (530–609), who "constantly worked at the *Hua-yen Sūtra*" during the Chou suppression, hid in the Chung-nan Mountains and "led Dharma Master Ching-yüan to stay together with him in the forests and fields."[28] Tao-an "venerated the *Nirvāṇa Sūtra*" and "had an extensive knowledge of the *Great Perfection of Insight Treatise*."[29] Chih-tsang (541–625) in the face of the Chou suppression took up residence among the common people.[30] He "took the *Great Perfection of Insight Treatise* as the pinnacle of words." Hsüan-chüeh was a disciple of Hsüan-ching (d. 606). Hsüan-ching had studied the *Twenty-Five Thousand Prajñāpāramitā Sūtra* and the *Vimalakīrti-nirdeśa* under his master, Ho; at the time of the Chou suppression he hid away in the forests and practiced meditation.[31] He is also said to have attained to visions of the bodhisattva Maitreya. His disciple Hsüan-chüeh lectured in the capital Ch'ang-an on the Mahayana and was famed for his grasp of the *Mañjuśrī Prajñāpāramitā Sūtra*.[32]

Five of these names are relevant to sayings in *Record III*: Ching-yüan; Chih-tsang; P'u-an and Tao-an; and Hsüan-chüeh. Dhyana Master Yüan of the opening section of *Record III* (section 68) may be Ching-yüan; the Dharma Master Tsang of 69 may be Chih-tsang; the Dhyana Master An of 71 may be either P'u-an or Tao-an; and Dhyana Master Chüeh of 74 may be Hsüan-chüeh. The commonalties of this group are: studies of the *Great Perfection of Insight Treatise*, the *Prajñāpāramitā Sūtras*, the *Nirvāṇa Sūtra*, and the *Vimalakīrti-nirdeśa*; attention to dhyana practice; some asceticism; and experience with the Chou suppression of Buddhism. All were active in the last decades of the sixth century and the first decades of the seventh, which suggests how very old some of the material in *Record III* may be. In *Record III*, it should be noted, the frequency of colloquial usages lessens drastically.[33] The reason for this reduction is unclear, but is likely to be of significance.

All four of the sayings in question are consistent with the Madhyamaka background of the above figures. The opening saying of *Record III* is classic Madhyamaka: "Dhyana Master Yüan says: 'If you know that all dharmas are ultimately void, then knower and known are also void; the knowing of the knower is also void; and the dharmas that are known are also void. Therefore: "Dharmas and knowing are both void; this is called the voidness of voidness." Therefore, the *Buddha Store Sūtra* says: "The Buddhas of the past preached that all dharmas are ultimately void. The Buddhas of the future will preach that all dharmas are ultimately void."'" "Voidness of voidness" refers to the teaching that taking voidness as a view rather than as the relinquishing of all views makes a being untransformable. Thus this opening saying of *Record III* makes exactly the same point as the opening saying of *Record I*, the sayings in both cases setting the tone for what is to come. In the case of the other three sections, the themes are equally those of Madhyamaka: No dharma can be apprehended; the person who has long walked the path is not examining voidness any further; mind is not connected to any dharma; and so forth.

The exchanges between Tripiṭaka Dharma Master, Bodhidharma, and the deluded one (sections 79–80) are about voidness as the middle between the two extreme views of it-is-ness and it-is-not-ness. The deluded one holds that the six consciousnesses create the defilements of greed, hostility, and stupidity. Bodhidharma responds that the defilements seem to arise but that in fact, from the perspective of the truth of the highest meaning, there is no arising. The deluded one emphasizes that dharmas do conventionally exist and charges that Bodhidharma is entertaining a nihilistic voidness, one that denies the existence of dharmas in the conventional sense—that is, denies the everyday world of convention. Bodhidharma responds that the defiled six consciousnesses are the locus of enlightenment. Two citations from the *Vimalakīrti-nirdeśa* follow, making the points that the pearl is obtained in the sea of defilements and that sentient beings are in Buddha lands. It is likely that the *Vimalakīrti* citations are the work of a commentator, and the choice of the *Vimalakīrti* is consistent with the Śūnyavāda slant of the *Records* as a whole.

Hui-k'o has only one saying in *Record III* (section 82): "Because common men lack understanding, they say that the past differs from the present and say that the present differs from the past. Furthermore, they say that, apart from the four elements [of earth, water, fire, and wind], there is in addition the Dharma Body. When you understand, the five aggregates right now are the perfect, pure nirvana, and this body and mind are endowed with the ten thousand practices. Truly, this is proclaimed as the great thesis. If you have such an understanding, you see the bright, pure pearl in the sea of defilements, and you are capable of illuminating the darkness of all sentient beings in radiance."

This saying appears in Yen-shou's *Record of the Mirror of the Thesis* as the saying for the second patriarch, the Great Master K'o, in the list of the seven Buddhas of the past, the twenty-seven patriarchs of India, and the six patriarchs of China, showing its importance for the standard patriarchal lineage.[34] It seems to be echoing a passage in the *Chao Treatise* of Seng-chao, the very famous early Madhyamika.

The one saying for Master Yüan in *Record III* (section 90) reinforces his image as a Chinese Vimalakīrti: "Dhyana Master Yüan says: 'All the sutras and treatises are dharmas that produce mind. If you produce a mental focus on the path, then ingenious artifice will give rise to knowledge and a complement of events. If mind is not produced, what need is there for cross-legged sitting dhyana? If ingenious artifice does not arise, why toil over right mindfulness? If you do not raise the thought of enlightenment and do not seek insight and understanding, then you will exhaust both phenomena and principle.'" This is the only mention of cross-legged sitting dhyana (*tso-ch'an*) in the *Records* as a whole, and it turns out to be rhetorical. Its locus classicus is the *Vimalakīrti-nirdeśa*, where the Buddha sends off his disciple Śāriputra to inquire about Vimalakīrti's illness, and Śāriputra responds:

World-honored One! I dare not go to him to inquire about his illness. Why? I remember I was in the past in the midst of the forest practicing quiet sitting beneath a tree. At the time Vimalakīrti came up to me and said: "This sitting is not necessarily quiet sitting. Now, quiet sitting is to manifest neither body nor thought in the three realms. That is quiet sitting. Manifesting all deportments without rising from the extinction samadhi is quiet sitting. Manifesting all the affairs of the common man without setting aside the Dharma of the path is quiet sitting. When the mind abides neither internally nor externally, that is quiet sitting. When one practices the thirty-seven limbs of enlightenment while being immobile in the midst of views, that is quiet sitting. When one enters nirvana without cutting off the defilements, that is quiet sitting. If you can sit in this way, you are one who is sealed by the Buddhas."[35]

If Master Yüan is the Vimalakīrti figure who explains that the physical act of sitting in cross-legged posture is not necessarily quiet sitting, that quiet sitting is the nonproduction of thought, then who is Śāriputra, the literalist addicted to sitting in cross-legged posture deep in the forest? He had to be others in the Bodhidharma circle who reified cross-legged sitting beneath a tree. They had succumbed to what Yüan calls "ingenious artifice" and lost the meaning of Bodhidharma's coming from the West.

By asking what is the need for the (very gradual) mediation of the practice of sitting for the practitioner who is in no-thought, Yüan becomes, in the parlance of the later Ch'an tradition, a representative of the all-at-once or immediate teaching of the Southern School, the Ch'an analogue of the Mahayana, and those in the Bodhidharma circle to whom his rhetoric was directed become representatives of the inferior step-by-step or gradualist teaching of the Northern School, the analogue of the Hinayana. This would make the sixth patriarch Hui-neng, the founding hero of the Southern School and the most famous name in the traditional story of Ch'an after that of Bodhidharma, a descendant in rhetoric of Master Yüan, for, echoing Yüan, Hui-neng in the *Platform Sūtra of the Sixth Patriarch* (*Liu-tsu t'an-ching*) says: "In this teaching 'sitting' means without any obstruction anywhere, outwardly and under all circumstances, not to activate thoughts."[36] Hui-neng is portrayed in the traditional story as illiterate, very young, and not even fully Chinese by birth—all characteristics that would place him in a position of inferiority to Shen-hsiu, the learned, elderly, and accomplished champion of the Northern School. The *Records* show us that the Hui-neng of the traditional story is an exemplar of one who is free of Master Yüan's "ingenious artifice."

Appendix A

....

The Stratigraphy of the
Tun-huang Ch'an Manuscripts

What Japan and the West know as Zen literature consists of records of the sayings and dialogues of the masters, biographical transmission-of-the-lamp records, case collections providing topics for meditation practice, detailed codes for the regulation of the community's everyday life, rules for cross-legged sitting in the Zen style, poetic inscriptions, various versions of the ox-herding pictures that illustrate the stages of practice in terms of herding an ox, poetry collections, and lineage charts. A host of Japanese monks who made the pilgrimage to China in order to train there and a handful of eminent Chinese monks who ventured to Japan to aid in the spread of Ch'an carried this literature in printed form to Japan during the Southern Sung and Yüan Dynasties, the thirteenth and fourteenth centuries. Let us refer to this literature as "neo-Ch'an" literature, on the model of the term *neo-Confucianism*.

The discovery in the early part of this century of a small, walled-up cave within the Mo-kao Grottoes located outside the oasis town of Tun-huang in Northwest China has led to the retrieval of a lost early Ch'an literature of T'ang Dynasty times (618–907). This hidden subcave, usually known as cave no. 17, was found to be stuffed to the ceiling with Buddhist manuscripts and art.[1] It had been sealed up around 1000 C.E., but no one knows for certain why. Some have suggested that pious Buddhists wished to save the contents from the destructive fury of invaders.

The most likely reason, however, is connected to technological advance. In China proper the new technology of printing was quickly embraced by the Buddhists to spread their message and reached the backwater Tun-huang about the year 1000. Once printed canons replaced the old manuscript copies in the libraries of the Tun-huang monasteries, something had to be done with the manuscripts. They could not simply be discarded, since, paper being at a premium, that might lead to the profane use of sacred materials. The answer was to protect them by placing them in a small, subsidiary cave and walling it up. This cave seems to have remained undisturbed until modern times, and the arid climate of the extreme Northwest preserved the contents. Soon after it was opened, rumors spread. In little time a steady stream of European and Japanese teams arrived and carried off much of its contents to the libraries of their countries.

In the decades following, a cadre of East Asian scholars scanning the major European, Chinese, and Japanese collections of Tun-huang manuscripts found manuscripts bearing Ch'an works no one had heard of.[2] These works were not part of the neo-Ch'an corpus; indeed, they could not be, for they had been lost before that corpus was assembled and printed. In time, microfilms and catalogues of the major collections became available and facilitated further discoveries of lost Ch'an texts, principally by Japanese scholars. This process of discovery has continued down to recent years, and there is the possibility that still more manuscripts will turn up. However, in spite of decades of editions and studies, the implications of these Ch'an manuscripts as a whole for the study of the origins of Ch'an have not yet been fully appreciated.

About three hundred Chinese manuscripts relating to Ch'an have so far been discovered in the Tun-huang collections.[3] Many are fragments of scrolls, and we have a number of scrolls bearing the same works. The total number of separate works included in these manuscripts is roughly one hundred, and it is from these one hundred titles that a list of the earliest works must be extracted. Though three hundred manuscripts may sound like a large number, it is a remarkably small percentage of the Tun-huang "library," which amounted to tens of thousands of Chinese and Tibetan manuscripts, as well as a very small number in Central Asian and Indic languages.

These three hundred manuscripts are, in the main, the informal scrolls of individuals, apparently executed for private use.[4] They appear to have functioned as the memoranda of private individuals (in "private hands").

Many have the look of quick copies, quite erratic and sometimes even sloppy. Most utilize the verso of a manuscript. In numerous cases we find various Ch'an texts copied out in a continuum. These characteristics point to the conclusion that they were not part of any formalized monastic curriculum in the Tun-huang monasteries. For unknown reasons they found their way into cave no. 17 along with the much larger remains of one or more monastic libraries, which are in the steady, and sometimes elegant, hands of standard-style professional scribes. We must try to resist unconsciously shoehorning these manuscripts into the scenario of neo-Ch'an literature. Codicology, which focuses on such aspects as the type of paper and writing instrument, the spacing of the columns, handwriting styles, and recto texts (usually official documents with a date), can give us a good idea of when a manuscript was copied. By isolating those texts on manuscripts that appear to have been copied earliest and by double-checking for what little evidence of dating we find in the texts themselves, we can find our way to a tentative list of the earliest texts.

Codicological work by a Japanese scholar outside the field of Zen studies distributes Ch'an manuscripts into three chronological strata:

1. 750–780, a period during which Chinese cultural influence still held sway at the remote oasis center
2. 780s to c. 860, the period of Tibetan occupation of Tun-huang and its aftermath, during which Tun-huang's cultural fabric was severed from that of China
3. the 900s, when Tun-huang was brought once again under Chinese rule by a powerful local Chinese family; sometimes referred to as the Return-to-Righteousness Army period in reference to the victorious local Chinese army; in spite of Tun-huang's being in Chinese hands once again, the cultural link to China proper was not fully restored.[5]

Tibetologists, principally Japanese, working on the European Tun-huang collections in recent decades have turned up Tibetan manuscripts relating to Ch'an, so that we now have over forty fragmentary manuscripts of this type.[6] The history of Tun-huang plainly tells us when the Tibetan Ch'an manuscripts were copied: either during the period of Tibetan occupation or perhaps during its immediate aftermath, when use of the Tibetan language and script must have lingered in the former colony even though the Tibetan administration had disappeared. Tibetan Ch'an lore has also survived in another form: in two Rdzogs-chen texts from central Tibet.[7] The Rdzogs-chen (Great Perfection) is a branch of the Rnying-ma-pa (Ancient School), which flourished in Tibet and Tibetan-controlled areas during the late eighth and ninth centuries. The new Indian traditions that took hold in Tibet from the tenth century onward did not consider it a fully authentic expression of Buddhism. In fact, the orthodox scholastics of the new schools held that Rdzogs-chen was utterly contaminated by the heretical teachings of Chinese Ch'an. Of the two Rdzogs-chen texts with Ch'an material, one is a recently discovered copy of a block print from eastern Tibet, and the other is a literary treasure (gter ma), a well-known genre of Tibetan literature. The latter purports to be an eighth-century text hidden away in central Tibet and rediscovered in the fourteenth. Both the Tibetan Tun-huang manuscripts and the two Rdzogs-chen books are useful in the study of early Ch'an texts because they provide us with Tibetan translations of portions of at least nine of those texts, including the anthology translated in this volume. Neither students of early Ch'an nor Tibetologists interested in early Tibetan Buddhism can afford to ignore this corpus.

Political and cultural influence from the Chinese center was strongest at Tun-huang during the Sui and T'ang Dynasties down to the time of the An Lu-shan Rebellion (755–763). In spite of the turbulence aroused in North China by the rebellion, Chinese cultural influence at the oasis must have remained more or less intact down to the Tibetan conquest. The second- and third-stratum materials came into being when Tun-huang was quite remote from China and thus when the Central Asian crossroads character of the oasis was dominant. The Tibetan Ch'an manuscripts serve to remind us how much, particularly during the Tibetan occupation period, the religion of Tun-huang was the religion of the Silk Road and therefore how it must be approached as part of a continuum extending across the Western Region to such distant places as the city-state of Kucha. One of the characteristics of the Buddhism of this continuum was a receptivity to both Indian and Chinese currents. This was a truly eclectic environment, so it should come as no surprise that its Buddhism was not purely Chinese.

At least in some cases, what was being copied during the two centuries of the Tibetan period and the Return-to-Righteousness Army period in the numerous monasteries of Tun-huang and among lay Buddhists in the area would have been conditioned by an Inner Asian atmosphere. Consequently, we should consider the possibility that at least some of the second- and third-stratum manuscripts represent documents of not a purely Chinese Ch'an but rather a Chinese Ch'an transmuted into an Inner Asian Ch'an.[8] This scenario, of course, has far-reaching implications when we use the Tun-huang Ch'an manuscripts to reconstruct the literary history of Ch'an. Since they may not be altogether representative of what circulated in China proper, we may be drawn into some sort of archival fallacy.

This danger is probably smallest in the case of the first stratum, manuscripts from which are generally on thin, high-quality hemp paper similar to that used in the areas of the imperial capitals of China proper. This fact suggests at least a residual cultural link to the Chinese heartland. The middle-stratum manuscripts, on the other hand, are on thick, coarse paper in larger sheets, and the Chinese brush has been replaced by the Tibetan-style wooden pen—both paper and pen being local products. This shift is only natural since Tun-huang in the late eighth century was cut off from China and hence from a supply of brushes and high-quality hemp paper. The third-stratum manuscripts are on the same sort of large, coarse, thick paper that appeared in the wake of the Tibetan conquest and that continued to be used after the Tibetans in turn had been ejected by Chinese forces. The use of local writing materials suggests that the pool of Ch'an texts found on the last two strata may derive from the local religious situation. At any rate, these strata are less likely than the first to directly reflect developments in the Buddhist world of China, so we should use them more cautiously in reconstructing such developments.

The first stratum of Ch'an manuscripts, those copied between about 750 and 780, clearly bears the earliest texts. Though we cannot be certain of the length of the time lag between their compilation in China proper and their copying at the remote outpost Tun-huang, or the copying in North China and transportation into Tun-huang, internal evidence in two of them indicates compilation dates in the early eighth century. Most of them were probably compiled in the late seventh and early eighth centuries and copied at Tun-huang some decades later. Here is a list of texts that are found on manuscripts classified as early stratum.[9] With some confidence we can say that these are among the oldest Ch'an books available to us:

1. The three *Records* of the *Bodhidharma Anthology*[10]
2. *Former Worthies Gather at the Mount Shuang-feng Stūpa and Each Talks of the Dark Principle* (*Hsien-te chi yü shuang-feng shan t'a ko t'an hsüan-li*)
3. *Treatise on Perfect Enlightenment* (*Yüan-ming lun*)
4. *Essentials of Cultivating Mind* (*Hsiu-hsin yao lun*)
5. *On Examining Mind* (*Kuan-hsin lun*)
6. Three short treatises attributed to the fifth- to sixth-century figure Seng-ch'ou: *Dhyana Master Ch'ou's Idea* (*Ch'ou ch'an-shih I*); *Dhyana Master Ch'ou's Medicinal Prescription for Curing the Outflows* (*Ch'ou ch'an-shih yao-fang liao yu-lou*); and *Treatise on the Mahāyāna Mind-Range* (*Ta-ch'eng hsin-hsing lun*)
7. *Record of the Transmission of the Dharma Treasure* (*Ch'uan fa-pao chi*; datable to sometime after 713)
8. *Record of the Laṅkā Masters and Disciples* (*Leng-chia shih-tzu chi;* datable to 719–20)[11]

Some of these texts continued to be copied at Tun-huang in the subsequent two periods, but others did not. This means that the copying of certain very early texts went on at Tun-huang long after it had ceased in China proper, so here lies part of the secret of the value of the Tun-huang manuscripts for early Ch'an studies.

The second stratum, those manuscripts copied during the subsequent Tibetan-occupation period, probably reflects Tibetan interests and tastes, at least when viewed from the perspective of China proper. These manuscripts and the Tibetan Ch'an manuscripts are both written on the same sort of coarse paper and often with the same instrument, the Tibetaṇ wooden pen, an instrument somewhat less elegant than the Chinese brush—the equivalent of a ballpoint rather than a fountain pen. The fusion of Chinese and Tibetan Buddhist culture during this period is nowhere more evident than in a Chinese Ch'an text written in the horizontal Indian palm-leaf style introduced by the Tibetans, and in another Chinese Ch'an text laboriously spelled out in Tibetan transliteration.[12] Middle-stratum manuscripts constitute a major portion of all the Chinese Ch'an manuscripts so far discovered in the collections, certainly many more than those of the first stratum.

Here is a list of Chinese Ch'an texts on manuscripts classified as middle stratum and a selection of Tibetan Ch'an-related manuscript materials, which are of the same era. For convenience, abbreviated and tentative titles are often used here and below. The Chinese portion of the list includes only texts that appear for the first time in the middle stratum; that is, it excludes those that have already appeared on the early-stratum list. The Tibetan list is simply a tentative survey of a diffuse and fragmentary literature.

CHINESE

1. *On Cutting Off Examining* (*Chüeh-kuan lun*) under the name of Bodhidharma
2. Three works attributed to Shen-hui: *Platform Talks* (*T'an-yü*); *Treatise on Settling Is and Is-Not* (*Ting shih-fei lun*); and *Meaning of the Verifications of Shen-hui's Dialogues* (*Wen-ta tsa-cheng I*)
3. *Treatise on All-at-Once Awakening to the True Thesis* (*Tun-wu chen-tsung lun*)
4. *Essential Judgments on All-at-Once Awakening to the True Thesis* (*Tun-wu chen-tsung yao-chüeh*)
5. *Judgments on the True Principle of All-at-Once Awakening to the Mahāyāna* (*Tun-wu ta-ch'eng cheng-li chüeh*)
6. Collections of verses and songs such as *Lines on Understanding the Nature* (*Liao-hsing chü*); *Revolution of the Five Watches of the Night in Which the Southern School Settles the False and the Correct* (*Nan-tsung ting hsieh-cheng wu-keng chuan*); and *Difficulties in Traversing the Path* (*Hsing-lu nan*)
7. A "Ch'an sutra": *Ch'an Gate Sūtra* (*Ch'an-men ching*)
8. *Record of the Dharma Treasure through the Generations* (*Li-tai fa-pao chi*; datable to sometime after 775)[13]

TIBETAN

1. *Master Mo-ho-yen's Ch'an All-at-Once Entrance Gate* (*Mkhan po Ma-ha-yan gi bsam gtan cig car 'jug pa'i sgo*)
2. *Explanation of the Essence of Ch'an by Master 'Gal-na-ya* (*Mkhan po 'Gal-na-yas bsa[m] gtan gi snying po bshad pa'*)
3. Untitled sayings of Ch'an masters
4. *Treatise on Ch'an* (*Bsam brtan gyi lon*)

5. *Insight Luminosity* (Gsal ba shes rab)

6. *The Dharma of Quieting Mind of Ch'an Master Hsiang-mo Tsang* (*Bsam gtan kyi mkhan po Bdud-'dul-kyi-snying-po'i sems bde bar gzhag pa'i chos*; may be a translation of a lost Chinese original entitled *Hsiang-mo Tsang ch'an-shih an-hsin fa*)

7. *The Dharma of Quieting Mind of Ch'an Master Wo-lun* (*Bsam gtan gyi mkhan po Nyal-ba'i-'khor-lo sems bde bar bzhag pa'i* [*chos*]; may be a translation of a lost Chinese original entitled *Wo-lun ch'an-shih an-hsin fa*)

8. Translation of a section of the Chinese *Judgments on the True Principle of All-at-Once Awakening to the Mahāyāna* (no. 5 above)

9. Translation of part of the Chinese *Record of the Laṅkā Masters and Disciples* (no. 8 in the early-stratum list)

10. Translation of the Chinese *Essential Judgments on All-at-Once Awakening to the True Thesis* (no. 4 above)

11. Translation of a portion of the "Ch'an sutra" *Thunderbolt Samādhi Sūtra* (*Chin-kang san-mei ching*)[14]

The third stratum, those materials copied during the tenth century, seem out of China proper's Ch'an orbit. We find none of the texts that at that time in China were becoming the mainstream of neo-Ch'an literature. A summary of the texts found on manuscripts classified as third stratum runs as follows:

1. *Ch'an Master Bodhidharma's Method of Examining* (*P'u-t'i-ta-mo ch'an-shih kuan-men*)

2. *Ch'an Master Bodhidharma's Treatise* (*P'u-t'i-ta-mo ch'an-shih lun*)

3. *Treatise on No-Mind* (*Wu-hsin lun*)

4. Shen-hui's *All-at-Once Awakening to Non-arising Insight Songs* (*Tun-wu wu-sheng pan-jo sung*)

5. *Five Teaching Devices of the Mahāyāna* (*Ta-ch'eng wu fang-pien*), and others of the teaching-devices series

6. *Treatise on the Mahāyāna Northern School* (*Ta-ch'eng pei-tsung lun*)

7. *Ten Questions on the Ch'an Plan* (*Ch'an-ts'e shih-tao*)

8. *Ch'an Master Wo-lun's Gazing-at-Mind Dharma* (*Wo-lun ch'an-shih k'an-hsin fa*)

9. *Essential Judgments on the Ch'an Secret* (*Ch'an-men pi yao-chüeh*)

10. Praises, meditations for the five watches of the night, and songs

for the hours of the day such as the *Twelve Poems on the Ch'an Gate* (*Ch'an-men shih-erh shih*)

11. *Verses of Ch'an Master Wo-lun* (*Wo-lun ch'an-shih chi*)
12. Vajrayana-related works such as the *Mahāyāna Medicinal Checkpoint* (*Ta-ch'eng yao-kuan*)
13. *Sagely Descendants Collection* (*Sheng-chou chi*; datable to 899)[15]

It is clear from the above list that during the tenth century Ch'an literature at Tun-huang was isolated from new developments in China, which were concentrated in far-away South China. These new developments hinge on a break in the Ch'an textual tradition in the late ninth century due to political disturbances and social destruction in North China. What survived was edited and printed in the great monastic centers of South China, supplemented by a vast array of new compilations, and eventually carried to Japan. This is neo-Ch'an literature. In the isolated oasis town, on the other hand, those doing the copying continued reproducing T'ang texts that were no longer circulating in China, and Ch'an continued to mix with Indian esoteric Buddhism, which had long been moribund in China.[16] Cave no. 17 serves as a magnificent fossil repository for the study of early Ch'an literature. It has given us the beginnings of Ch'an literature.

Appendix B

··

Toward a Literary History
of Early Ch'an

Neo-Ch'an generated many lineage charts, and the genealogical urge has never subsided. A Zen encyclopedia published in Japan in 1979 contains a lineage chart starting with Śākyamuni Buddha that in small print goes on for almost fifty pages.[1] Such charts are necessary for a school of Buddhism that claims to silently transmit Buddha Mind from generation to generation, each generation sealing the enlightenment of the next. In search of the first step toward a literary history of early Ch'an, let us draw up lineage charts for texts—the *Biography* and *Record II/Record III*—rather than for a founding patriarch, as has always been the case.[2] And instead of providing a string of names with attached biographies, let us line up a string of textual quotations. We can watch the quotations and the characters therein develop and grow. Here, then, is the first half of a chart:

T'an-lins's *Biography*

|

Bodhidharma entry and Hui-k'o A in Tao-hsüan's *Continued Biographies* (645)

|

Record of the Transmission of the Dharma Treasure (post-713)

|

Annals of the Laṅkā Followers and Their Dharma
(the lost *Leng-chia jen-fa chih*; post-708–9)

|

Record of the Laṅkā Masters and Disciples
(719–20; incorporated much of the above *Annals*)

|

Record of the Dharma Treasure through the Generations
(*Li-tai fa-pao chi*; shortly after 775)

|

Transmission of the Treasure Forest (*Pao-lin chuan*; 801)

|

Sagely Descendants Collection (899)

|

Patriarchal Hall Collection (952)

|

Record of the Transmission of the Lamp of the Ching-te Era (*Ching-te chu'an-teng lu*; 1004)

FIGURE 2.

Now let us look at a lineage chart for *Record II* and *Record III*:

Vimalakīrti-nirdeśa's bodhisattva sayings on nonduality

|

Record II and *Record III*

|

*Former Worthies Gather at the Mount Shuang-feng Stūpa
and Each Talks of the Dark Principle*

|

Sayings of the Great Laṅkā Masters in *Record of the Laṅkā Masters and Disciples*

|

Sayings of Wu-chu in the *Record of the Dharma Treasure through the Generations*

|

Essentials of Mind Transmission (*Ch'uan-hsin fa yao*)
and *Wan-ling Record* (*Wan-ling lu*) by the layman P'ei Hsiu

|

Sung Dynasty neo-Ch'an recorded-sayings literature

FIGURE 3.

The *Biography* and *Records* are patriarchal ancestors of the two main genres of Ch'an literature: the transmission records, which are not histories but do utilize the biographical (*chuan*) format of the secular histories; and the recorded-sayings books, which are ultimately traceable in format to the *Analects* of Confucius (*Lun-yü*), a seemingly informal record of conversations and actions of the master designed to catch his personality rather than provide a statement of his doctrine. Ch'an literature broke with the inherited Indian Buddhist literary genres—the formal or scientific treatise (sastra) and the systematic commentary (*bhāsya, vṛtti,* etc.)—and reverted to native genres, but remained faithful to the Indian Buddhist content. The *Biography* and *Records* are utterly Buddhistic in thrust and utterly Chinese in genres, style, and language patterns. This is the beginning of the great achievement of Ch'an literature, one not found in other Buddhist cultures, except for those on China's periphery, such as the Korean, Japanese, and Vietnamese, and thus within the cultural sphere of Chinese Ch'an.

Our focus is on the genealogical tree of *Record II* and *Record III*. These are the successors to the ninth chapter of the *Vimalakīrti-nirdeśa*, the sayings of the various bodhisattvas on nonduality. Just as in the case of Bodhidharma, the *Vimalakīrti* is the Indian who becomes the first patriarch of China, the first patriarch of the recorded-sayings genre. Whereas the linguistic format of the two *Records* is either question and answer (*wen-ta*) or such-and-such master says (*yüeh*), that of the *Vimalakīrti* is such-and-such bodhisattva says (*yüeh*) until we reach the crescendo of Vimalakīrti's silence. Here are the sayings of two of the bodhisattvas in the *Vimalakīrti*:

Lion Bodhisattva says: "Sin and merit are dual. If you comprehend the natu e of sin, then it is no different from merit. With the thunderbolt wisdom you come to understand that these characteristics have neither bondage nor liberation. This is entrance into the Dharma gate of nonduality." Lion-Mind Bodhisattva says: "Having the outflows and having no outflows are dual. If you apprehend all dharmas, then you will not produce a thought of either the outflows or no outflows. Do not be attached to characteristics and do not abide in no-characteristics. This is entrance into the Dharma gate of nonduality."[3]

The masters of the *Records* are also bodhisattvas speaking on nonduality. Here is Chih, the associate of Master Yüan, in *Record III* (section 87):

> Dhyana Master Chih says: "All dharmas are Buddha dharmas; that is the so-called Dharma eye. All behavior and activities are enlightenment. Following mind, you will go straight to the path of the Buddhas. Do not be alarmed. Do not be frightened. All loci are equal."

The successor of these two *Records* is a rather strange, small text entitled *Former Worthies Gather at the Mount Shuang-feng Stūpa and Each Talks of the Dark Principle*, a collection of sayings (each with the same introductory verb, *yüeh*, as *Record III*) for twelve figures at an imaginary memorial gathering for the "fifth patriarch" Hung-jen at his stupa on Mount Shuang-feng just north of the Yangtze River in Hupeh. It is a very brief recorded-sayings text but lacks any colloquial forms and is designed to provide a particular slant on the genealogy of the embryonic tradition:

> Monk Pārśva says: "The teachings of the canon are to be taken as commentary on the mind ground. Sit silently in empty fusion."
>
> Aśvaghoṣa Bodhisattva says: "Mind is the same as space. Space is no mind. This mind is also that way."
>
> Dhyana Master Ch'ao says: "The correct and incorrect are equally usable."
>
> Dhyana Master Buddha says: "The extreme principle is wordless. The sagely mind is unimpeded."
>
> Reverend K'o says: "Correct mindfulness is uninterrupted and intrinsically pure."
>
> Superior Man Yü says: "Realize the real and lose objects. Quiet anxieties and have no thought."
>
> Master Min says: "When mind is pure without anxieties, Dharma will spontaneously appear."
>
> Dhyana Master Neng says: "The mind range is sameness, uniformity, and without admixture."
>
> Dhyana Master Hsien says: "Correct thoughts so that they do not arise. Concentration and insight are to be used equally."
>
> Master Tao says: "Stimulating thoughts is bondage. No thought is release."
>
> Dhyana Master Tsang says: "Empty deception does not exist, yet it is real. But it is still not the locus in which to rest mind." Also: "When one enters meditation, one corrects thoughts and objects. When one exits from meditation, one examines illusions and reflections."
>
> Dhyana Master Hsiu says: "In the pure locus gaze at purity."[4]

Here we have Indian patriarchs. It is said that Pārśva's name ("lying on one's side" or "slouching") came from his zeal in practice: he never lay down on his side.[5] Note that his saying refers to the practice of sitting. Aśvaghoṣa was known in China as the author of the treatise entitled *Awakening of Faith in the Mahāyāna* (*Ta-ch'eng ch'i-hsin lun*). As in the case of Pārśva, the content of the Aśvaghoṣa saying is significant. It emphasizes space, calling to mind the *Awakening of Faith*, which teaches that in a state of enlightenment the very substance of mind is equal to space.[6]

The fourth worthy, Dhyana Master Buddha, was the teacher of Seng-ch'ou, whom Tao-hsüan compared to Bodhidharma in his critique of meditation styles at the end of the section on meditation practitioners in his *Continued Biographies of Eminent Monks*. Dhyana Master Buddha was the first head of Shao-lin Monastery on Mount Sung outside the capital Lo-yang at its founding in the late fifth century. He is in the slot where we would expect to find Bodhidharma, perhaps suggesting some sort of blurring of the two names. His saying brings to mind entrance by principle, and, in fact, the great compendium *Record of the Mirror of the Thesis* attributes entrance by principle to a Dhyana Master Buddha rather than to Bodhidharma.[7] Reverend K'o and Superior Man Yü are Hui-k'o and Tao-yü, respectively—the two disciples of Bodhidharma according to T'an-lin. Those familiar with the succession as it is presented in the traditional story will note the presence of one of the most famous names in Ch'an, the "sixth patriarch" Hui-neng, and his opponent in the verse duel of the *Platform Sūtra of the Sixth Patriarch*, Shen-hsiu. However, this document clearly antedates the creation of that polarity, for there is no hint of an all-at-once/step-by-step duel.

In the patriarchal lineage of the recorded-sayings genre the next generation is a text we might provisionally entitle *Sayings of the Great Laṅkā Masters*. It does not exist independently, and the title is simply provisional and for the sake of convenience. The *Record of the Laṅkā Masters and Disciples*, one of the two earliest transmission records extant, contains entries for the seven generations of the succession. Due to its Laṅkāist tendencies, it places Guṇabhadra as the first patriarch and Bodhidharma as the second, the Guṇabhadra rendering of the *Laṅkāvatāra Sūtra* being the one favored in Laṅkāist circles. Each of the entries for the seven generations ends with a section of sayings introduced by the phrase "the

Great Master says" (ta-shih yün). In general these sayings differ in style from the rest of the transmission record.

The sayings for the first two generations, Guṇabhadra and Bodhidharma, refer to their making inquiries about things or pointing to things and asking their meaning.[8] These contain minimal colloquial elements. The sayings for the next three generations (the standard sequence of Hui-k'o, Seng-ts'an, and Tao-hsin) are hardly noteworthy and lack any colloquial patina. By far the most colloquial sayings are for the sixth and seventh generations, Hung-jen and Shen-hsiu. These sayings sections may have circulated as an independent work; perhaps they were a part of the earlier and now lost Annals of the Laṅkā Followers and Their Dharma, much of which was incorporated into the Record of the Laṅkā Masters and Disciples.

The colloquial vocabulary of the Hung-jen sayings, particularly the second-person pronoun, is strongly reminiscent of Record II and Master Yüan. The format of the Sayings of the Great Laṅkā Masters, the master doing the questioning or making the statement devoid of any response on the part of disciples, is close to Record III. Let us look at the Hung-jen material:

> The Great Master says: "There is a one-person house that is all filled with shit, weeds, and dirt. What is it?"
> Also: "You have swept away the shit, weeds, and dirt and tidied things up so that there is not one thing. What is it?"
> Also: "When you are doing sitting, on a level surface sit with your back straight, broadly loosen body and mind, and at the distant horizon gaze at the one character [or the single horizontal stroke of the character 'one']. You will make spontaneous progress. For novices caught up in a throng of objective supports, gaze at the one character within the mind. When doing sitting after realization, the impression is like that of being located on a solitary, tall mountain in the midst of a broad field. You are sitting on exposed ground at the top of the mountain and gazing off into the distance on all four sides. It is limitless. When doing sitting, broadly loosen body and mind to fill up the world and abide in the Buddha realm. The pure Dharma Body is limitless. The impression is also like this."
> Also: "When you are right in the midst of realizing the Dharma Body, who is experiencing that realization?"
> Also: "A Buddha has the thirty-two marks. Does a jug also have the thirty-two marks? Do soil, wood, tiles, and stones also have the thirty-two marks?"

Also, he would take fire tongs, one long and one short, display them, and ask: "Which is long and which short?"

Also, when he would see someone lighting memorial candles or doing the many things of everyday life, he would always say: "This one is creating a dream, performing the art of sleight of hand." Or he would say: "Without doing anything or performing anything, every single thing is the great, complete nirvana."

Also: "Understand that arising is a nonarising dharma. It is not that there is a no-arising apart from arising dharmas. Nāgārjuna says: 'No dharma arises from self; no dharma arises from another; neither from both self and other; nor without cause. Therefore, we know they are nonarising.' If dharmas arise from conditions, they lack essence. If they lack essence, how could these dharmas exist? It is also said: 'In space there is neither a middle nor an end. The body of the all the Buddhas is also like this.' My sanctioning of your clear vision of the Buddha Nature is precisely this."

Also: "When you are right in the midst of doing cross-legged sitting dhyana inside the monastery, is your body also doing sitting dhyana beneath the trees in the mountains? Are all soil, wood, tiles, and stones capable of doing sitting dhyana? Are soil, wood, tiles, and stones also capable of seeing forms and hearing sounds, putting on a monk's robe and taking up a begging bowl?" The *Laṅkā Sūtra*'s speaking of the "Dharma Body of objects" is precisely this.[9]

The Shen-hsiu sayings are:

The Great Master says: "The *Nirvāṇa Sūtra* says: 'One who expounds well the one character is called a master of the rules of discipline.' That line appears in the sutra, but realizing it lies within the mind."

Also: "Is this mind an existent mind or not? What kind of mind is it?"

Also: "Are the forms that you see existent forms or not? What kind of forms are they?"

Also: "Do you hear the sound of the striking of the bell? At the time of its striking, does the sound exist? Before the striking does the sound exist? What kind of sound is the sound?"

Also: "Does the sound of the striking of the bell exist only within the monastery? Does the sound of the bell also exist throughout the worlds of the ten directions?"

Also: "'The body extinguishes, but the shadow does not extinguish.' 'The bridge flows, but the water does not flow.' In the method of my teaching everything comes down to the two words *substance* and *function*.

This is called 'the gate of twofold profundity.' It is also called 'turning the wheel of Dharma.' It is also called 'fruit of the path.'"

Also: "Before you see, you see, and when you see, you see it over again."

Also: "The *Necklace Sūtra* says: 'The bodhisattva is illuminating and quiescent, a Buddha quiescent and illuminating.'"

Also: "A mustard seed enters Mount Sumeru, and Mount Sumeru enters a mustard seed."

Also: When he saw birds fly by, he would ask: "What is that?"

Also: "Are you capable of doing cross-legged sitting dhyana on the tip of a dangling tree branch?"

Also: "Are you capable of passing directly through a wall?"

Also: "The *Nirvāṇa Sūtra* says: 'There is a Limitless Body Bodhisattva. He comes from the east.' Since the bodhisattva's bodily measurements are limitless, why does he come only from the east? Why doesn't he come from the west, the south, the north? Maybe it is impossible."[10]

In all three of the *Records* cross-legged sitting dhyana (*tso-ch'an*) is mentioned only once, in a saying of Master Yüan that states that it is unnecessary if one has already achieved the state wherein thoughts do not arise. But here it is a frequent topic. Now we have Shen-hsiu, so famous in the traditional story as the champion of the inferior gradualist teaching, asking if it can be practiced on the tip of a dangling tree branch. If the practitioner answers yes, he will fall and perhaps die. If he answers no, he is going against the practice. How is he to respond?

Perhaps we find a similar dilemma in the fifth case of the case collection *No-Gate Checkpoint*: "The master Hsiang-yen said: 'It is like a person up in a tree. He holds a tree branch in his mouth, without seizing a branch with his hands or planting his feet on one. Below the tree there is someone who asks the meaning of Bodhidharma's coming from the West. If he does not respond, he is evading the person's question, and if he responds, he will lose his life. At a time like that how does one respond?'"[11] Tracing such literary motifs across time may tell us more than would an exclusive focus on when Shen-hsiu left home for the Buddhist life, when he took up residence here or there, who wrote his funerary inscription, and so forth.

Next we come to the sayings of Wu-chu, which constitute a substantial portion of the late eighth-century transmission record entitled *Record of the Dharma Treasure through the Generations*. Here is a dialogue between

Wu-chu and a large group of officials attached to the imperial armies of Szechwan:

> One day when the Master was drinking tea, thirty secretaries and imperial functionaries of the military government happened to come by for an audience. Having taken their seats, they inquired: "The Master has a great liking for tea." The Master said: "It is so." He then recited from the *Verses on Tea*:
>
>> "Luminous plants grow in dark valleys,
>> Fit to be a catalyst for entering the path.
>> Mountain dwellers pick the leaves,
>> And the exquisite flavor flows into cups.
>>
>> In the quietude it settles false thoughts,
>> And the enlightened mind illuminates the platform of
>>   understanding.
>> Without expenditure of human energy and strength,
>> Immediately the Dharma gate swings open."
>
> The secretaries at this point asked: "Why does the Master not teach people to read the sutras, practice Buddha-mindfulness, and engage in forms of worship? We disciples do not understand." The Master said: "I have realized the ultimate of nirvana, and I teach people to do likewise. I do not utilize the incomplete teachings of the Tathagata. I send around self-liberation in order to awaken novices. They are already people who have attained true samadhi." Having finished speaking, the Master was stern and immobile. The secretaries and functionaries in unison said: "There has never been such a thing!"[12]

What is noteworthy here is not the teachings content, the Pao-t'ang ("Protect the T'ang Dynasty") house's jettisoning of all Buddhist praxis, or the language patterns. It is the scene. This is the earliest example we have of a tea-drinking scene as the background for a Ch'an dialogue.[13] In neo-Ch'an literature it is quite commonplace. Also, the disciples being treated to tea are part of the military establishment, a situation that parallels the later relationship between the renowned master Lin-chi I-hsüan and a powerful military figure in the Northeast. The recorded-sayings genre is beginning the process of coming out of the cloister and meeting a variety of laypeople of the secular world.

The next generation in the recorded-sayings lineage is the *Essentials of Mind Transmission* and *Wan-ling Record* for the ninth-century Ch'an master Huang-po Hsi-yün of Hung-chou in the South. The initial compiler P'ei Hsiu (797–870) stands between two famous figures of Ch'an, Tsung-mi and Huang-po. In his writings Tsung-mi carried on a consistent critique of the teachings of Huang-po's Hung-chou house. P'ei served Tsung-mi as a devoted lay disciple until the latter's death in 841, wrote prefaces to a number of Tsung-mi's works, and composed the master's funerary inscription.

P'ei never diverged from his deep admiration for Master Mi, though, within a year of the death of the master, he was stationed in the South and sought out Huang-po. P'ei was known for his literary talent and his calligraphy, as well as for a devotion to Buddhism so deep that many scorned it as excessive.[14] From his middle years onward he was a vegetarian, constantly involved with Buddhistic practices, and the bearer of a Dharma name. He was the perfect fusion of active official, learned scholar, calligrapher, and Buddhist practitioner—a fusion that calls to mind what Tsung-mi might have become had he not decided upon a Ch'an career. P'ei states in the preface to this Huang-po record:

> In Hui-ch'ang 2 [842] when I was stationed as an examiner in Chung-ling, I invited the master to come down from Mount Huang-po and proceed to the prefectural seat in order to take up residence at Lung-hsing Monastery. Morning and evening I questioned him about the path. In Ta-chung 2 [848] when I was stationed as an examiner in Wan-ling, I again went to politely ask the master to come to the prefectural seat and peacefully dwell at the K'ai-yüan Monastery. Morning and evening I received his Dharma. I retired to write it down. I recorded but one or two of ten things he said. I have worn this as a mind seal and have not dared to publicize it. But now I fear that the essential meaning of the spiritual master will not be heard by future people, and consequently I have taken it out and handed it over to his monk disciples, T'ai-chou and Fa-chien. They returned to Kuang-t'ang Monastery on the old mountain, Huang-po, and asked the venerables and monks of the Dharma assembly whether there are discrepancies between it and what they personally heard many times in past days.[15]

This preface, dated 857, is the earliest account we have of the compilation of a recorded-sayings book. P'ei's notes, which were probably quite simple and short, involved two encounters with Huang-po.[16] Today's two texts are in fact the result of the work of monk disciples on Mount Huang-po who contributed their own notes and edited the whole.

It is significant that the core was the product of a layman. In this case the lay world went into the cloister and brought back the beginnings of a book. It is also significant that the *Wan-ling Record*, which was not independent in the beginning, is not directed toward practicing Ch'an monks but is an exposition of Ch'an for laypeople.[17]

The *Essentials of Mind Transmission* and *Wan-ling Record* became very popular among the scholar-officials (*shih ta-fu*) of the subsequent Sung Dynasty and in the warrior society of Kamakura and Muromachi Japan.[18] One of the Hōjōs, military rulers in Kamakura times, is said to have had a copy at his side as he practiced cross-legged Zen sitting.[19] This recorded-sayings text spoke to more than just Ch'an monks. Because of its theoretical cast and freedom from technicalities appropriate to Ch'an monks it attracted general readers with an interest in Ch'an.

Let us look at one passage from the *Essentials of Mind Transmission*:

Question: "How can one not fall into the fifty-two stages of the bodhi-sattva?" The master says: "Merely eat your rice all day long without chewing a grain of it. Walk all day long without stepping on a bit of ground. Then there will be no characteristics such as self and person. Though all day not divorced from the everyday world, he is not deluded by objects. Such a one is called the self-existent person. Moment after moment he sees no characteristics at all. Do not recognize the three times of past, present, and future. The past has not gone; the present is not here; and the future will not come. To quietly sit cross-legged and trust fate without getting caught up is called liberation. Strive! Strive! Of the thousands of followers of this method of ours only four or five can manage this. If one doesn't think about this, the day will come when he is visited by calamity. Therefore, it is said: 'By exerting effort in the present life you must settle the matter. Who can afford to be visited by a surplus of calamities for many eons?'"[20]

Here are two passages from the *Wan-ling Record*:

Minister P'ei asked the master: "Of the four to five hundred people in the mountain here with you, how many have obtained your Dharma?" The master said: "The number of those who have obtained it can't be fathomed. Why? The path lies in awakening in the mind. How could it have to do with words and speech? Words and speech are just things used to tell children what to do." ... Question: "Will it be all right if one traverses this path in the no-mind mode?" The master says: "No-mind is traversing this path. What is this superfluous talk about whether it will be all right or not? For example, in a case where you momentarily produce just one thought, immediately there will be sense objects. If you are without even one thought, immediately sense objects will be forgotten. When mind spontaneously extinguishes, there is nothing more to be pursued."[21]

The underlying themes in both of these works can be found in the *Records*: Dharma is speechless; seeing characteristics is tantamount to seeing demons; insight cannot be shown through speech; delusion about the realm of objects leads to self-deception; those who do not understand say that the past differs from the present and the present differs from the past; have nothing to be apprehended in traversing this path; and so forth. Minister P'ei's recorded-sayings book for Huang-po has brought the *Records* to stylistic fulfillment.

It is an understatement to say that the Sung Dynasty recorded-sayings literature is enormous, and when we add those recorded-sayings works compiled in the subsequent Yüan and Ming Dynasties, the volume is simply staggering. The *Manji Continued Buddhist Canon (Manji zokuzō)*, which was published in Japan early in this century, in its section containing separate records lists well over two hundred titles, some consisting of many fascicles.[22] It turns out that in the long run those who championed silent transmission of Buddha Mind published many more words than did the doctrinal schools of Buddha Word.

From this vast sea of neo-Ch'an recorded-sayings texts let us pluck one Sung Dynasty work, the *Recorded Sayings of Ch'an Master Fen-yang Wu-te*. As mentioned earlier, the recorded-sayings collection of Fen-yang (947–1024) is of extraordinary importance in the history of Ch'an literature, since it contains the earliest case collection we have. One of its most fascinating cases is found in the first of the three collections contained in the middle fascicle. It centers on the T'ang Dynasty figures Minister P'ei Hsiu and Huang-po. This P'ei Hsiu case deserves quotation, if only to suggest the processes, the conventions, by which some cases were built up. Here we have a hilarious pun playing off the quieting-mind (*an-hsin*) case between Bodhidharma and the second patriarch Hui-k'o found as the first case in the same collection.[23] The quieting-mind exchange of *Record II* has surfaced once again, this time as a play on words. The word *an* ("quieting") happens to be part of the term for the assigning of a Dharma name (*an-ming*) after one has received the precepts:

> Minister P'ei brought in a Buddha image. He knelt before Huang-po and said: "Please, master, give me a Dharma name" [or "Please, master, quiet name"]. Huang-po called out: "P'ei Hsiu!" Hsiu responded: "Yes!" Huang-po said: "My giving you a Dharma name is over" [or "My quieting name for you is over"]. P'ei thereupon bowed.
>
> > Before the master he knelt and asked for the giving of a Dharma
> > name [or asked for quieting name].
> > Suddenly out of the blue [the master] gave a shout.
> > If not for Minister P'ei, who would have dared to respond?
> > Immediately it caused the deaf and blind to hear.[24]

In this case the topic for meditation (*hua-t'ou*), which according to neo-Ch'an pronouncements is to be "held up" twenty-four hours a day no matter what the practitioner is doing, is clearly P'ei's immediate verbal response to being called by Huang-po. "Yes!" does not quite catch it. It is the sound one makes upon receiving a question or an order from a superior, very much like the Japanese *hai!* or *hā!*

Now let us examine one of Fen-yang's dialogues:

> The master was doing sitting in his private quarters. At the time monks and laymen were standing in attendance. Outside there was a person whose name was unknown to all. He came in, bowed, and raised a question: "What is the master's house style?" The master said: "My house is broad. There is no type lacking in it." The student did not yet comprehend the deep purport of the master. He begged the master to give him a device by which he could smash the sword point into a lump. The master said: "The lion's seat is quiet, and inside his private quarters he holds in his hand a dragon-shaped staff." "What is it used for?" The master said: "To smash obstinate, stupid stones and to select precious, glistening stars." "What are precious, glistening stars?" The master said: "I am walking in a desolate weed patch, and you have entered the deep forest." This person bowed, got up, went out the gate, and disappeared. No one knows his whereabouts.[25]

Fen-yang's recorded-sayings text is a watershed. In subsequent examples of the genre the commentarial impulse grows stronger and literary tendencies gain the ascendancy.[26] Though such tendencies had been there from the beginning—that is, from the *Records* onward—Fen-yang's collection looks backward and belongs more to the colloquial language of the T'ang records than to the self-conscious style of literary composition typical of the recorded-sayings texts of the Sung.

The evolution of the recorded-sayings genre is not a steady one. It proceeds more or less in accordance with what certain Darwinians call punctuated equilibrium. Long periods of nothing happening are interrupted by bursts of rapid change. Where are the bursts? Two of them are to be found in the Master Yüan sections of *Record II* and P'ei Hsiu's recorded-sayings book for Huang-po. These two stand out not just for the vibrancy of their colloquial language but also for the forcefulness with which the master emerges for the reader. We come to know something of the personalities of Yüan and Huang-po. This is certainly not the case with the *Former Worthies Gather at the Mount Shuang-feng Stūpa and Each Talks of the Dark Principle* or the *Sayings of the Great Laṅkā Masters* in the *Record of the Laṅkā Masters and Disciples*.

The compiler of the Yüan material in *Record II* and P'ei Hsiu are far apart in time but not in accomplishment. Yüan's words were virtually forgotten for centuries, except perhaps in distant Tibet, where his sayings continued to circulate in tantric circles, and are hardly known today outside scholarly circles. P'ei's draft, after being reworked by monk disciples of Huang-po, could hardly have been more successful. It was included in an edition of the canon printed in Huang-po's native prefecture in 1148 and has ever since held the status of a Ch'an classic.[27] Huang-po has to this day occupied a prominent position in the Ch'an pantheon. Master Yüan, on the other hand, quite quickly fell into oblivion in terms of history, biography, and genealogy charts, surviving only as a literary figure thanks to Tun-huang manuscript research. He may, however, be our earliest "Zen master."

Notes

Introduction

1. Sekiguchi Shindai, *Daruma daishi no kenkyū* (Tokyo: Shunjūsha, 1969), 3.

2. The theoretician is the Lin-chi master Ta-hui Tsung-kao (1089–1163). *Ta-hui p'u-chüeh ch'an-shih yü-lu*, T 47:921c; Araki Kengo, trans., *Daie sho*, Zen no goroku 17 (Tokyo: Chikuma shobō, 1969), 51.

3. Bernard Faure, "Bodhidharma as Textual and Religious Paradigm," *History of Religions* 25, no. 3 (1986): 187–98.

4. John C. Maraldo, "Is There Historical Consciousness within Ch'an?" *Japanese Journal of Religious Studies* 12, nos. 2–3 (June–September 1985): 145.

5. Yanagida Seizan, ed., *Sodōshū*, Zengaku sōsho 4 (Kyoto: Chūbun shuppansha, 1974), 31–39. The information concerning Bodhidharma's original name and subsequent name change, however, comes from the *Ching-te ch'uan-teng lu* (1004), T 51:216a and 217a. There the older brothers are identified as Vitimiratāra and Puṇyatāra. The last element, -tāra, means "carrying across, a savior, protector."

6. Suzuki Daisetsu, *Tonkō shutsudo shōshitsu issho* (Kyoto: privately published, 1935). The following year he published an edition and interpretation: Suzuki Daisetsu, *Kōkan shōshitsu issho oyobi kaisetsu furoku: Daruma no zempō to shisō oyobi sono ta* (Osaka: Ataka bukkyō bunko, 1936).

7. Burton Watson, *Early Chinese Literature* (New York: Columbia University Press, 1962), 127.

8. Yanagida Seizan, "Goroku no rekishi," *Tōhō gakuhō* 57 (March 1985): 320, 322–23, and 344: "In fact, within the Tun-huang manuscript *Long Scroll of the Treatise on the Two Entrances and Four Practices* the special characteristic of Bodhidharma's recorded sayings lies in the *Miscellaneous Record II* portion, which today virtually no one pays any attention to. If we seek for the significance of the

emergence of Zen Buddhism in independent texts called 'recorded sayings,' *Miscellaneous Record II* is truly worthy of the designation 'recorded sayings.'.... It is in the post-Baso period that a true rehabilitation of the recorded-sayings literature begins. *Miscellaneous Records II* and *III* of the Tun-huang manuscript *Treatise on the Two Entrances and Four Practices* are the forgotten ancestors of the recorded sayings.... To repeat, the assumption that the new Zen Buddhism of the post-Baso period took the words of the *Miscellaneous Records* as a foundation and thereby gave birth to independent dialogues and recorded sayings seems to hit the mark in this case." *Baso* refers to the lineage of Ma-tsu Tao-i (709–88), which leads to Lin-chi I-hsüan. Yanagida's hypothesis has far-reaching implications, for he is suggesting that the *Records* were resurrected by the Lin-chi school and used as the prototype for such texts as the *Chen-chou Lin-chi Hui-chao ch'an-shih yü-lu* (*Recorded Sayings of Ch'an Master Lin-chi Hui-chao of Chen Prefecture*; T no. 1985).

9. Franklin Edgerton, *Buddhist Hybrid Sanskrit Grammar and Dictionary* (1953; reprint, Delhi: Motilal Banarsidass, 1970), 1:1–2, gives a number of close reflexes of this very old passage in the context of a discussion of early Buddhism's use of the popular spoken languages of various regions. The *P'i-ni mu ching* (T 24:822a), a translation of the lost *Vinaya-mātṛkā* (*Summary of Discipline*), has two Brahman monks approaching the Buddha and saying: "'Among the disciples of the Buddha, there are those of different surnames, those of different countries, and those of different prefectures and districts. Their pronunciations are not the same; their speech is improper. All of them are destroying the Buddha's true meaning. All that we ask of you, World-honored One, is that you let us rely on the *Chando-citi-śāstra* to collect the Buddha sutras and edit the texts in order to make the pronunciation eloquent and the meaning fully evident.' The Buddha tells the monks: 'My Dharma has nothing to do with beautiful language. Just make sure the meaning of the teachings is not lost. This is my thinking. You should speak the teachings according to whatever pronunciations the various sentient beings can take in and understand.'"

10. Sekiguchi, *Daruma daishi no kenkyū*, 11: "Heretofore the accepted opinion has been that only the *Two Types of Entrance*—that is, the *Two Entrances and Four Practices in One Roll*—can be viewed as truly the Dharma talks of the Great Master Bodhidharma." Sekiguchi examines the six traditional texts attributed to Bodhidharma and follows the consensus. Of the four texts attributed to Bodhidharma found among the Tun-huang manuscripts, he designates the *P'u-t'i-ta-mo ch'an-shih lun* (see appendix A, note 15) an authentic Bodhidharma work. John R. McRae, *The Northern School and the Formation of Early Ch'an Buddhism* (Honolulu: University of Hawaii Press, 1986), 101–2, states: "Only one work, it is generally agreed, can legitimately be attributed to Bodhidharma: the *Erh-ju ssu-hsing lun* (*Treatise on the Two Entrances and Four Practices*).... After decades of discoveries in the collections at London, Paris, and Peking and after much research in

Japan, China, and elsewhere on the meaning of the Tun-huang finds, our best and almost only source for the earliest teachings of Ch'an remains, ironically, the one text that has been available all along." McRae includes the *Records* in the material that he does not treat. He comments that he has "used only that portion of the miscellaneous material [of the Tun-huang manuscript *Long Scroll*] that appears to be of arguably early vintage."

11. For a summary of the exegeses of wall-examining, see McRae, *The Northern School*, 112–15.

12. The translation works from the edition in Yanagida Seizan, trans., *Daruma no goroku*, Zen no goroku 1 (Tokyo: Chikuma shobō, 1969), which is hereafter abbreviated as DG. Yanagida's edition is based on five Tun-huang manuscripts and the version in the 1907 Korean collection entitled *Sŏnmun ch'waryo* (hereafter abbreviated as SC). SC contains the *Two Entrances, First Letter, Second Letter,* and *Record I.* It can be found in Yanagida Seizan, ed., *Kōrai-bon*, Zengaku sōsho 2 (Kyoto: Chūbun shuppansha, 1974), 14–25 (hereafter abbreviated as KB). I have adopted the section numbers of DG running from 1 to 74. Discovery of two manuscripts subsequent to the publication of DG allows us to extend the anthology to section 91. Altogether we now have nine manuscripts (for information on Tun-huang Ch'an manuscript studies, see appendix A):

Peking *su* 99: *Biography; Two Entrances; First Letter; Second Letter; Record I; Record II;* and a portion of *Record III*

Stein Ch. 2715: end of the *First Letter; Second Letter; Record I; Record II;* and a portion of *Record III*

*Stein Ch. 3375: end of the *Biography; Two Entrances; First Letter;* and most of the *Second Letter*

Pelliot Ch. 3018: portions of *Record I* and *Record II*

*Pelliot Ch. 4634: portions of *Record I* and *Record II*

*Stein Ch. 1880: portion of *Record I*

Stein Ch. 7159: *Two Entrances; First Letter; Second Letter;* and a portion of *Record I*

Pelliot Ch. 2923: small portion of *Record I;* all of *Record II;* and a portion of *Record III*

Pelliot Ch. 4795: small fragment of *Record III*

The three asterisked numbers were originally a continuum. DG is based on the first five; the last two were published after DG and give us considerably more of *Record III.* From the midst of section 74 to the beginning of section 87 my translation works from the transcription of a portion of Pelliot Ch. 2923 contained in Tanaka Ryōshō, "Ninyū shigyōron chōkansu (gi) kenkyū oboegaki," *Komozawa daigaku bukkyō gakubu kenkyū kiyō* 38 (March 1980): 58–60 (hereafter abbreviated as NSC); and Tanaka Ryōshō, *Tonkō zenshū bunken no kenkyū* (Tokyo: Daitō shuppansha, 1983), 177–79 (hereafter abbreviated as TZBK). Pelliot Ch. 2923 begins in the midst of section 48 and breaks off at the beginning of section 87. From section 87 to section 91 my translation works from the transcription of the fragment Pelliot Ch. 4795 contained in Tanaka Ryōshō, "Bodaidaruma ni kansuru tonkō shahon sanshu ni tsuite," *Komozawa daigaku bukkyō gakubu kenkyū kiyō* 31 (March 1973): 164; and TZBK, 182. It also appears in NSC, 62. Pelliot Ch. 4795, which begins in the midst of section 87 and breaks off in section 91, is full of lacunae. There is also a popular treatment without the Chinese text or annotations: Yanagida Seizan, trans., *Daruma*, Jinrui no chi-teki isan 16 (Tokyo: Kōdansha, 1981), 129–312. I have dubbed sections 68–91 *Record III* for two reasons. They are named sayings, as opposed to the named and anonymous dialogues of *Record II* (sections 50–67), and thus constitute a stylistic unit. Also, Tibetan texts have sections 68–91 as a discrete unit, though the order is jumbled (see chapter 3, note 20). For a list of quotations from the anthology found in the *Tsung-ching lu* (hereafter abbreviated TCL), see chapter 4, note 7. The *Ching-te ch'uan-teng lu*, T 51:458b–c, has the *Biography* and the *Two Entrances*. The Japanese collection *Shōshitsu rokumon*, T 48:369c–370c, has the *Two Entrances* and part of *Record I* under the title *Anshin hōmon* (*Method for Quieting Mind*). A Gozan edition of the late Kamakura period is a reprint of a Sung edition. See Shiina Kōyū, "Shōshitsu rokumon to Daruma daishi sanron," *Komozawa daigaku bukkyō gakubu ronshū* 9 (November 1978): 208–32. For an English translation, see John Alexander Jorgenson, "The Earliest Text of Ch'an Buddhism: The Long Scroll" (master's thesis, Australian National University, 1979). McRae, *The Northern School*, 102–6, provides a translation of the *Biography, Two Entrances, First Letter*, and *Second Letter*. For a French translation, see Bernard Faure, *Le traité de Bodhidharma: Première anthologie du bouddhisme Chan* (Paris: Le Mail, 1986).

Translation of the Seven Texts
of the *Bodhidharma Anthology*

    1. TCL, T 48:942a–b, contains an exposition of entrance by principle introduced by "Dhyana Master Buddha says." Though the transcription of the name is different, perhaps this refers to the Indian dhyana master Buddha (Bhadra), the founding abbot of Shao-lin Monastery and the master of Seng-ch'ou, a contemporary of Bodhidharma. The *Bsam gtan mig sgron* (*Dhyāna of the Enlightened Eye*), an eastern Tibetan block print, contains a translation of entrance by principle introduced by "from the sayings of the Great Master Bodhidharmatāra": *mkhan po chen po Bod-dhe-dar-mo-ta-ras bshad pa las | yang dag pa la phyogs shing rtogs pa spangs te | lham mer gnas na | bdag kyang med gzhan yang med | ma rabs dang 'phags*

pa mnyam zhing gcig ste | mi 'gyur bar brtan par gnas na | de phan chad yi ge dang bstan pa'i rjes su mi 'brang ngo | | 'di ni yang dag pa'i don gyi rnal du phab pa rnam par rtog pa med pa | zhing zhing bya ba med pa ste | de ni don la mi 'jug pa'o | | See Gnubs-chen Saṅs-rgyas-ye-śes, *Rnal 'byor mig gi bsam gtan* or *Bsam gtan mig sgron,* Smanrtsis shesrig spendzod, vol. 74 (Leh, Ladakh: S. W. Tashigangpa, 1974), fols. 57.5–58.2 (hereafter abbreviated as BGMS). This passage also appears at fol. 130.2–4. In addition to BGMS we also find material from the anthology in another central Tibetan text, the "Blon po bka'i thang yig" ("Decrees of the Ministers") section of the *Bka' thang sde lnga* (*Five Classes of Commands*). For a transcription, see Giuseppe Tucci, *Minor Buddhist Texts Part II,* Serie Orientale Roma, vol. 9 (1958; reprint, Kyoto: Rinsen Book Company, 1978), 68–81 (hereafter abbreviated as MBT). Since the *Bka' thang sde lnga* is so evidently corrupt, below I have relied solely on BGMS. Okimoto Katsumi, "Chibettoyaku *Ninyū shigyōron* ni tsuite," *Indogaku bukkyōgaku kenkyū* 24, no. 2 (March 1976): 40, also relies on BGMS rather than on the *Bka' thang sde lnga.* Okimoto uses Tōkyō daigaku shozō zōbun bunken no. 293 rather than the MBT text. For a discussion of Tibetan Ch'an lore, see appendix A, notes 6 and 7.

2. For the first, see *Lao Tzu* 63, and for the third, *Vimalakīrti-nirdeśa,* T 14:546a (hereafter abbreviated as VN). The BGMS translation of the four practices, fol. 173.5–6, is: *Ma-hā-yan gyi Bsam gtan rgya lung chen po las | spyod pa la 'jug pa ni spyod pa bzhi ste | gcig ni 'khon la lan ldon pa'i spyod pa'o | | gnyis pa ni rkyen gyi rjes su spyod pa'o | | gsum pa ni ci yang tshol ba med pa'i spyod pa'o | | bzhi pa ni chos dang mthun pa'i spyod pa'o | |* The explication of each practice follows. The Tibetan claims to be quoting from the *Great Chinese Injunctions on Ch'an* of the Chinese Ch'an master Mo-ho-yen (Mahayana), the famous figure of the Council of Tibet.

3. Unidentified.

4. *Nirvāṇa Sūtra,* T 12:677a–b.

5. *Lotus Sūtra,* T 9:14c.

6. Unidentified.

7. VN, T 14:540a.

8. Probably from the *Nirvāṇa Sūtra,* T 12:450a–451a. The *Mi-le ta-ch'eng fo ching,* T 14:430b, gives it as the verse of impermanence rather than the Snow Mountains verse.

9. TCL, T 48:603b, contains this letter, introduced by "as Layman Hsiang says."

10. *Chung-lun,* T 30:18c.

11. This and the next sentence are based on the *Chung-lun,* T 30:24c.

12. The opening part of this section draws upon Seng-chao's *Chao-lun,* T 45:153a–154c and 157a–161b. TCL, T 48:950c, contains the last portion introduced by "the *Mahāyāna Entering the Path and Quieting Mind Dharma* says" (*Ta-ch'eng ju-tao an-hsin fa yün*).

13. The BGMS translation of this section, fols. 130.4–131.2, is: *yang mi zhig gis smras pa | chos so cog yod pa ma yin no | | bshad pa khyod kyis med par mthong ngam | yod pa las med par gyur na | med pa la yod par 'gyur pas | de nyid khyod kyis yod pa'o | | mi zhig gis smras pa | bdag gi chos so cog ma skyes par mthong ngo | bshad pa khyod kyis ma skyes par mthong ngam | skyes pa las skyes par 'gyur na | ma skyes pa la skyes par 'gyur pas | de nyid khyod kyis skyes pa'o | | yang smras pa | bdag gi | chos so cog la sems med par mthong ngo | bshad pa khyod kyis sems med par mthong ngam | sems las med par gyur na | sems med pa las yod par gyur pas | de nyid khyod kyi sems yin no | |*

14. The first two sentences of this section, followed successively by portions of sections 13, 49, 19, 20, 24, 25, 26, 27, 28, 30, 31, 33, 34, 42, and 48, appear in TCL (T 48:939b–c) as one quotation introduced by "the master composed the *Method for Quieting Mind* [*An-hsin fa-men*], which says." "The master" refers to "the first patriarch of this land, Bodhidharmatāra." The BGMS translation of this section, fol. 131.2–4, is: *mkhan po chen pos bshad pa | mi shes na mi chos la 'brang | shes na ni chos mi la 'brang ngo | | shes na ni rnam par shes pa gzugs su 'du | bslad na ni gzugs rnam par shes pa la 'du'o | | gzugs kyi rgyu las rnam par shes pa bskyed pa ma lags | te | de ni gzugs mi mthong ba zhas bya | ces 'byung ngo | |*

15. The final quotation marks for the Tripiṭaka Dharma Master saying have been placed here because this is where the BGMS translation ends. The last sentence appears as a sutra quotation in section 77, but the sutra is unidentified. The remainder of the section may be commentary.

16. The answer seems to be based on VN, T 14:548b. See also *Nirvāṇa Sūtra*, T 12:510a.

17. T 15:751b.

18. The phrase *tzu-hsin hsien-liang* (*svacitta-dṛśya*) appears in the Guṇabhadra translation of the *Laṅkāvatāra Sūtra* (T 16:495b and 498b). It is not used in the other *Laṅkāvatāra* translations. See Daisetz Teitaro Suzuki, *An Index to the Lankavatara Sutra* (Kyoto: Sanskrit Buddhist Texts Publishing Society, 1934), 190–91. It also appears in section 19.

19. This simile, with slightly different phrasing, appears in the *Nirvāṇa Sūtra*, T 12:443a and 494a.

20. *Fo-shuo hsiang-fa chüeh-i ching*, T 85:1337a. The *Chung-lun*, T 30:32c, says: "All the Buddhas rely on the two truths in order to speak Dharma to sentient beings. The first is the worldly, conventional truth, and the second is the truth of the highest meaning."

21. The second half of this line appears in the *Nirvāṇa Sūtra*, T 12:443a.

22. *Lao Tzu* 41. The following comment appears in Stein Ch. 2715 in small characters. It is not in SC (KB, 17) or in Peking *su* 99, the only other versions we have of this section.

23. Based on VN, T 14:555c.

24. VN, T 14:540a.

25. Based on VN, T 14:540a and 546a.

26. DG suggests that there may be a passage missing here.

27. Section 69 quotes this as a sutra passage, but the sutra is unidentified.

28. Echoes the first of the four practices, that of requiting injury.

29. *Śrīmālā Sūtra*, T 12:221c.

30. The next two sentences appear in TCL (T 48:897a) introduced by "the patriarchal master says."

31. For these two hells, see *Ta chih-tu lun*, T 25:176c–177a.

32. See *Ta chih-tu lun*, T 25:176a and 177a–b.

33. Unidentified.

34. Source unidentified.

35. *Mencius*, Chih-hsin shang.

36. *Huai-nan Tzu*, Yao-lüeh.

37. *Lieh Tzu*, Huang-ti: "That which ordinary knowledge knows is shallow."

38. *Chuang Tzu*, Tsai-yu.

39. The term *ch'un-pu* ("plainness") appears in *Chin-shu*, Wu-ti chi-lun and Liu Hung chuan; *ch'iao-wei* ("ingenious artifice") in *Chuang Tzu*, Tao-chih.

40. VN, T 14:551c.

41. DG, 119, has emended Stein Ch. 2715, Peking *su* 99, and SC (KB, 19) to the colloquial *yü-mo*.

42. From *Chuang Tzu*, Ch'iu-shui.

43. VN, T 14:540b.

44. This sentence and "Self means ego" below appear in TCL (T 48:848a) introduced by "as the Great Master Dharma says."

45. In section 2 this line appears as an unidentified sutra quotation that serves to explicate the first of the four practices.

46. Following the punctuation of Suzuki, *Kōkan shōshitsu isho oyobi kaisetsu*, 1:18.

47. The next three sentences appear in TCL (T 48:848a) introduced by "as the Great Master Dharma says." It is continuous with the saying from the previous section.

48. VN, T 14:549a.

49. Based on VN, T 14:549a.

50. VN, T 14:544c. The order differs in the sutra.

51. From Seng-chao's commentary on VN, the *Chu wei-mo-chieh ching*, T 38:374a.

52. VN, T 14:540b.

53. VN, T 14:540b. This line immediately precedes the previous quotation.

54. Based on VN, T 14:542b.

55. Based on VN, T 14:542c.

56. VN, T 14:539c: "Not cutting off the defilements and entering nirvana is quiet sitting."

57. See VN, T 14:547c.

58. Following Peking *su* 99, which has a line missing in Stein Ch. 2715: *ho i-ku sheng-szu hsing chi-shih nieh-p'an* ("Why? Birth-and-death in essence is identical to nirvana"). Since this is a repetition, DG, 137, deletes it. SC (KB, 21) also varies: "It is like not awaiting the cutting off of fire to enter heat. Therefore, he does not await the cutting off of birth-and-death to enter nirvana. Why? Birth-and-death in essence is identical to nirvana. The hearer cuts off. . . ."

59. Seng-chao's *Chao-lun*, T 45:151a: "Near and yet you cannot know them. Just this is the nature of things."

60. See Kuo Hsiang's commentary on the *Chuang Tzu*, *Chuang-tzu chu*, Hsiao-yao yu.

61. *Chuang Tzu*, Hsiao-yao yu.

62. Pelliot Ch. 3018 begins with this question. The first sixteen lines of this manuscript are an unidentified Buddhist text. Where the two sheets have been pasted together we have the title *P'u-t'i-ta-mo lun* (*Bodhidharma Treatise*) and the beginning of section 31.

63. *Lao Tzu* 70.

64. *Lao Tzu* 64.

65. *Chao-lun*, T 45:151c: "Past and now always exist because they are unmoving."

66. Though the order is different, this is a quotation from VN, T 14:545b.

67. The remainder of this section appears in TCL (T 48:482a) introduced by "the first patriarch, the Great Master, says."

68. This line appears in TCL (T 48:482a) as part of the quotation from the preceding section.

69. Based on VN, T 14:543a.

70. *Lieh Tzu*, Huang-ti.

71. VN, T 14:551c: "Mañjuśrī said: 'According to my opinion, in all dharmas there are neither words nor speech, neither showing nor knowing. It is free of all questions and answers. This is the Dharma gate of nonduality.'"

72. *Mencius*, Chih-hsin shang.

73. Source unidentified.

74. Based on *Chung-lun*, T 30:2b. The line "Therefore, we come to know nonarising" below is also part of this verse.

75. The source of the following is unidentified.

76. Following SC (KB, 23).

77. Based on *Chung-lun*, T 30:3b.

78. *Sarvadharmāpravṛtti-nirdeśa*, T 15:751b.

79. VN, T 14:541b.

80. See the *Abhidharma-mahāvibhāṣā-śāstra* (?), T 27:692c.

81. Translated in the light of the VN passage, which is partially quoted below. This passage (T 14:544a) contains the line *yu-ju ju-lai fu-t'ien chih hsiang wu so fen-pieh* ("like the marks of a Tathagata's merit field, indistinguishable"). On Buddhas, solitary Buddhas, and arhats as merit fields, see *Ta chih-tu lun*, T 25:84c–85a.

82. Based on VN, T 14:544a: "Vimalakīrti then received the necklace [from the bodhisattvas] and divided it into two parts. Holding one part, he gave it to the lowest beggar in this assembly. Holding the other part, he offered it to the Invincible Tathagata. All of the assembly looked at the Invincible Tathagata of Radiance Land and saw the necklace on that Buddha change into a four-pillared treasure platform. The four sides with majestic ornaments did not conceal one another. At that time Vimalakīrti manifested a supernormal transformation and spoke these words: 'If the giver with an equal mind gives to the lowest beggar, it is like the marks of a Tathagata's merit field, indistinguishable. It is equal to great compassion and seeks no reward. This is called complete Dharma giving.'"

83. Following SC (KB, 24).

84. VN, T 14:545b.

85. Following SC (KB, 24).

86. Following the punctuation of Suzuki, *Kōkan shōshitsu isho oyobi kaisetsu*, 1:27.

87. The wave simile is prominent in the *Laṅkāvatāra Sūtra*. A typical example is the following from the Guṇabhadra translation, T 16:484a: "Mahāmati, it is like a fierce wind blowing over the great ocean. The wind of external objects whirls over the mind ocean, and waves of consciousness are continuous." See also T 16:496a.

88. Pelliot Ch. 2923 and 3018 have Dharma Master Yüan; Pelliot Ch. 4634 and Peking *su* 99 have simply Dharma Master.

89. The *Laṅkāvatāra Sūtra*, T 16:487a, says: "The hearer without interruption sees the eighth stage, and the production of the defilements is cut off, but the habit-energy defilements are not cut off." See also T 16:497b, 526c, and 540a.

90. *Dīrghāgama*, T 1:17c–18a, contains the refrain "relying on the sutras, relying on the discipline, relying on the Dharma." *Ta chih-tu lun*, T 25:125a: "When the Buddha was about to enter nirvana, he said to all the monks: 'From this day forth you should rely on Dharma and not rely on people. You should rely on the meaning and not rely on the words. You should rely on insight and not rely on knowledge. You should rely on the sutras of explicit meaning and not rely on those of implicit meaning.'"

91. The term *ching-shen* ("spirit") occurs in *Chuang Tzu*, K'e-i, and in *Lieh Tzu*, T'ien-tuan. Szu-ma Ch'ien's preface to his *Shih-chi*, T'ai-shih-kuan tzu-hsü, says: "The Taoists enable one to have his spirit concentrated and unified."

92. The *Sarvāstivāda-vinaya-vibhāṣā* (?), T 23:510a, lists the butchering of sheep as the first of the twelve wicked things. The *Daśā-dhyāya-vinaya* (?), T 23:359b, having listed five places associated with women to which a monk should not go, says: "There are five further places a monk should not go. What are the five? The house of a thief; the house of a low-caste person; the house of a butcher; the house of a prostitute; and a house that deals in wine." See also the *Lotus Sūtra*, T 9:37c, and the *Laṅkāvatāra Sūtra*, T 16:561c.

93. VN, T 14:545a: "That sick bodhisattva should have this thought: 'If this sickness of mine is neither real nor existent, the sickness of sentient beings is also neither real nor existent.' When performing this examination, if toward sentient beings you produce great compassion with a loving view, then you should reject it." Kumārajīva's commentary, the *Chu wei-mo-chieh ching*, T 38:378a, adds: "Seeing that sentient beings exist, you give rise to love attachments in the mind, and because due to these compassion is produced, it is called the great compassion with a love view."

94. VN, T 14:540a, expresses the idea that "expounding the Dharma lacks both expounding and explaining."

95. VN, T 14:545b: "What is called bondage and what is called liberation? To covet the taste of dhyana is the bondage of the bodhisattva. To live by teaching devices is the liberation of the bodhisattva."

96. VN, T 14:540a.

97. Supplying the negative *pu* from Pelliot Ch. 3018.

98. Supplying the negative *pu*. Though no manuscript has it, this line seems to be parallel to the one in the previous section. The punctuation of Pelliot Ch. 3018 includes the *chih* with the previous unit and thus reads: "Sins lack any characteristic of form that can be known. What shall I bring?"

99. Following Pelliot Ch. 2923 and 3018. This pattern appears above. DG, 220, follows Peking *su* 99. Again the negative *pu* has been supplied, though no manuscript has it.

100. *Ekottarāgama*, T 2:551a.

101. Based on VN, T 14:540a.

102. This story, down to "neither sin nor merit," appears in TCL (T 48:941b) as the words of Dhyana Master Yüan. TCL's blurring of Yüan and K'o is suggestive.

103. In the sutra, T 16:486a–b and 525b–c, the order is: Outpouring Buddha (*niṣyanda-buddha*); Dharma Buddha; and Magical-Creation Buddha (*nirmita-buddha*). Here we have the addition of Knowledge Buddha, which probably derives from the *jñāna-buddha* mentioned at 481b and 482b of the Guṇabhadra translation.

104. The Guṇabhadra translation, T 16:503a, states: "The Buddha said to Mahāmati: 'The Tathagatas of the three times have two types of comprehension

of Dharma. They are preaching comprehension [*deśanā-naya*] and self-realization comprehension [*siddhānta-naya*]. Preaching comprehension means: Following that which the minds of sentient beings respond to, the Tathagatas preach the sutras of the various devices. This is called preaching comprehension. Self-realization comprehension means that the practitioner is free of the various false thoughts manifested by his own mind. It means that he does not fall into the categories of oneness/difference or both/neither and transcends all thought, mind, and mind consciousness. In the sagely realm of self-awakening he is free of causal and seeing characteristics.'" In its list of the three Buddhas the Guṇabhadra translation describes the Dharma Buddha in the following terms: "The Dharma Buddha is free of self-nature and the mind characteristics. That which the self-awakened sage takes as an objective support is erected and carried out." This clearly relates the Dharma Buddha to the self-realization comprehension.

105. Unidentified. The name suggests the *Laṅkāvatāra Sūtra*.

106. Unidentified.

107. This sutra quotation may end with the previous sentence. Several passages in the *Sarvadharmāpravṛtti-nirdeśa* resemble this quotation. For instance, T 15:795b: "If greed lies neither within nor without and does not lie in the east, the south, the west, or the north, or in the four corners, or above or below—that is, in the ten directions—then it is nonarising." See also 755b. At 753b the sins of karmic obstacles are discussed.

108. Following Peking *su* 99.

109. This may be Fa-hsien (577–653) of Ching-chou (Hupeh). According to his entry in the *Hsü kao-seng chuan* (T 50:599c–600a; hereafter abbreviated as HKSC), Fa-hsien trained in dhyana under Chih-i in Ching-chou before training under Tao-hsin at East Mountain. Fa-hsien had a dream in which a strange monk ordered him to go to East Mountain and see Tao-hsin. He obeyed the monk's command. He was at East Mountain during the second quarter of the seventh century. The early eighth-century transmission record *Ch'uan fa-pao chi* says: "Fa-hsien of Ching-chou and Shan-fu of Ch'ang-chou [Kiangsu] both faced northward and received [Tao-hsin's] Dharma." See Yanagida Seizan, trans., *Shoki no zenshi I*, Zen no goroku 2 (Tokyo: Chikuma shobō, 1971), 380. Thus Fa-hsien was a major disciple of Tao-hsin. The *Hsien-te chi yü shuang-feng shan ko t'an hsüan-li* (*Former Worthies Gather at the Mount Shuang-feng Stūpa and Each Talks of the Dark Principle*) translated in appendix B includes a saying attributed to a Dhyana Master Hsien. Tsung-mi's *Chung-hua ch'uan hsin-ti ch'an-men shih-tzu ch'eng-hsi t'u* (*Chart of the Master-Disciple Succession of the Ch'an Gate Which Transmits the Mind Ground in China*) lists Hsien of Ching-chou as a student of Tao-hsin. (The original title of this work was *P'ei Hsiu shih-i wen* or *Questions of the Imperial Redactor P'ei Hsiu*.) See Kamata Shigeo, trans., *Zengen shosenshū tojo*, Zen no goroku 9 (Tokyo: Chikuma shobō, 1971), 289; and Ishii Shūdō,

"Shinpuku-ji bunko shozō no *Hai Kyū shūi mon* no honkoku," *Zengaku kenkyū* 60 (1981): 82.

110. Unidentified.

111. This may be the Madhyamika Ching-yüan. See chapter 4. The BGMS translation of this section, fol. 122.4–6, is: *bsam gtan gyi mkhan po Kha shan shis bshad pa | gal te chos so cog yun du stong par shes na shes pa dang shes pa'i stong par shes par nus pa'i ye shes kyang stong pa ste | de bas na chos dang ye shes kun kyang stong pa yin pas | de ni stong pa nyid kyang stong pa yin no | |* The Tibetan does not include the sutra quotation, which may be commentary.

112. Based on the *Chu wei-mo-chieh ching*, T 38:372c, a Kumārajīva comment.

113. A contraction of T 15:794b.

114. This may be the Madhyamika Chih-tsang (541–625); see chapter 4. Another possibility is the Fa-tsang of Shu-chou (Anhwei), listed as a disciple of Tao-hsin in Tsung-mi's *Questions of the Imperial Redactor P'ei Hsiu* (Kamata, *Zengen shosenshū tojo*, 289; Ishii, "*Hai Kyū shūi mon*," 83 n. 37). The *Former Worthies Gather at the Mount Shuang-feng Stūpa and Each Talks of the Dark Principle*, translated in appendix B, has two sayings of a Dhyana Master Tsang. TCL, T 48:941b13–15, has a portion of this saying introduced by "Dhyana Master Tsang says." The BGMS translation of this section, fols. 122.6–123.2, is: *mkhan po Dzan shan tis bshad pa | chos so cog la thogs pa med pa ni | chos lam spyod pa ma yin no | | de ci'i phyir zhe na |mig gis gzugs so cog mthong na | mig gis gzugs so cog thob par mi rung | tshogs drug char ded pa 'dra bas | mdo sde las | ci yang thob pa med pa ni | sangs rgyas kyi lung ston to | | yang chos so cog thob par mi rung ba nyid kyang thob par mi rung ngo | |* The Tibetan includes both sutra quotations.

115. Unidentified.

116. Unidentified.

117. Unidentified. The BGMS translation of this section, fol. 123.2–3, is: *mkhan po Yen shan shis bshad pa | mig gis mthong ba'i gnas nyid bden pa'i mtha' yin te | chos so cog kyang bden pa'i mtha' yin no | de las gzhan du btsal du ci yod | |* This closely follows the Chinese.

118. This may be the Madhyamika P'u-an (530–609) or his fellow student Tao-an; see chapter 4. TCL, T 48:941b17–20, has this saying introduced by "Dhyana Master An says." The BGMS translation of this section, fol. 123.3–6, is: *mkhan po A shen shis bshad pa | sems drang po ni chos lam yin no | | de ci'i phyir zhe na | drang por phye | drang por dran | drang por spyod na | de yan chad stong pa la mi spyod cing thabs mi 'tshol ba'i phyir | de ni gtan du chos lam spyod pa yin no | | mdo sde las kyang | drang por blta ba la ni mthong ba med | | drang por thos pa la ni nyan pa med | | drang por dran pa la ni sems pa med | drang por len pa la ni spyod pa med | | drang por bshad pa la ni 'phro ba med | |* This closely follows the Chinese.

119. From VN, T 14:542c.

120. Unidentified. DG, 243, suggests that it may not be a Buddhist text.

121. Unidentified. The BGMS translation of this section, fols. 123.6–124.1, is: *mkhan po Bo-len shan shis smras pa | chos kyi ngo bo nyid la the tshom med de | gcig car bsgom pa la ni the tshom ma za cig | mdo ste las | chos so cog ngo bo nyid kyi sems med pa'i phyir | de bzhin nyid do | | de bzhin nyid kyi phyir ngo bo nyid kyi sems med do | |* This diverges considerably from the Chinese: "Dhyana Master Bo-len says: 'In the Dharma Nature there is no doubt; in the all-at-once cultivation do not doubt. From the sutra: "Because dharmas have no mind of self-nature, they are Thusness; because they are Thusness, they have no mind of self-nature."'"

122. Unidentified.

123. Unidentified. Pelliot Ch. 2923 reads: *ching yün pen wu-hsin ku ju-hsin ju-hsin ku pen-wu.* However, the copyist has crossed out the two underlined characters. Peking *su* 99—and DG, 244, which is based on it—are missing these two characters. It is probable that the copyist of Pelliot Ch. 2923 was originally correct, but, confused by the apparent repetition, crossed out the two characters. This is confirmed by the Tibetan translation, which contains only one sutra quotation. The Tibetan suggests that a *hsin* at the end has been dropped in both Peking *su* 99 and Pelliot Ch. 2923. It is supplied in brackets.

124. Unidentified.

125. Unidentified. The BGMS translation of this section, fol. 124.2–4, is: *mkhan po Hang shan shis bshad pa | yong zhig byed do cog kun kyang de bzhin nyid do | | gzugs mthong ba dang | sgra thos pa yang de bzhin nyid do | chos so cog kyang de bzhin nyid do | ci'i phyir na 'gyur ba med cing tha dad pa med pa'i phyir ro | | mdo sde las | sems can yang de bzhin nyid | 'phags pa yang de bzhin nyid | chos so cog kyang de bzhin nyid yin no | |* This deletes everything from "transformation or variation" to the sutra quotation.

126. Based on VN, T 14:542b.

127. This may be the Madhyamika Hsüan-chüeh, a disciple of Hsüan-ching (d. 606); see chapter 4. TCL, T 48:941b20–23, has this saying introduced by "Dhyana Master Chüeh says." A line is added to the sutra quotation: *hsin yu i-ch'ieh fa ko pu hsiang-chih* ("Mind and all dharmas do not know one another"). The BGMS translation of this section, fol. 124.4–5, is: *mkhan po Kag shan shis bshad pa | gal te sems ci la yang mi rtog par go na | de nyid chos lam gyi srol yin no | de ci'i phyir zhe na | mig gis gzugs so cog mthong ba'i tshe na | mig gi ngo bo nyid grol thar pa'o | | tshogs drug char mthun te | mdo las chos so cog la gting ma rtogs pa'i phyir |*

128. From here onward the translation works from the transcription of a portion of Pelliot Ch. 2923 in NSC, 58–60, and TZBK, 177–79. The remainder of this sentence does not appear in Stein Ch. 2715 and Peking *su* 99.

129. NSC, 58, and TZBK, 177, are missing *yen* ("eyes").

130. Stein Ch. 2715 ends here with: *lun i-chüan* ("Treatise in one roll") and Peking *su* 99 ends here with an amusing poem by the copyist. "I present a five-character poem:

> Today I finished copying out this book.
> Why has the payment not been sent?
> Who is the undependable fellow?
> Averting our faces, we do not look at each other."

It seems that the copyist, displeased at not being paid for his work, sent an unusual poem of parting.

131. NSC, 58, and TZBK, 177, mistranscribe *ching* for *fa*.

132. *Mahāprajñāpāramitā Sūtra* (?), T 6:600c: "Forms do not cooperate, and so forms are unconnected to one another. Forms are unconnected to one another, and so forms are nonarising."

133. Unidentified. TCL, T 48:941b11–13, has a portion of this saying introduced by "Dhyana Master Fan says." The BGMS translation of this section, fols. 124.5–125.1, is: *gal te chos so cog cig pa yin pa'i phyir na | de grol thar ba yin no | | yid kyi chos yin spyod yul yang chos yin | chos kyi chos la sdig mi byed | bsod nams mi byed na rang grol thar pa'o | | yang chos | kyi chos la bcings pa dang | grol thar pa mi mthong ngo | |* No name is provided, and the sutra quotation is not identified as such.

134. Unidentified.

135. The BGMS translation of this section, fol. 125.1–2, is: *mkhan po Shi shan shis bshad pa | chos so cog thogs pa med do | | de ci'i phyir zhe na | chos so cog la nges pa med pas | | de nyid theg pa med cing zhi ba rdzogs pa yin pa'i phyir te |*

136. Unidentified. The *Ching-te ch'uan-teng lu*, T 51:219c, has four disciples of Bodhidharma, each giving a saying that illustrates his or her level of understanding. They are Tao-fu; Ni Tsung-ch'ih (the nun Dharani); Tao-yü; and Hui-k'o. Bodhidharma tells the first, "You have attained my skin"; the second "You have attained my flesh"; the third, "You have attained my bone"; and the fourth, "You have attained my marrow." The nun Tsung-ch'ih's saying is: "According to present understanding, they rejoiced in seeing the Land of Akṣobhya Buddha. Having seen it once, they did not see it again." This is the first portion of one of the sutra quotations of this nun Yüan-chi section. The earliest text in which Tsung-ch'ih is mentioned in the context of Bodhidharma's body parts is the late eighth-century Pao-t'ang house transmission record *Li-tai fa-pao chi*: "The Great Master said: 'In the state of T'ang there are three people who have obtained my Dharma. One person has obtained my marrow; one person has obtained my bone; and one person has obtained flesh. The one who has obtained the marrow is Hui-k'o; the one who has obtained the bone is Tao-yü; and the one who has obtained the flesh is the nun Tsung-ch'ih." T 51:181a; Yanagida Seizan, trans., *Shoki no zenshi II*, Zen no goroku 3 (Tokyo: Chikuma shobō, 1976), 68. Like Yüan this nun comes down to us as a literary figure. TCL, T 48:941b23–25, has a portion of this saying introduced by "The nun Yüan-chi says." The BGMS translation of this section, fol. 125.2–6, is: *chos so cog la zla med pas | de nyid rang gi*

ngo bo grol thar pa'o | ci'i phyir na mig gis gzugs mthong ba'i tshe na | mi mthong ba med la yid kyis rnam par shes pa'i tshe mi shes pa med bslad pa'i tshe na shes pa med | shes pa'i tshe na bslad pa med | rmi lam gyi tshe na tshor ba med | tshor ba'i tshe na rmi lam med pa'i phyir ro | mdo las | phal pa mang pos sangs rgyas A-sham mthong nas | phyis ma mthong ba dang | chos so cog la mig dang rna ba'i zlā med do | | de ci'i phyir zhe na | chos kyis chos mi mthong | chos kyis chos mi shes pa'i phyir ro | yang gzags [gzugs] kyi rgyu las rnam par shes pa ma skye na | gzugs mi mthong ba yin no | | There is no name, and it has both sutra quotations.

137. *Fang-kuang pan-jo ching,* T 8:105c: "All dharmas are nonreacting."

138. Based on one of the following: *Fang-kuang pan-jo ching,* T 8:105b–c; *Twenty-Five Thousand Prajñāpāramitā Sūtra,* T 8:363b–c; or *Eight Thousand Prajñāpāramitā Sūtra,* T 8:578b.

139. Unidentified. This line appears in section 8 of *Record I* as part of a Tripiṭaka Dharma Master saying.

140. Unidentified. The BGMS translation of this section, fols. 125.6–126.1, is: *mkhan po Am shan shis bshad pa | rig pa la gtsang dme med do | | sems la mun pa med do | | sems kyis chos mi shes na | chos kyis bdag bcings kyi | shes pa yang med la | bslad par shes pa med de | de ni shes pa chen po'o | |* This is quite compressed.

141. Pelliot Ch. 2923 reads: *ch'ing pu-tung i nieh-p'an.* I have deleted the negative *pu.*

142. Unidentified. NSC, 59, and TZBK, 178, have Yin's saying as section 79 (106) and merge Tripiṭaka Dharma Master's saying with the following dialogue between him and the deluded one into one section (80 or 107). DG has Tripiṭaka Dharma Master's saying as a response to Yin (DG's section 80) and the remainder as the next section (81). The translation here follows the former model. The BGMS translation of this section, fol. 126.1–2, is: *mkhan po In shan shis bshad pa | | gzhan las bshad pa rnam par shes pa drug mi bden pa'i 'du shes yin no | rnam bzhis blang dor byas pa dang | de'i ming ni bdud kyi las zhes bya'o | |*

143. The BGMS translation of the first Bodhidharma saying, fol. 126.2–4, is: *mkhan po chen pos bshad pa | 'du shes g'yos pa'i tshe g'yo ba med na de nyid sangs rgyas kyi chos yin no | sems yang dag pa dang mnyam snyoms pa dang | byang chub kyi sems la 'jug pa kyang chos kyi ngo bo nyid dang gcig tu mthun pa ste | bslad pa'i mi ni rnams par shes pa drug gis | mya ngan 'khrugs pa byed zhes 'chad | |* The dialogue between Tripiṭaka Dharma Master and the deluded one is missing.

144. Based on VN, T 14:549b.

145. VN, T 14:538a. The material including this sentence and running down to "deluded interpretations" appears in TCL (T 48:953a11–13) introduced by "Tripiṭaka Dharma Master says."

146. Unidentified. This could conceivably refer to Hung-jen, the leader of East Mountain during the third quarter of the seventh century. The BGMS translation of this section, fols. 128.6–129.1, is: *mkhan po shan shis bshad pa | bdag gi*

yid kyi yang dag pa'i chos shes | na | de'i don la zab mi zab dang | g'yo mi g'yo med de |
chos lam dang mi 'gal bas thob pa dang | stong ba'i gnas mi mthong ngo | | No name is
given, and it covers only the first three sentences.

147. TCL, T 48:939c29–940a3, has the first four sentences of this section
introduced by "the second patriarch, the Great Master K'o, says." This is the
saying for Hui-k'o in TCL's list of the seven Buddhas, the twenty-seven patriarchs of India, and the patriarchs of China. The BGMS translation of this section,
fol. 129.1–3, is: *mkhan po Hye-khas bshad pa | mkhas da ltar gyi lnga phung nyid yongs*
su rdzogs pa'i mya ngan las 'das par shes shing | lus dang sems ni spyod do cog dang
ldan pa ni | gzhung chen po dang ldan pa yin te | gal te de ltar shes na mya ngan gyi
nang na rnam par dag pa'i rin po ches mthong zhing sems can thams cad kyi mun pa
bsal bar yang byed do | | This constitutes the last three sentences of the section.

148. See *Chao-lun*, T 45:151c. NSC, 59, and TZBK, 178, emend the *yü* of Pelliot
Ch. 2923 to *wei* (the second "say") in the light of TCL, T 48:940a1.

149. Unidentified. The BGMS translation of this section, fols. 129.3–130.1, is:
mkhan po Lang shan shis bshad pa | chos rnams kyi don rig na bden pa nan thun pa
dang | tha dad pa yang med do | | mngon pa dang mi mngon pa'i tshig ni | btsums pa
dang | phye ba med pa rnam pa gnyis yod de | btsums pa'i don ni sems g'yo ba mi
mthong | spyod pa dang shes pa la mi rtog cing byed do cog lang [?] mi gnas te | ngo bo
nyid kyi sangs rgyas kyi chos la gnas pa'o | sems phye na yul gzhan la gtogs pa ste | de
ni khe g'yogs kyi man ngag zhes kyang bya ste | rgyu dang 'bras bur 'dus pa'o | | yin pa
dang ma yin pas bcings pa rang dbang ma thob phye ba'i don zhes bya'o | | This con-
stitutes the whole of the section. The two modes are referred to as "closed"
(*btsums pa*) and "opened" (*phye ba*). The *mchan bu* style of annotation glosses the
former as *ma 'phro* ("not emanating") and the latter as *'phro* ("emanating").

150. Unidentified. The BGMS translation of this section, fol. 130.1–2, is: *mkhan*
po Mahā shan shis bshad pa | shes pa'i tshe na ni 'jig rten dang 'jig rten las 'das pang
[?] *mi stong pa 'ba' zhig yod du zad kyi | bden par na 'jig rten dang 'jig rten las 'das pa*
thob pa med do | | This is only the sentence about void names.

151. Unidentified sutra.

152. TCL, T 48:941b25–26, has the first sentence down to "Buddha dharmas."
It is introduced by "Dhyana Master Yao says." The BGMS translation of this
section, fol. 126.4–6, is: *mkhan po Hya'u-gya'u shan gyis bshad pa | sems dang rnam*
par shes pa'i rang bzhin ngo bo nyid kyi yang dag par yin par rtogs na | sems kyi dmigs
pa'i gnas so cog sargyas [sangs rgyas] kyi zhing dang mya ngan las 'das pa yin te | sems
kyi yul lo cog tu rtogs pas | sangs rgyas kyi yul lo cog tu rtog pa sangs rgyas chos ma yin
pa med do | |

153. There seems to be something missing here. The Tibetan translation
above may offer a hint. It reads: "Master Hya'u-gya'u says: 'If you understand
that the self-nature of thought and the consciousnesses is reality, then the loci of
the objective supports of mind are Buddha fields, nirvana. By examining objects

of mind, there are no cases in which it is not the examination of Buddha objects, Buddha dharmas.'" Perhaps the Chinese originally read something like: "Mind reflects on the ten thousand objects, and there are no cases in which it is not reflection on Buddha objects, Buddha dharmas."

154. This line is probably from a sutra, with the first-person pronoun referring to the Buddha. Pelliot Ch. 2923 has an extra *wu*.

155. Unidentified. The BGMS translation of this section, fols. 126.6–127.3, is: *bsam gtan gyi mkhan po Shi shan gyis bshad pa | ma rabs dang | 'phags | pa'i sgo gnyis thog ma med pa nas lugs gcig ste | ma rabs ni | 'phags pa'i rgyu zhes bya ste | 'phags pa ni ma rabs kyi 'bras bu zhes bya'o | | rgyu dang 'bras bu gcig la gcig ltos pas | dge mi dge las mi 'da' ste | dge'o cog ni 'phags pa'i ye shes las 'byung | mi dge ba ni blun po las 'byung ngo | | mdo sde las | nga dang gang zag med mos kyi | dge dang mi dge'i las mi gtor | zhes pas | khrims lnga bsrun na nges par mi lus thob | stong pa la rtog ste | chos lam spyad na nges par dgra bcom pa'i 'bras bu thob | |* "Dhyana Master Shi says: 'The two gates of the common man and the sage have been of one mode from without beginning; the common man is the so-called cause of the sage, and the sage is the so-called effect of the common man. Cause and effect are to be viewed as one, and so virtuous and nonvirtuous karma are not abandoned. Virtues arise from the sage's knowing; nonvirtue arises from the idiot. From the sutra: "Though there is neither the self nor the person, virtuous and nonvirtuous karma are not thrown out, and so those who maintain the five precepts certainly obtain a human body. Those who examine voidness and cultivate the path will certainly attain the fruit of arhat."'"

156. In the light of the Tibetan I have emended the *o* ("evil") of Pelliot Ch. 2923.

157. Unidentified sutra. From here onward, whenever lacunae have been tentatively reconstructed from the Tibetan of BGMS, the reconstructions are given in italics.

158. Unidentified source. It is unclear where this quotation ends. The translation in BGMS ends here, and so I have placed the final quotation mark at this point.

159. Pelliot Ch. 2923 breaks off after "All dharmas are Buddha." From here onward the translation works from the transcription of Pelliot Ch. 4795 contained in Tanaka, "Bodaidaruma ni kansuru," 164; and TZBK, 182. (It also appears in NSC, 62.) Pelliot Ch. 4795 is a small fragment of eleven lines in very poor shape. Ellipsis points indicate those cases in which reconstruction was impossible. The Tibetan translation of section 87 in BGMS allows us to connect these two Pelliot Ch. numbers with certainty. The BGMS translation of this section, fol. 127.4–5, is: *mkhan po Shi shan shis bshad pa | chos so cog kun kyang sangs rgyas kyi chos yin par shes na de nyid chos kyi mig ces bya | g'yos shing byas so cog kun byang chub yin pas yang dag pa'i sems bzhin du sangs rgyas kyi chos lam du phyin te mi dngangs mi skrag*

na gnas so cog kun kyang 'dra'o | | "Dhyana Master Shi says: 'If you know that all dharmas are Buddha dharmas, that is the so-called Dharma eye. All moving and activity are enlightenment, and so, in conforming with the mind of reality, you will arrive at the path of the Buddha Dharma. If you are not terrified and not frightened, all loci will be equal.'" Chih is presumably the Tao-chih of section 76 and the Chih who is an associate of Yüan in sections 52–53 of *Record II*.

160. *Vajracchedikā Sūtra*, T 8:751b: "Therefore, the Buddha said that all dharmas are Buddha dharmas."

161. *Mañjuśrī Prajñāpāramitā Sūtra*, T 8:727c: "If one can hear of such a deep perfection of insight, his mind will not be alarmed or frightened, will not sink or be regretful."

162. Reading *ya* as *yeh*.

163. Tanaka, "Bodaidaruma ni kansuru," 164, and TZBK, 182, transcribe the Tun-huang nonstandard character *i* ("also") as *hu* ("mutual"). See Chin Yung-hua, ed., *Tun-huang su-tzu so-yin* (Taipei: Shih-men t'u-shu kung-szu, 1980), 4.

164. Unidentified. The BGMS translation of this section, fols. 127.5–128.1, is: *mkhan po Phag-do shan shis bshad pa | kun rdzob kyi bden pa yod pas stong pa ma yin | dgra bcom pa'i 'bras bu med pas na yod pa ma yin pa | bden pa gnyis ni gnyis kyi phyir gcig ma yin | 'phags pas gzigs na stong pas na gnyis su med pa'o* | |

165. The BGMS translation of this section, fol. 128.1–2, is: *mkhan po 'Dzi shan shes bshad pa | bslad pa'i mis ni sdig med pa'i las sdig tu mthong ngo | shes pa'i mis ni sdig gis gnas nyid la sdig med par rig go* | | "Dhyana Master 'Dzi says: 'The corrupted person sees sinless karma as sin. The man of understanding knows that in the locus of sin there is sinlessness.'" Luo Charngpeir, *T'ang wu-tai hsi-pei fang-yin*, Academica Sinica, National Research Institute of History and Philology Monographs Series A, no. 12 (Shanghai: Kuo-li chung-yang yen-chiu yüan li-shih yü-yen yen-chiu so, 1933), 23, gives *tzu* (Morohashi no. 30095) as a potential reconstruction in the T'ang Northwest dialects of Tibetan *dzi*.

166. The BGMS translation of this section, fol. 128.2–4, is: *mkhan po Yan shan shes bshad pa | mdo sde dang bshad pa kun kyang sems g'yo ba'i chos yin no | gal te chos lam gyi sems g'yos pa yin na yang de g'yo rgyu'i sems g'yos pa'o | gzhan lta smos kyang ci dgos | gal te sems mi g'yo na | bsam gtan bsgom ci dgos | g'yo rgyu'i sems mi g'yo na | drang por bsam zhing nyon mongs ci dgos | gal te byang chub kyi sems mi g'yo zhing shes rab dang shes pa mi tshol na las dang don thams cad zad do* | | "Dhyana Master Yan says: 'All the sutras and treatises are dharmas of mind movement. If the mind of the Dharma path is set in motion, it is mind movement that wanders about. How much more so for others [i.e., thoughts other than that of the Dharma path]? If mind does not move, what need is there for dhyana practice? If the wandering mind does not move, what need is there to be troubled by right mindfulness? If you do not set in motion the thought of enlightenment and do not seek insight and understanding, then you will exhaust both phenomena and principle.'"

167. This may be the Dhyana Master Lang of Huang-mei, the location of East Mountain, who is listed as a disciple of Tao-hsin in Tsung-mi's *Questions of the Imperial Redactor P'ei Hsiu* (Kamata, *Zengen shosenshū tojo*, 289; Ishii, "*Hai Kyū shūi mon*," 83 n. 37). TCL, T 48:941b26–28, has the portion running from "whatever" to "cut them off" introduced by "Dhyana Master Lang says." The bracketed words are supplied from TCL. The BGMS translation of this section, fol. 128.4–6, is: *bsam gtan gyi mkhan po Han shan shis bshad pa | sems ni chos lam gyi ngo bo yin | lus ni chos lam gyi snod yin | dge ba'i bshes gnyen ni rkyen gyis byung ba yin no | | sems bde na yul yang bde ste | mtha' gnyis la blang dor med na khams bco brgyad la blta'o | |* "Dhyana Master Han says: 'Mind is the self-nature of the Dharma path. Body is the vessel of the Dharma path. The good friend appears due to conditions. If mind is pure, objects are also pure. When there is neither grasping nor rejecting of the two extremes, you will be gazing at the eighteen elements.'"

168. TZBK, 182, deletes the *se* ("form"). There is probably a copyist's error here.

169. Unidentified source.

170. Pelliot Ch. 4795 breaks off here.

Commentary on the *Biography, Two Entrances*, and *Two Letters*

1. The early eighth-century transmission record *Leng-chia shih-tzu chi* allows us to identify the Dharma Master as Tripiṭaka Dharma Master Bodhidharma and T'an-lin as the compiler of the *Biography* and *Two Entrances*. In its Bodhidharma entry the *Leng-chia shih-tzu chi* quotes these two pieces in their entirety and introduces them with the title *Lüeh-pien ta-ch'eng ju-tao szu-hsing ti-tzu T'an-lin hsü* (*Brief Explanation of the Four Practices of Entering the Path of the Mahāyāna: Preface by Disciple T'an-lin*). At the end of this quotation we find a very intriguing line: "These four practices were spoken by Dhyana Master Dharma himself; as to the rest, Disciple T'an-lin recorded the master's words and actions and made a collection of one roll, calling it the *Bodhidharma Treatise [Ta-mo lun]*." The question is: What does "the rest" refer to? Mostly likely it is *Record I*. T 85:1284c25–26 and 1285b15–17; Yanagida, *Shoki no zenshi I*, 127 and 133.

2. For the later Ch'an view, see the *Ch'uan-fa cheng-tsung chi* of Ch'i-sung (1007–72), T 51:744a. This is continued in modern scholarship. HKSC, T 50: 552b19–20, states: "At the time of the Chou suppression of the Dharma [574–577], together with fellow trainees of K'o [*yü K'o t'ung-hsüeh kung*], T'an-lin protected sutras and images." This line has often been read as: "together with his fellow trainee K'o." Ui Hakuju, *Zenshūshi kenkyū* (1935; reprint, Tokyo: Iwanami shoten, 1966), 1:62, has a more likely reading: *Eka no dōgaku tomo ni* ("together with fellow trainees of Hui-k'o").

3. For the *Tsu-t'ang chi*, see Yanagida, *Sodōshū*, 36. The *Ching-te ch'uan-teng lu* is T 51:219b1–2.

4. T 51:999c, 1000b, and 1004a. See W. F. J. Jenner, *Memories of Lo-yang: Yang Hsüan-chih and the Lost Capital (493–534)* (Oxford: Clarendon Press, 1981), 151 and 171–72; and Yi-t'ung Wang, *A Record of Buddhist Monasteries in Lo-yang: By Yang Hsüan-chih* (Princeton: Princeton University Press, 1984), 13, 20–21, and 57. The intriguing line, of course, is *po-szu kuo hu-jen* ("a Persian Central Asian"). According to Berthold Laufer, *Sino-Iranica* (1919; reprint, Taipei: Ch'eng Wen Publishing Company, 1978), 194–95, the term *hu* relates to Central Asia and particularly to peoples of Iranian extraction. What we seem to have is an Iranian speaker who hailed from somewhere in Central Asia.

5. Hu Shih, "P'u-t'i-ta-mo k'ao," in *Hu Shih wen-ts'un* (Taipei: Yüan-t'ung t'u-shu kung-szu, 1953), 3:294, and in *Ko Teki zengakuan*, ed. Yanagida Seizan (Kyoto: Chūbun shuppansha, 1975), 54. Hu's pioneer article appeared in 1927. The pole on Yung-ning's great stupa, at which the Iranian Bodhidharma marveled, was damaged by a big wind in 526; the monastery served as a military encampment site in 528 and again in 529; and the whole complex was burned down in 534 by a fire that is said to have continued smoldering for three months.

6. It also includes a biographical entry for a Seng-fu (464–525), who trained under a Dharma in the North (T 50:550a–c). At the beginning of the first of his six chapters on meditation practitioners, Tao-hsüan provides a list of twenty-three names for the main entries of the chapter. Bodhidharma and Hui-k'o are the fifth and sixth, respectively, and they are clearly to be taken as master and leading disciple. We have in embryo the standard Ch'an lineage chart. Such charts not only enshrine but also exclude. The first name in the list is Seng-fu, a name that probably should have been between Bodhidharma and Hui-k'o. Why Tao-hsüan put it there we do not know, but in time the effect of his arrangement was to gloss over Seng-fu's role in the tradition. The entry states: "There was a Dhyana Master Dharma who was good at clarifying the practice of examining [*kuan-hsing*]. Seng-fu came around and disturbed Dharma in the grottoes and asked deep and extensive questions. Seng-fu subsequently became his follower and left home." Later he lectured in the South and in Szechwan. The question is whether this Dharma is the South Indian Bodhidharma in the fifth slot on Tao-hsüan's list. Tao-hsüan does not explicitly identify them, and this was probably intentional on his part. See Yanagida Seizan, "Daruma zen to sono haikei," in *Hokugi bukkyō no kenkyū*, ed. Ōchō Enichi, 2d ed. (Kyoto: Heiraku-ji shoten, 1978), 135. It seems that Tao-hsüan recognized this identity but felt compelled to play it down in order not to compromise the idea of a Bodhidharma/Hui-k'o lineage. Tao-hsüan in effect makes Seng-fu a "side" successor of Bodhidharma, and Hui-k'o the direct successor—an arrangement that is mirrored in the treatment of Seng-fu in later Ch'an literature. There under the name Tao-fu he is listed as the recipient

of Bodhidharma's skin, Hui-k'o having obtained the very marrow of the master's bones. An example is *Ching-te ch'uan-teng lu*, T 51:219b–c. See Kawajima Jōmyō, "Sōfuki ni tsuite," *Indogaku bukkyōgaku kenkyū* 25, no. 2 (March 1977): 146–47; and Satomichi Tokuyū, "Bodaidaruma to sono shūhen (1): Dōiku to Sōfuku ni tsuite," *Tōyō daigaku tōyōgaku kenkyūjo kiyō* 12 (1978): 117–21. For a very useful index to HKSC, see Makita Tairyō, ed., *Tō kōsōden sakuin*, 3 vols., Chūgoku kōsōden sakuin, vols. 2–4 (Kyoto: Heiraku-ji shoten, 1973 and 1975).

7. T 50:551b–c.

8. Jorgenson, "The Earliest Text," 160, suggests that Sung here is not necessarily a time indicator, but may refer only to place. If so, Tao-hsüan's Bodhidharma could have arrived later than 479, during the Liang Dynasty.

9. Yanagida, "Goroku no rekishi," 320, suggests that Tao-hsüan had a strong propensity to overlook the *Record* material and to consider only T'an-lin's preface and exposition as this injunctions roll (*lu ch'i yen-kao chüan*).

10. Hu Shih, "Leng-chia tsung k'ao," in *Hu Shih wen-ts'un* (Taipei: Yüan-t'ung t'u-shu kung-szu, 1953), 4:210, and in *Ko Teki zengakuan*, ed. Yanagida Seizan (Kyoto: Chūbun shuppansha, 1975), 170. See also Yanagida Seizan, *Shoki zenshū shisho no kenkyū* (Kyoto: Hōzōkan, 1967), 3–27.

11. Hu, "Leng-chia tsung k'ao," 211 (171).

12. T 50:551c27–552a27. This constitutes about thirty lines of the T text. The remainder is fifty-five lines.

13. *Analects*, Wei-cheng: "At forty I was without confusion." This is the suggestion of Yanagida, "Daruma zen to sono haikei," 139.

14. Satomichi, "Bodaidaruma to sono shūhen (1)," 118–19. Did Bodhidharma die there peacefully in sitting posture after having bequeathed his final injunctions to his disciples? An event mentioned in secular sources suggests a different but somewhat far-fetched scenario. There was an infamous mass political execution carried out at Ho-yin, also known as Lo-pin, in 528, just about the time the Hui-k'o entry has Bodhidharma dying. The one detail that might link Tao-hsüan's Bodhidharma to this event is that a Seng-fu, perhaps the one who engaged in the practice of examining under a Dharma, lost an uncle in the battle between rebel and loyalist forces some time before the mass executions carried out by the victorious insurgents. Since this uncle of a Seng-fu was a loyalist leader, it is possible that, once the insurgents had won, they rounded up everyone associated with that uncle, including the Buddhist master of his nephew the monk. A Dharma might have gotten caught up in the retribution through his association with his disciple Seng-fu. This scenario does not contradict the atmosphere of the entry and is supported by the mention of a lack of a proper funeral for Bodhidharma. Corpses of eminent masters were not simply stashed in riverbank caves; they had elaborate funerals. For a report of the execution of a Buddhist monk at the site, see T 50:683a7.

15. T 50:552a–c. The Layman Hsiang letter is the *Second Letter* of the *Bodhidharma Anthology*.

16. Yanagida, *Shoki zenshū shisho no kenkyū*, 21, and Yanagida Seizan, "Bodaidaruma *Ninyū shigyōron* no shiryō kachi," *Indogaku bukkyōgaku kenkyū* 15, no. 1 (December 1966): 321.

17. T 50:666b. Guṇabhadra, also known as Mahayana, was a Central Indian who arrived in Kuang-chou (Canton) by ship in 435 and was subsequently active at Nanking. (This is exactly the itinerary, incidentally, followed by the traditional story's Bodhidharma just a bit later.) Guṇabhadra's rendering of the *Laṅkāvatāra* is T no. 670. Three slogans are noteworthy. The "South India one-vehicle thesis" (*nan t'ien-chu i-ch'eng tsung*) may be linked to the fact that some in the Bodhidharma lineage during the early eighth century seem to have called themselves the Southern School (*nan-tsung*) because the Laṅkā tradition came from South India. The otherwise unknown Li Chih-fei's preface to Ching-chüeh's (683–?) commentary on the *Heart Sūtra* says: "The *Ancient Dhyāna Instructions* [*Ku ch'an-hsün*] says: 'At the time of Emperor T'ai-tsu of the Sung, Tripiṭaka Dhyana Master Guṇabhadra took the *Laṅkāvatāra Sūtra* to transmit the lamp. It arose from South India and is called the Southern School. Next it was transmitted to Dhyana Master Bodhidharma. Next it was transmitted to Dhyana Master Hui-k'o.'" For the text, see Yanagida, *Shoki zenshū shisho no kenkyū*, 596. The second slogan is "forgetting words, forgetting thoughts, nonapprehension, and correct examining are the thesis" (*wang-yen wang-nien wu-te cheng-kuan wei tsung*). Here it is the thesis of the Bodhidharma lineage, but the nonapprehension correct-examining thesis is a name for the thesis of San-lun, and the South India one-vehicle thesis is connected to this. See Hirai Shun'ei, "Shoki zenshū shisō no keisei to sanronshū," *Shūgaku kenkyū* 5 (1963): 78; and Hirai Shun'ei, *Chūgoku hannya shisōshi kenkyū: Kichizō to sanron gakuha* (Tokyo: Shunjūsha, 1976), 334 and 407. Chi-tsangs's *San-lun hsüan-i*, T 45:10c, mentions the nonapprehension correct-examining thesis. The third slogan, "spoke of the dark principle but did not produce written records" (*k'ou-shuo hsüan-li pu-ch'u wen-chi*), shows up as "did not produce written records but spoke of the dark principle" (*pu-ch'u wen-chi k'ou-shuo hsüan-li*) in the Hung-jen entry of Ching-chüeh's *Leng-chia shih-tzu chi* (T 85:1289b20–21; Yanagida, *Shoki no zenshi I*, 269) and as "did not produce written records" (*pu-ch'u wen-chi*) in the entry for Ts'an, Hui-k'o's successor (T 85:1286b8–9; Yanagida, *Shoki no zenshi I*, 167). This slogan may be the seed of the most famous of all Ch'an slogans, "transmitting from mind to mind and not relying on the written word" (*i-hsin ch'uan-hsin pu-li wen-tzu*), which is attributed to Bodhidharma. As such it appears throughout the works of Tsung-mi: *General Preface to the Collection of Explanations of the Ch'an Source* (T 48:400b19–20; Kamata, *Zengen shosenshū tojo*, 44); *Questions of the Imperial Redactor P'ei Hsiu* (Kamata, *Zengen shosenshū tojo*, 296; Ishii, "Hai Kyū shūi mon," 83); and *Yüan-chüeh*

ching ta-shu ch'ao (*Digest of the Great Commentary on the Perfect Enlightenment Sūtra*) (ZZ 1, 14, 3:275b). Editors in the late seventh century may have plucked the name Ts'an from this list and plugged it into their own transmission account in order to provide a genealogical bridge from Hui-k'o to Tao-hsin. The Seng-ts'an entry in the *Leng-chia shih-tzu chi* (T 85:1286b7–8; Yanagida, *Shoki no zenshi I*, 167) explicitly quotes HKSC when giving the line "After Dhyana Master K'o: Dhyana Master T'san." Nothing is known of any of the names on this list except Old Master Na, who appears in Hui-k'o B.

18. T 50:553b–555b. This lengthy and detailed entry is more than five times as long as the Bodhidharma entry. For treatments of Seng-ch'ou, see Yanagida, "Daruma zen to sono haikei," 150–57, and Yün-hua Jan, "Seng-ch'ou's Method of Dhyana," in *Early Ch'an in China and Tibet*, Berkeley Buddhist Studies Series, no. 5, ed. Whalen Lai and Lewis R. Lancaster (Berkeley: Lancaster Publications, 1983), 51–63. According to the entry (T 50:553c), Seng-ch'ou visited the founding abbot of Shao-lin Monastery, Buddha or Bhadra, shortly after its opening in 496. After Seng-ch'ou made his presentation, the abbot said: "You are the greatest in dhyana training east of the Pamirs." Seng-ch'ou received the transmission and subsequently dwelled at Sung-yüeh Monastery nearby. Epigraphy relating to Shao-lin records more about Seng-ch'ou than Bodhidharma. Seng-ch'ou was famous for separating fighting tigers with his tin staff (T 50:553c–554a and 559b).

19. T 50:596c. "Sayings left behind" (*li-yen*) is a classical phrase meaning a transmitted text. It could refer to the injunctions roll that Tao-hsüan mentions at the end of his Bodhidharma entry. The theme of rejecting both sin and merit may come from the *Records*. The Seng-ch'ou entry (T 50:553c) states that he relied on the teaching of the four foundations of mindfulness (of body, feelings, mind, and dharmas) of the "Sheng-hsing" chapter of the *Nirvāṇa Sūtra* (T 12:447b and 689a). *Chuang Tzu*, Wai-wu, compares getting the fish and forgetting the trap to getting the idea and forgetting the words.

20. Here is a provisional list of material from the *Bodhidharma Anthology* found in BGMS, the *Bka' thang sde lnga*, and Tibetan Tun-huang manuscripts. See appendix A, notes 6 and 7.

FROM BGMS

fol. 57.5: entrance by principle of section 2 introduced by "from the sayings of the Great Master Bodhidharmatāra" (*mkhan po chen po Bo-dhe-dar-mo-ta-ras bshad pa las*)

fols. 122.4–130.2: sections 68; 69; 70; 71; 72; 73; 74; 75; 76; 77; 78; 79; 80; 85; 86; 87; 88; 89; 90; 91; 81; 82; 83; and 84; that is, *Record III*

fol. 130.2: entrance by principle of section 2 introduced by "from the *Rgya lung chen po*" fol. 130.4: section 7 of *Record I* introduced by "also a person says" (*yang mi zhig gis smras pa*)

fol. 131.2: section 8 of *Record I* introduced by "the Great Master says" (*mkhan po chen pos bshad pa*)

fol. 173.5: entrance by practice of section 2 introduced by "from Ma-hā-yan's *Bsam gtan rgya lung chen po*"

Two other quotations from the *Rgya lung chen po* do not appear in the *Bodhidharma Anthology* as we have it:

fol. 177.5: a cultivation in which one perceives the luminosity of a Buddha-body (*sku'i 'od gsal*), introduced by "from the *Rgya lung chen po*"

fol. 179.1: one of a set of dialogues added to the end of the *Chüeh-kuan lun*, introduced by "from the *Rgya lung*"

FROM THE *Bka' thang sde lnga*

fol. 19b.4; MBT, 69.5: cites the title "Dharmatāra's *Rgya lung chen mo*"

fol. 21b.1; MBT, 70.27: entrance by principle of section 2 introduced by "spoken by the Great Master Bodhidharmatāra" (*mkhan chen Bo-dhi-dha-rmo-tta-ras gsungs*)

fols. 23b.3–25a.3; MBT, 74.10–76.17: sections 68–91 (missing 80) of *Record III* in the same order as BGMS but without 78

fol. 25a.3; MBT, 76.17: section 7 of *Record I*

fol. 25a.4; MBT, 76.20: section 8 of *Record I* introduced by "the Great Master Dharmatāra says" (*mkhan po chen po Dha-rmo-ttā-ras bshad*)

FROM PELLIOT TIB. 116

fol. verso 41.2: entrance by principle of section 2 introduced by "from the sayings of Bodhidharmatāra, the first of the sevenfold lineage" (*bdun rgyud kyi dang po Bo-de-dar-ma-ta-las bshad pa las*)

FROM PELLIOT TIB. 821

fol. 5.1: entrance by principle of section 2 introduced by "from the sayings of Bodhidharmatāra, the first of the sevenfold lineage"

The *Chüeh-kuan lun* quotation under the title *Rgya lung* (*Chinese Injunctions*) in BGMS is a translation of a dialogue about killing illusory sentient beings found at the end of the *Chüeh-kuan lun* in three of its six Tun-huang manuscripts (Pelliot Ch. 2885; Pelliot Ch. 2045; and Peking *jun* 84). For the passage, see Yanagida Seizan and Tokiwa Gishin, eds., *Zekkanron* (Kyoto: Zen bunka kenkyūjo, 1976), 99–100.

21. BGMS, fols. 57.5–58.2. For a transcription, see chapter 2, note 1. The same passage also appears at fol. 130.2–4 with *lham mer gnas pa*. The *Bka' thang sde lnga* has it with *lham mer gnas* (fol. 21b.2; MBT, 70.28).

22. Pelliot Tib. 116, fol. verso 42.1, has *lham mer gnas na*.

23. This portion of the Mahāyoga thesis is found in BGMS at fol. 59.3–4: *chos thams cad ni rang rig par gsal ba nyid bden pa gnyis med pa | byed pa pos ma byas pa dang | yong gis 'od gsal ba | dbyings ye shes gnyis su med pa ste |* The following portion of the Atiyoga thesis is at fol. 60.4: *rang rig pa ma bzhag ma g'yos ma bslad ma zhugs par lhan ne lhang nge [= lham me lham me] ye gsal bar ci zhig bsgom |*

24. Hayashi Taiun, "Bodaidaruma den no kenkyū," *Shūkyō kenkyū* n.s. 9, no. 3 (1932): 66–68, has collected the relevant passages from the translation records, sutra prefaces, and the *Li-tai san-pao chi*. According to translation records and sutra prefaces, T'an-lin participated in the following projects: a 540 translation of a sutra from the *Ratnakūṭa* collection by Tripiṭaka Dharma Master Vimokṣaprajñarṣi (?), who was assisted by his disciple Gautama Prajñāruci (T 12:115b); a 541 translation of a Vasubandhu sutra commentary done at the Chin-hua Monastery by Tripiṭaka Dharma Master Vimokṣaprajñarṣi and the Indian Brahman Gautama Prajñāruci (T 26:273c); a 541 translation of a Vasubandhu commentary on the *Dharmacakra-pravartana Sūtra* done at the Chin-hua by Dharma Master Vimokṣaprajñarṣi and his disciple Gautama Prajñāruci (T 26:355c); a 541 translation of Nāgārjuna's *Vigraha-vyāvartanī* done at the Chin-hua by Tripiṭaka Dharma Master Vimokṣaprajñarṣi together with the Indian Brahman Gautama Prajñāruci (T 32:13b); a 541 translation of Vasubandhu's *Karmasiddhi-prakaraṇa* by the same two translators (T 31:777b); a 542 translation of an *avadāna* by Gautama Prajñāruci (T 3:390c); a translation of the *Saddharma-smṛtyupasthāna Sūtra* by the Brahman Gautama Prajñāruci (T 17:1b); and the *Shun-chung lun*, a 543 translation of a Madhyamaka work attributed to Nāgārjuna and Asaṅga (T 30:39c). According to the *Li-tai san-pao chi*, T 49:86a–87a, T'an-lin participated in ten projects. Of translations by Bodhiruci we find: a Vasubandhu commentary on the *Lotus Sūtra*, for which T'an-lin wrote the preface; and a Vasubandhu commentary on the *Dharma-cakra-pravartana Sūtra*. There is an *avadāna* by Buddhaśānta. Of translations by Gautama Prajñāruci we find: a 539 translation of the *Saddharma-smṛtyupasthāna Sūtra* done at Yeh; a sutra from the *Ratnakūṭa* collection that was done in 541 at the Chin-hua; a sutra, the *Mangalaṣṭaka*; an *avadāna* done in 542 at the Chin-hua; a translation of the *Caturdharmaka Sūtra* done at the Chin-hua; a 538 translation of Nāgārjuna's *Vigraha-vyāvartanī*; and a 541 translation of Vasubandhu's *Karmasiddhi-prakaraṇa* done at the Chin-hua. This list amounts to eighty-two rolls. The *Li-tai san-pao chi* remarks that, at the same time Gautama Prajñāruci was translating in Yeh, Bodhiruci was rendering some of the same texts (T 49:87a). Vimokṣaprajñarṣi was a native of Oḍḍiyana. He arrived in Lo-

yang in 516 with his disciple Gautama Prajñāruci; in 541 they traveled together to Yeh. Gautama Prajñāruci was a native of Benares. Bodhiruci, a native of central India, arrived in Lo-yang in 508. He worked up until 534–37 in Lo-yang and then in Yeh. Buddhaśānta, an Indian, was active in Lo-yang and Yeh during the period 525–39.

25. Translation records and catalogues use such phraseology as the following: "Facing the translator was Sramana T'an-lin's brush" (T 12:115b); "Sramana T'an-lin faced the translator and recorded" (T 26:355c); "Facing the translator was Sramana T'an-lin receiving with his brush" (T 32:13b); and "T'an-lin received with his brush and composed the preface" (T 49:86a).

26. This commentary, compiled between 605 and 617, quotes the commentary of T'an-lin/Armless Lin/Lin-kung at: T 37:21c; 22a; 22b; 29b; 38b; 39a; 43a; 45b; 52c; 54b; 58b; 73a; and 89c. In some of these—for instance, T 37:22a and 22b—T'an-lin refers to the Sanskrit original of the sutra. Concerning matters of translation terminology, Chi-tsang relied heavily on the famous translator Paramārtha and T'an-lin, which places T'an-lin in illustrious company. See Hayashi, "Bodaidaruma den no kenkyū," 68–69.

27. T 51:743c–744a.

28. References are to the fifteen-section Guṇabhadra translation, which was the one used in Chinese commentaries. The letter and prediction are T 12:217a–b; the ten undertakings are 217b–c; the three great vows are 218a; the interpretation of the four noble truths as an explanation of the Tathagatagarbha is 221b–c and 222b; and the Buddha's final pronouncement to Śrīmālā is 223a. For an English translation, see Alex Wayman and Hideko Wayman, trans., *The Lion's Roar of Queen Śrīmālā* (New York: Columbia University Press, 1974).

29. For a diagram showing how Hui-yüan's *Sheng-man ching i-chi* (ZZ 1, 30, 4) breaks down the fifteen chapters of the sutra, see Ono Gemmyō, ed., *Bussho kaisetsu daijiten* (1933–36; reprint, Tokyo: Daitō shuppansha, 1964–67), 5:359. The lost second roll of this commentary turned up among the Tun-huang manuscripts, Pelliot Ch. 2091 and 3308. For a chart of K'uei-chi's *Sheng-man ching shu-chi* (ZZ 1, 30, 4), see Ono, *Bussho kaisetsu daijiten*, 5:360. For Chi-tsang's breakdown, see T 37:27b.

30. T 37:21c.

31. A work with a similar title (*Ju-tao an-hsin yao fang-pien fa-men*) and description is mentioned in the *Leng-chia shih-tzu chi* (T 85:1286c21; Yanagida, *Shoki no zenshi I*, 186). The last portion of section 6 of *Record I* is quoted in TCL (T 48:950c) under the title *Ta-ch'eng ju-tao an-hsin fa*. There has been much debate concerning the verse(s). Japanese scholars differ on where to locate the beginning and end. For a summary of these opinions, see Jorgenson, "The Earliest Text," 370–76. I have followed Jorgenson and begun with *tso-ch'an*.

32. T 47:142c.

Commentary on the *Records*

1. For an excellent biography, one that goes a long way toward solving the problem of Tsung-mi's Ch'an filiation, see Peter N. Gregory, *Tsung-mi and the Sinification of Buddhism* (Princeton: Princeton University Press, 1991), 27–90. See also Kamata Shigeo, *Shūmitsu kyōgaku no shisōshi-teki kenkyū* (Tokyo: Tōkyō daigaku shuppankai, 1975), 52–72; and Jan Yün-hua, *Tsung-mi* (Taipei: Tung ta t'u-shu kung-szu yin-hsing, 1988), 1–42. Gregory (315–25) lists thirty-one works by Tsung-mi, though some are listed twice under different titles.

2. T 48:413a; Kamata, *Zengen shosenshū tojo*, 254.

3. The opening line of the first fascicle of TCL, T 48:417b, runs: "The patriarchs make known the principle of Ch'an, transmitting the correct thesis of silent alignment; the Buddhas extend the gate of the teachings, setting up the great purport of the canonical explanations." This is the theme of the *General Preface to the Collection of Explanations of the Ch'an Source* (T 48:399c; Kamata, *Zengen shosenshū tojo*, 33): "The canonical teachings are the sutras and treatises left behind by the Buddhas and bodhisattvas. Ch'an is the poetic lines and verses composed by the various good friends on the path. The Buddha sutras open outward, catching the thousands of the beings of the eight classes, while Ch'an lines and verses pinch up an abridgment, being oriented to one type of karmic ability found in this land of China." Yen-shou was from Ch'ien-t'ang (Hang-chou) and became an official. At twenty-eight he took ordination under a disciple of Hsüeh-feng I-tsun (822–908) and eventually became the third generation of the Fa-yen lineage. He practiced Ch'an and Buddha recitation. His *Sung kao-seng chuan* entry is T 50:887a–b. His official career provides another similarity with Tsung-mi, as the latter was preparing for such a career but opted for Ch'an.

4. T 48:924a.

5. Yün-hua Jan, "Two Problems concerning Tsung-mi's Compilation of Ch'an-tsang," *Transactions of the International Conference of Orientalists in Japan* 19 (1974): 46, remarks that Sekiguchi Shindai first suggested in a conversation that Tsung-mi's collection had been absorbed into that of Yen-shou.

6. The transmission belt between Tsung-mi and Yen-shou could have been a disciple of Hsüeh-feng I-tsun. A 1576 Korean edition of the *General Preface to the Collection of Explanations of the Ch'an Source* has an undated postscript added at the time of the Sung printing (Kamata, *Zengen shosenshū tojo*, 260; KB, 149). It tells how a copy in the hand of the illustrious calligrapher P'ei Hsiu, Tsung-mi's closest disciple, eventually made its way to Wu-yüeh (Kiangsu/Chekiang) via Ch'an Master Wei-ching, who may be Nan-yüeh Wei-ching, a disciple of Hsüeh-feng I-tsun. The southerner Wei-ching is an excellent candidate for one disposed to ensure the transmission of Tsung-mi's collection. His *Sung kao-seng chuan* entry, T 50:818b–c, speaks of his propensity for Hua-yen teachings, for which

Tsung-mi had a strong affinity. Yen-shou took ordination under another student of I-tsun and eventually was invited to a monastery in Wu-yüeh.

7. Here is a provisional list of quotations from the entire *Bodhidharma Anthology* found in TCL:

T 48:482a: sections 33–44 of *Record I* introduced by "the first patriarch, the Great Master, says"

603b: section 4, the *Second Letter*, introduced by "as Layman Hsiang says"

848a: sections 25–26 of *Record I* introduced by "as the Great Master Dharma says"

897a: section 18 of *Record I* introduced by "the patriarchal master says"

939b–c: sections 8; 13; 49; 19; 20; 24; 25; 26; 27; 28; 30; 31; 33; 34; 42; and 48 of *Record I* introduced by "the master compiled the *Method for Quieting Mind*, which says" (*shih shu An-hsin fa-men yün*), "master" referring to "the first patriarch of this land Bodhidharmatāra" (*tz'u-t'u ch'u-tsu P'u-t'i-ta-mo-to-lo*).

939c–940a: section 82 of *Record III* introduced by "the second patriarch, the Great Master K'o, says" (*ti-erh tsu K'o ta-shih yün*)

941b: sections 75; 69; 62; 71; 74; 77; 85; and 91 of *Record II* and *Record III*

942a–b: section 2, the *Two Entrances*, introduced by "Dhyana Master Buddha says"

950c: section 6 of *Record I* introduced by "the *Method of Entering the Path and Quieting Mind of the Mahāyāna* says" (*Ta-ch'eng ju-tao an-hsin fa yün*)

953a: section 80 of *Record III* introduced by "Tripiṭaka Dharma Master says" (*san-tsang fa-shih yün*)

The sheer size of TCL has slowed research on it. A great step forward is the publication of the text in electronic form: Urs App, ed., *ZenBase CDI* (Kyoto: International Research Institute for Zen Buddhism, 1995). Yen-shou's *Hsin-fu chu* (ZZ 2, 16, 1) also contains some quotations from the anthology.

8. T 48:939b–c. The seven Buddhas of the past and the twenty-seven patriarchs of India are covered at T 48:937c–939b.

9. Ching-chüeh's commentary on the *Heart Sūtra*, which dates to 727, quotes the *An-hsin lun* (*Treatise on Quieting Mind*), and the quotation corresponds to a sutra quotation in section 68 of *Record III*. See Yanagida, *Shoki zenshū shisho no kenkyū*, 601. There is thus a strong possibility all the *Records* material went under the title *Method for Quieting Mind*. Also Ching-chüeh's *Leng-chia shih-tzu chi* appears to quote the *Records*: T 85:1287a6–7 (sections 36 and 22 of *Record I*; sections 73 and 87 of *Record III*); T 85:1287b14 (section 56 of *Record II*).

10. Here is a tentative list: *pu* at the end of sentences indicating a question; *i-ko* ("one"); *tan-shih* ("if"); *sui-chi* ("even though"); *tzu-shih* ("from the outset"); *tsai* of *hsing-tsai* ("ventures off"); *nan-nü* ("youths"); *han* ("fellow"); *ni* ("you");

ch'u-wu ("no matter what may come"); *ch'u-shih* ("no matter what may happen"); *a-shei* ("who"); *feng-wu* ("no matter what may come"). Three works are indispensable for the study of colloquial language in Ch'an texts. Yoshitaka Iriya, Ruth F. Sasaki, and Burton F. Watson, "On Some Texts of Ancient Spoken Chinese" (Kyoto, 1954), is an English translation, with comments and emendations, of Henri Maspero, "Sur quelques textes anciens de chinois parlé," *Bulletin de l'École Français d'Extrème-Orient* 14, no. 4 (1914): 1–36. This article draws its examples from five texts: *P'ang chü-shih yü-lu; Ch'uan-hsin fa yao* and *Wan-ling lu; Lin-chi lu;* and *Chao-chou yü-lu.* I have adopted its terminology. Ōta Tatsuo, *Chūgoku rekishi bumpō* (1958; reprint, Kyoto: Hōyū shoten, 1978), is a historical grammar of spoken Chinese with a wealth of examples. Iriya Yoshitaka and Koga Hidehiko, eds., *Zengo jiten* (Kyoto: Shibunkaku shuppan, 1991), is a superb dictionary of Ch'an colloquial language.

11. The Japanese, who inherited the Sung Dynasty recorded-sayings literature, divorced as they were from spoken Chinese, treated these books as a literary language akin to that of the Chinese classics—in other words, as a literature to be parsed, rearranged in Japanese word order with the addition of Japanese particles, and studied. Only in recent times has a Japanese specialist in the colloquial of T'ang China pointed out many of the traditional "literary" misreadings of colloquialisms in Zen texts that have been faithfully transmitted in the Zen monasteries of Japan for centuries. According to Iriya Yoshitaka, trans., *Rinzairoku* (Tokyo: Iwanami shoten, 1989), 228, the problem has been the traditional habit of doing *kundoku* readings, in literary format, of Zen texts filled with colloquial forms.

12. For an English translation, see Burton Watson, trans., *The Vimalakīrti Sūtra* (New York: Columbia University Press, 1997). Also see Charles Luk, trans., *The Vimalakīrti Nirdeśa Sūtra* (1972; reprint, Boston: Shambhala, 1990). For a translation done from a Tibetan translation, see Robert A. F. Thurman, trans., *The Holy Teaching of Vimalakīrti* (University Park and London: Pennsylvania State University Press, 1976). For a French translation from the Tibetan with reference to the Chinese versions, see Étienne Lamotte, trans., *L'enseignement de Vimalakīrti* (Lɔuvain: Publications Universitaires, 1962). For an English translation of Lamotte, see Sara Boin, trans., *The Teaching of Vimalakīrti* (London: Pali Text Society, 1976).

13. T 14:544b.

14. T 14:551c.

15. T 30:18c.

16. Here is a tentative list: *hui-shih* ("surely"); *ni* ("you"); *pei* (passive construction); *tou* (strengthens negative); *na* ("how"); *jo-wei* ("how"); *mou-chia* ("I"); *i-ko* ("one"); *shang-tzu* ("even"); *a-shei* ("who"); *ni-chia* ("you"); *t'ou* (suffix as in *pi-tzu-t'ou,* "brush"); and *a-ning* ("how").

17. Yanagida, "Goroku no rekishi," 322.

18. Yanagida and Tokiwa, *Zekkanron*, 87.

19. Yanagida, "Goroku no rekishi," 325, claims that Yüan was advancing the teachings of Lin-chi I-hsüan (d. 866) centuries before Lin-chi and that Lin-chi's message is no more than a reshuffling of the Yüan of the *Records*. It is clear that in terms of both content and style the Yüan passages of *Record II* remind one of the *Lin-chi lu*. Yüan claims that possession of the energy of liveliness is a guarantee against being put in thralldom by people or the Dharma. If we substitute belief in oneself and strong resolution, the resolution of the manly man, for Yüan's physical energy, we have Lin-chi. Both are talking about spirit, mettle, pluck, pep. Both claim that they have no teaching to give to others. Whereas Yüan says words and letters will deceive you, Lin-chi claims they will tire you out without bringing any benefit. Here is Lin-chi speaking: "Those about to train in the path must believe in themselves. Do not seek outside yourself.... Followers of the path! If you want to apprehend real Dharma, you must first of all be a resolute man. If you are pliant and vacillating, it won't work. A cracked vessel is inadequate for storing clarified butter; one who is a great vessel must, more than anything else, not be deceived by other people.... If you seek the Buddha, you will be gathered in by Buddha-demons; if you seek the patriarchs, you will be bound by patriarch-demons.... Followers of the path! If you wish to achieve an understanding of real Dharma, all you must do is not be taken in by the deceptions of other people.... I have not one Dharma to give to people; it is merely curing disease and loosening bonds.... Do not seek in the written word. Your mind will be stirred, you will become tired out, and you will inhale cold air, to no benefit." T 47:499a, 499c, 500b, and 502c; Yanagida Seizan, trans., *Rinzai-roku*, Butten kōza 30 (Tokyo: Daizō shuppan, 1972), 118–72. Even the language patterns are similar: use of the second-person pronoun *ni* and the passive construction with *pei*.

20. T 48:941b.

21. Yanagida, "Goroku no rekishi," 338–41; Yanagida, *Sodōshū*, 37 and 40.

22. Daizōkyō gakujutsu yōgo kenkyūkai, *Taishō shinshū daizōkyō sakuin*, vol. 27, *Shoshū-bu 3* (Tokyo: Taishō shinshū daizōkyō kankōkai, 1983), 5.

23. T 47:607c.

24. T 48:298a; Hirata Takashi, trans., *Mumonkan*, Zen no goroku 18 (Tokyo: Chikuma shobō, 1969), 146.

25. The Ho lineage portion of the chart derives from Hirai, *Chūgoku hannya shisōshi kenkyū*, 282. The HKSC entry for Hui-pu (518–87), another entry from the original layer, also links San-lun and Hui-k'o. Hui-pu, a student of San-lun under Dharma Master Seng-ch'üan of Chih-kuan Monastery on Mount She (northeast of Nanking in Kiangsu), came from the South to Yeh and received instruction from Hui-k'o. Hui-pu's entry (T 50:480c) says: "He constantly took pleasure in

cross-legged sitting dhyana and was far removed from clamor and disturbance. He vowed not to lecture and took protecting and holding the Dharma as his mission. Finally he traveled northward to Yeh and came into contact with things he had never heard of. At Dhyana Master Hui-k'o's place he eventually comprehended Hui-k'o's famous views. He then by means of words awakened to the intent. Hui-k'o said: 'What the Dharma Master has stated can be said to destroy self and eliminate views. There is no going beyond this.' Hui-pu then loosed his mind on the lecture mat and completely revealed the principles of the thesis. He made a complete inspection of the meanings of the texts, and one after the other all were in his mind. He also wrote essays and commentaries to the extent of six pack-animal loads, which were carried back to the area called South-of-the-Yangtze. And he sent them to Lang-kung [a student of Seng-ch'üan], who had him lecture on them. Because there were omissions, he went again to the Northern state of Ch'i, extensively copied out what was missing, and returned to present it to Lang. He stored up nothing beyond his robe and bowl. He specialized in cultivating mindfulness and insight and lingered alone in the pine forests."

The biography of Pao-kung (542–621) mentions Hui-pu (T 50:512c): "At the beginning of the Chih-te era of the Ch'en Dynasty [583–86] Hui-pu of Mount She went north to Yeh. When he first returned, he wanted to open a dhyana monastery. He earnestly requested Pao-kung to gather a party of pure practitioners. Pao-kung bowed to Hui-pu's call and immediately set about the responsibility. He established the ranks of administrators and drew in people to train in a dhyana lineage. And so the practice style of the Hsi-hsia Monastery has never dropped off. Even now it is endlessly praised in song. Pao-kung also followed Hui-pu to listen to the three treatises and was good at understanding the dark words. All his previous doubts one by one dissipated." Thus, it seems that Hui-k'o's dhyana was transmitted at the Hsi-hsia Monastery in the Nanking region down to Tao-hsüan's time. See Yanagida, *Shoki zenshū shisho no kenkyū*, 21 and 29 n. 5. Pao-kung later went to Ch'ang-an and was in contact with Tao-hsüan.

26. We have no HKSC entry for Ho; he is known only through the entries for his disciples Ching-ai (T 50:625c20–21) and Hsüan-ching (T 50:569b20 and 26–27). Ui, *Zenshūshi kenkyū*, 1:76, suggests that he was lecturing at the Pai-kuan Monastery in Ying-yang (Honan) before 550 and probably died around the time of the Chou suppression in 574. Ui also suggests that his ascetic practice was not as severe as Na's and Hui-man's since he dwelled at one monastery and had a scholarly style.

27. T 50:625c28–626a1 and 626c18–20.

28. T 50:681a12–16. This Ching-yüan may be the Ching-yüan of Chih-hsiang Monastery in the Chung-nan Mountains for whom there is an entry, T 50:511b–12a.

29. T 50:628a15.

30. T 50:586c9–10 and 23.

31. T 50:569b20 and 27–28; 569c8.

32. T 50:569c17–18.

33. A tentative list includes only *na* ("how") and *tou* (strengthens the negative).

34. T 48:939b–940a.

35. T 14:539c.

36. T 48:339a4–5; Philip B. Yampolsky, *The Platform Sutra of the Sixth Patriarch* (New York: Columbia University Press, 1967), 8 (from the back) and 140.

Appendix A

1. For the key points of Fujieda Akira's theory on the origin of the Tun-huang cave "library," see Akira Fujieda, "Une reconstruction de la 'Bibliothèque' de Touen-houang," *Journal Asiatique* 269 (1981): 67; and Fujieda Akira, *Tun-huang hsüeh t'ao-lun* (Tientsin: Nan-k'ai ta-hsüeh li-shih hsi, 1981), 79–80. The scenario runs as follows. During the ninth and tenth centuries the family of the émigré from Northwest China Wu Hsü-chih played a leading role in Tun-huang Buddhism. Since the Tibetans occupied Tun-huang from the 780s to about 860, Wu's sons were raised in a Tibetan-speaking environment. Both became Buddhist monks. Wu Fa-ch'eng (known in Tibetan as 'Gos Chos-grub) was appointed Great Reviser-Translator Sramana of the office established by the Tibetans for the translation of Chinese Buddhist texts, and his younger brother Wu Hung-pien, a politician monk, served as Monastic General-in-Chief of the Tun-huang monastic community. After Hung-pien's death in 850, for the next 150 years the Wu family continued annually to make sacrifices to him in one of their family caves (nos. 16, 17, and 18) within the Mo-kao cave complex. This complex, consisting of about four hundred caves hollowed out in irregular tiers along the face of a precipitous cliff, lies twelve miles southeast of the Tun-huang oasis, separated from the town by barren desert. The printing revolution reached the Tun-huang monasteries about the year 1000. At that time the Wu family ceased their annual sacrifices to their ancestor Hung-pien, took the outdated manuscript canon (*ching-tsang*) of a local monastery (probably the San-chieh, known in Tibetan as the Pam-kye), a cache of Tibetan manuscripts that no one could any longer read, and some miscellanea (including the Ch'an texts?), put them into the sacrificial chamber (no. 17), and permanently walled it up. (Some manuscripts bear the seal of the Pao-en Monastery, and Fujieda thinks they may have been borrowed by the San-chieh and not returned.) They used Hung-pien's memorial cave as a burial ground for "sacred waste." Nine centuries later a Taoist monk by the name of Wang was living in cave no. 16, a fairly large cave. A protruding section of its north wall

concealed the hidden chamber of no. 17. One way or another Wang accidentally discovered it. Fujieda's theory is the best available to us.

The story of the subsequent stream of Westerners and Japanese who arrived and carted off thousands of manuscripts to the libraries of their home countries is quite well known. The most famous of this stream by far is Aurel Stein, an enterprising archaeological explorer in the employ of the British in India, who arrived in March 1907 and soon heard a rumor about a cache of manuscripts. In time, Stein talked a mass of manuscripts out of Wang's hands and made a hefty donation for Wang's shrine. These materials were carried back to London, where they were deposited in the British Museum and the India Office Library. Early in 1908, the French Sinologist Paul Pelliot reached Tun-huang. Pelliot made a special effort to search out non-Buddhist texts; in the end he purchased more than three thousand Chinese rolls and more than two thousand Tibetan manuscripts. These now reside in the Bibliothèque Nationale in Paris. These activities came to the attention of the Ch'ing Dynasty authorities, and they ordered that the remainder of the manuscripts be brought to Peking and stored in the capital library. However, an enormous amount of material, mainly Tibetan, still remained at Tun-huang.

Among the twenty to thirty thousand manuscripts in the collections, less than three hundred have a date, the earliest being 406 and the latest 1002. There are approximately three to four thousand Tibetan manuscripts in the collections. The contents of the manuscripts are overwhelmingly Buddhistic, perhaps 90 percent of the whole. For a general treatment, including descriptions of all the collections and the formal characteristics of the manuscripts, see Akira Fujieda, "The Tunhuang Manuscripts, a General Description (Part I)," *Memoirs of the Research Institute for Humanistic Studies Zinbun* 9 (1966): 1–32. The catalogues of the main collections are as follows. For the Stein collection: Lionel Giles, *Descriptive Catalogue of the Chinese Manuscripts from Tunhuang in the British Museum* (London: Trustees of the British Museum, 1957); and Louis de la Vallée Poussin, *Catalogue of the Tibetan Manuscripts from Tun-huang in the India Office Library* (Oxford: Oxford University Press, 1962). For the Pelliot collection: Jacques Gernet and Wu Chi-yu, *Catalogue des manuscrits chinois de Touen-houang*, vol. 1 (Paris: Bibliothèque Nationale, 1970); Michel Soymie et al., *Catalogue des manuscrits chinois de Touen-houang*, vol. 3 (Paris: Bibliothèque Nationale, 1983); Michel Soymie et al., *Catalogue des manuscrits chinois de Touen-houang*, vol. 4 (Paris: Bibliothèque Nationale, 1991); Michel Soymie et al., *Catalogue des manuscrits chinois de Touen-houang*, vol. 5 (Paris: Bibliothèque Nationale, 1995); and Marcelle Lalou, *Inventaire des manuscrits tibétains de Touen-houang conservés à la Bibliothèque Nationale*, 3 vols. (Paris: Bibliothèque Nationale, 1939, 1950, and 1961). For the Peking collection: Ch'en Yüan, *Tun-huang chieh-yü lu* (Peiping: Kuo-li chung-yang yen-chiu yüan li-shih yü-yen yen-chiu so, 1931). Citations take the form: Stein Ch. 1880, Pelliot Ch. 3018,

Peking *su* 99, Pelliot Tib. 116, and so forth. For a table to convert Stein numbers into Giles's serial numbers, see Giles, *Descriptive Catalogue*, 303–31.

2. Tanaka Ryōshō, "Tonkō zenseki (kambun) kenkyū gaishi," *Tōkyō daigaku bungakubu bunka kōryū kenkyū shisetsu kenkyū kiyō* 5 (1981): 23–41, summarizes the discoveries and researches of the major scholars of the Tun-huang Ch'an manuscripts. Japanese scholarship has been voluminous since Yabuki Keiki in 1916 first discovered seven Ch'an manuscripts at the British Museum in London. The Chinese scholar Hu Shih in 1926 went to Europe and discovered four Ch'an manuscripts in the Paris and London collections. The Rinzai Zen layman Suzuki Daisetsu had a dual career: as a key figure in the spread of knowledge of Zen to the West through a number of English writings, and as a scholar of the Tun-huang Ch'an manuscripts. In 1935 Suzuki traveled to Korea, Manchuria, and China, and throughout the 1930s he published on Ch'an manuscripts in the Ryūkoku University (Kyoto) and Peking collections. In 1936 he went to Europe and brought back photographs of Ch'an manuscripts in the London and Paris collections. Simultaneously Kuno Hōryū was publishing his finds in the Paris collection. It would be hard to exaggerate the amount and quality of Yanagida Seizan's work on Tun-huang Ch'an manuscripts during the 1960s and 1970s. During that time Tanaka Ryōshō discovered numerous Ch'an manuscripts in the collections. Many other Japanese scholars have published in this area.

3. Tanaka Ryōshō, "Tonkō zenshū shiryō kōmoku betsu ichiran," *Sōtōshū kenkyūin kenkyūsei kenkyū kiyō* 1 (November 1969): 1–10, is a list of Ch'an manuscripts arranged under titles of texts. A preliminary descriptive catalogue is Tanaka Ryōshō, "Tonkō zenshū shiryō bunrui mokuroku shokō: I. Dentō shijōron," *Komazawa daigaku bukkyō gakubu kenkyū kiyō* 27 (March 1969): 1–17; "II. Zempō shūdōron (1)" 29 (March 1971): 1–18; "II. Zempō shūdōron (2)" 32 (March 1974): 30–49; and "II. Zempō shūdōron (3)" 34 (March 1976): 1–24. The two genres covered are transmission-of-the-lamp texts and dhyana-method texts. TZBK, 48–55, lists Ch'an manuscripts in the various collections. The "Tonkō zenshū kankei shiryō ichiran" in Yanagida, *Shoki zenshū shisho no kenkyū*, 51–53, is also a list of Ch'an manuscripts in the collections. Yanagida Seizan's "Zenseki kaidai," in *Zenke goroku II*, Sekai koten bungaku zenshū 36B, ed. Nishitani Keiji and Yanagida Seizan (Tokyo: Chikuma shobō, 1974), 453–66, treats Tun-huang Ch'an texts. For a broad survey by numerous Japanese scholars, see Shinohara Hisao and Tanaka Ryōshō, eds., *Tonkō butten to zen*, Tonkō kōza 8 (Tokyo: Daitō shuppansha, 1980).

4. Daishun Ueyama, "A Chronological Stratification of the Tun-huang Ch'an Manuscripts" (paper delivered at the CISHAAN Tun-huang/Turfan Seminar, Kyoto, Japan, 2 September 1983), 6–7.

5. Ueyama Daishun, "Tonkō ni okeru zen no shosō," *Ryūkoku daigaku ronshū* 421 (October 1982): 90–116, uses codicological criteria to arrange about 140 of the

most important Ch'an manuscripts into these three chronological strata. Ueyama Daishun, *Tonkō bukkyō no kenkyū* (Kyoto: Hōzōkan, 1990), 401–23, makes some corrections and additions to the initial article. The criteria include: analysis of paper (dimensions, appearance, color, width of columns, etc.); manuscript forms; handwriting; and recto texts (some manuscripts have dated administrative documents on the other side).

A few dated Ch'an manuscripts serve as benchmarks. Almost all administrative documents have other texts on the verso, usually Buddhist texts. Presumably, when the active life of official documents was over, they were removed from the office in question and subsequently used for other purposes, paper being at a premium at an outpost such as Tun-huang. When a Ch'an text appears on the verso of a dated administrative document, in order to determine the date of copying, it is necessary to have a rough estimate of the preservation period for documents. Since population records sent to the center during the early T'ang were kept for a period of fifteen years, Ueyama uses that figure.

Using the same 140 Ch'an manuscripts as a database, Ueyama, "A Chronological Stratification," 3–5, makes the following generalizations. Early-period manuscripts (750–780) are often on thin, high-quality paper, a typical example being Stein Ch. 2054, which Giles, *Descriptive Catalogue*, 186–87, describes as semicursive on thin, soft buff paper. During the middle period, the Tibetan occupation, Tun-huang was cut off from China proper and hence from its supply of brushes and high-quality hemp paper (*ma-chih*). Both were replaced by local products—the wooden pen introduced by the Tibetans, and a thick, coarse paper in larger sheets; also, Indian palm-leaf style manuscripts begin to appear. A representative example is Stein Ch. 4286, which Giles, *Descriptive Catalogue*, 187, describes as a mediocre manuscript on thick buff paper. During the late period of the tenth century the large, coarse, thick paper of the preceding Tibetan period continued in use; also, the calligraphy is frequently unskillful. An example is Stein Ch. 2679, which Giles, *Descriptive Catalogue*, 188, describes as a poor manuscript on coarse drab paper.

6. Daishun Ueyama, "The Study of Tibetan Ch'an Manuscripts Recovered from Tun-huang: A Review of the Field and Its Prospects," in *Early Ch'an in China and Tibet*, Berkeley Buddhist Studies Series, no. 5, ed. Whalen Lai and Lewis R. Lancaster (Berkeley: Lancaster Publications, 1983), 327–49, is a summary of Japanese discoveries and researches down to 1977. See also Daishun Ueyama, "Etudes des manuscrits tibétains de Dunhuang relatifs au bouddhisme de Dhyāna: Bilan et perspectives," *Journal Asiatique* 269 (1981): 288–95. Kimura Ryūtoku, "Tonkō chibettogo zen bunken mokuroku shokō," *Tōkyō daigaku bungakubu bunka kōryū kenkyū shisetsu kenkyū kiyō* 4 (1980): 93–129, is a preliminary descriptive catalogue that lists Tibetan Ch'an manuscripts in the Pelliot and Stein collections in numerical order. In most cases the Tibetan Ch'an manuscripts

are in palm-leaf style with four or five lines per leaf and carefully written, which makes citation by line number feasible.

7. BGMS, by Gnubs-chen Sangs-rgyas-ye-shes (also known as Rdo-rje-yang-dbang-gter), is a treatise on dhyana and on four approaches to realization: step-by-step entrance (Kamalaśila's *Bhāvanā-krama*); all-at-once entrance (Ch'an); Mahāyoga; and Rdzogs-chen. Its discovery in India during the early 1970s by E. Gene Smith was very important for both Tibetology and Ch'an studies. According to Ancient School tradition, the author was born in 772 at Sgrags-phu in central Tibet. He studied with famous teachers from India, Nepal, Bru-zha (northwest of Tibet), and Tibet, including Vimalamitra and Kamalaśila. His practice centered on a visualization of the body of Mañjuśrī bodhisattva and recitation of the Yamāntaka mantra. Yamāntaka, the Destroyer of Yama the Lord of Death, is a fierce emanation of Akṣobhya Buddha. As the nine-headed Vajrabhairava, who is black in color and assumes the jumping posture, he is a fierce representation of Mañjuśrī. The "Blon po bka'i thang yig" ("Decrees of the Ministers") is one section of the Rdzogs-chen text *Bka' thang sde lnga* (*Five Classes of Commands*), a *gter-ma* discovered by O-rgyan-gling-pa (1323–79), one of the numerous discoverers of hidden literary treasures. The Ch'an portions of BGMS are found at fols. 57–58 and 118–86. MBT, 68–81, provides a transcription of the relevant portion of the *Bka' thang sde lnga* based on two editions, one of Sde-dge and the other of Potala. As Tucci remarks (MBT, 19), the corruption of the text is quite evident.

8. For what an Inner Asian Ch'an was like, we can look to two Tibetan manuscripts. Pelliot Tib. 996(1) describes an Inner Asian Ch'an lineage connecting Kucha, Tun-huang, and Tibet. It lists an otherwise unknown Chinese master, called Be'u-sing in Tibetan, who was active in Tun-huang and Kan-chou. Be'u-sing was the successor of an Indian master, A-rtan-hver, who is said to have migrated from India to Kucha on the northern route of the Silk Road. Be'u-sing's successor was a Chinese, known by the Tibetan name Man. Man traveled to China, and his successor was the Tibetan Nam-ka'i-snying-po or Tshig-tsa-nam-ka, who was active in the early ninth century. This lineage flourished from about 750 to 850 all across the Ho-hsi region occupied by the Tibetans. This was truly an international Zen.

Pelliot Tib. 996(2) provides a brief biography for another Inner Asian Ch'an master, Spug-ye-shes-dbyangs. He left home during the period 742–97 and trained under Chinese Ch'an masters for decades. Sometime in the early ninth century he wrote a work based on the teachings of the masters of India, China, and Tibet. Pelliot Tib. 818, the *Rnyal 'byor chen por sgom ba'i don* (*Meaning of Mahāyoga Cultivation*), is a fragment of this work, eighty-eight questions and answers, with each of the answers giving two or three sutra citations. Later, Spug-ye-shes-dbyangs was active in the Chinghai region and died there in 850 or 863, at the age of eighty, at the hut of Nam-ka'i-snying-po. His training was in both Ch'an and Mahāyoga. See Marcelle Lalou, "Document tibétain sur l'expansion du Dhyāna chinois," *Journal Asiatique* 131 (1939): 505–23.

9. I have compiled this and the following two lists by combing through the works of Ueyama Daishun cited in note 5 above.

10. Of the nine manuscripts containing material from the *Bodhidharma Anthology*, Ueyama, *Tonkō bukkyō no kenkyū*, 404–5 and 413–14, classifies Pelliot Ch. 3018 (portions of *Record I* and *Record II*) and Pelliot Ch. 4795 (a small fragment of *Record III*) as early stratum. He classifies all the others with the exception of Stein Ch. 7159 as middle stratum. Thus, of the seven texts in the anthology, only the *Records* are to be found on early-stratum manuscripts. This reinforces any claim that the *Records* are among our earliest Ch'an documents.

11. For each of these texts, with the exception of the *Records*, I will give a brief description of contents, an edition if available, and an English translation if available. Detailed information can be found in Tanaka, "Tonkō zenshū shiryō bunrui mokuroku shokō," and Shinohara and Tanaka, *Tonkō butten to zen*. For no. 2, see the description and translation in appendix B.

No. 3 was compiled by someone who relied on dhyana practice grounded in the *Ta-ch'eng ch'i-hsin lun* to realize the perfect teaching (*yüan-chiao*), as opposed to the gradual and sudden teachings. The perfect teaching is a meditative concentration in which one realizes that everything is equal to space. The opening reflects the opening of the *Two Entrances*. In place of principle and practice we find the categories of the *Ch'i-hsin lun*, the two gates of sentient-being mind: Thusness and arising-extinguishing. For an edition and translation, see McRae, *The Northern School*, 18–44 (from the back) and 149–71.

No. 4 is a recorded-sayings work for Hung-jen of East Mountain. It is composed of two parts, the former consisting of the master's answers to disciples' questions and the latter a collection of the master's statements interspersed with occasional questions and answers. The main motifs are: the metaphor of the sun obscured by clouds; guarding mind (*shou-hsin*); and two types of meditation practice, one involving the visualization of the sun at an appropriate distance and the other a slow and peaceful ripening of gazing (*shu-k'an*) until the movements of consciousness disappear. For an edition and translation, see McRae, *The Northern School*, 1–16 (from the back) and 121–32.

No. 5 is a work of Hung-jen's disciple Shen-hsiu. It came to be attributed to Bodhidharma and presented as a dialogue between Bodhidharma and Hui-k'o. It opens with a statement on examining mind (*kuan-hsin*) and the twofold function of mind—pure mind and defiled mind. It gives many metaphorical equivalents: the six bandits are the six consciousnesses; the three realms of Buddhist cosmology are the three poisons of greed, hostility, and stupidity; the three eons of the bodhisattva course are the mind of the three poisons, and so forth. The thrust is that mere external seeking without internal cultivation is useless. For an edition, see Suzuki, *Kōkan shōshitsu isho oyobi kaisetsu*, 2:184–232.

The first of no. 6 discusses quieting mind (*an-hsin*) in dialogue format. It seems to echo much in the *Records*. The second discusses eight medicines, such as one-third ounce of faithfully receiving the Dharma, two-thirds ounce of pure zeal, and so forth. One is to "grind up the above eight flavors with the kindness cutter and pulverize them in the samadhi mortar before processing them with a nonduality silk strainer." The third sets up two types of exertion—the gate of entering principle and the gate of producing function, clearly echoing the *Two Entrances*. In the functional mode the practitioner behaves and speaks in a manner that does not contravene the ways of the world. This approximates the first two of the four practices. This piece also contains the same sort of *Records* vocabulary. For transcriptions of the first two, see Yanagida Seizan, "*Dembōhōki* to sono sakusha: Pelliot 3559go bunsho o meguru hokushū zen kenkyū shiryō no satsuki, sono ichi," *Zengaku kenkyū* 53 (July 1963): 57–58 and 61–62.

No. 7 was compiled by the layman Tu Fei, who had a close relationship with disciples of Shen-hsiu. It records the transmission of Dharma down from Bodhidharma, providing biographical entries for Bodhidharma, Hui-k'o, Seng-ts'an, Tao-hsin, Hung-jen, Fa-ju, and Shen-hsiu. Thus it accords Fa-ju the preeminent position as Hung-jen's successor and makes Shen-hsiu the successor of Fa-ju. It criticizes wall-examining and the four practices as "provisional, one-corner formulations." For an edition, see Yanagida, *Shoki no zenshi I*, 327–435. For a translation, see McRae, *The Northern School*, 255–69.

No. 8 was compiled by Ching-chüeh, whose main master was Hsüan-tse. It records the transmission of the "lamp of dhyana," which illumines in silence, providing entries for Guṇabhadra, Bodhidharma, Hui-k'o, Seng-ts'an, Tao-hsin, Hung-jen, and Shen-hsiu. At the eighth generation it gives the names of four of Shen-hsiu's disciples. Fa-ju is deleted. The most striking innovation here is the inclusion of Guṇabhadra, the translator of the four-roll *Laṅkāvatāra Sūtra*, as the first patriarch, with Bodhidharma as his successor. It is not just a string of biographical entries, but a virtual compendium of proto-Ch'an lore. It contains sayings for certain patriarchs, quotes the whole of the *Biography* and *Two Entrances*, provides the earliest extant exposition of cross-legged sitting, and so forth. It emphasizes the concrete practice of "pure sitting" (*ching-tso*). For an edition, see Yanagida, *Shoki no zenshi I*, 47–326.

12. Pelliot Ch. 3922 is a palm-leaf style copy of the *Tun-wu chen-tsung yao-chüeh;* Pelliot Tib. 1228 is a Tibetan transliteration of the *P'u-t'i-ta-mo ch'an-shih kuan-men.*

13. For each of these texts I will give a very brief description of contents. For more information, see Tanaka, "Tonkō zenshū shiryō bunrui mokuroku shokō," and Shinohara and Tanaka, *Tonkō butten to zen*.

No. 1 is attributed to Bodhidharma. It is a dialogue between two fictional characters, a disciple named Yüan-men (Gate-of-the-Conditioned) and a master named Ju-li (Entrance-into-Principle). Discusses under what conditions one may break the precepts; advocates "just extinguishing your views."

The first of no. 2 is an early Shen-hui work. It states that one should not practice *ning-hsin* ("coagulation of mind") and *k'an* ("gazing"), that *pu-kuan* ("no-examining") is enlightenment. The emphasis is on *wu-chu* ("no abiding"). The second is in dialogue format. It stresses that Hung-jen transmitted the robe to Shen-hui's master Hui-neng, making him the sixth patriarch, and attacks the *k'an-ching* ("gazing at purity") of P'u-chi and Hsiang-mo Tsang. P'u-chi's falsely calling himself the Southern School is not to be allowed. There are two schools, Southern (Hui-neng) and Northern (Shen-hsiu/P'u-chi). P'u-chi's calling himself the seventh patriarch and Shen-hsiu the sixth is not to be allowed. It extols chanting the *Vajracchedikā Sūtra*. The third is Shen-hui's answers to a varied series of questions from monks and laymen.

No. 3 is a dialogue between two aspects of the same person, the layman Li Hui-kuang and Ch'an Master Ta-chao. It discusses *hsin pu-ch'i* ("mind not arising"). The preface is virtually identical to that of no. 4 below.

No. 4 is also a dialogue between two aspects of the same person, Hou-mo-ch'en Yen and Chih-ta. It takes off from the *Vajracchedikā Sūtra* passage *ying wu so-chu erh sheng ch'i-hsin* ("one should produce a thought that has nowhere to abide"). The emphasis is on *k'an wu-so* or *k'an wu so-ch'u* ("gazing at the locus of 'no'"). It highlights the sequential relationship between *k'an* ("gazing") and *chien* ("seeing"). If one gazes, then one comes to see.

No. 5 was compiled by the official Wang Hsi. It consists of two series of questions and answers detailing the teaching of Ch'an Master Mo-ho-yen, who went from Tun-huang to central Tibet about 786 at the invitation of the Tibetan emperor. It stresses *k'an-hsin* ("gazing at mind").

The first of no. 6 is in verse form with a preface and is attributed to an unknown master named Man. The emphasis is on *k'an* ("gazing") and *wu-ch'i wu-tung* ("no arising no moving"). The second consists of meditations or exercises for the revolution of the five watches of the night (7 P.M. to 5 A.M.), with one verse for each watch. It is a versification of Shen-hui's attack on the Northern School. The last contains songs on the difficulty of the road for both monks and laypeople.

No. 7 is an apocryphal sutra with a preface by one Hui-kuang. The Buddha says: "Good sons! In cross-legged sitting dhyana one stops views, and in voidness there is not a thing. If you view a Buddha as having various rays of light and the thirty-two marks, these are all perverted views and entanglement in Māra's net." It is quoted in such Ch'an texts as the *Tun-wu yao-men*, no. 8 below, and TCL.

No. 8 is a record of Szechwan Ch'an by the followers of Pao-t'ang Wu-chu. It opens with the dream of Emperor Ming of the Later Han Dynasty. There are entries for six successive patriarchs: Bodhidharmatāra, Hui-k'o, Seng-ts'an, Tao-hsin, Hung-jen, and Hui-neng. These are followed by biographical entries for the major figures of Szechwan Ch'an: Chih-hsien; Ch'u-chi; Wu-hsiang (i.e., the Korean Priest Kim, the fountainhead of the Ching-chung lineage); and Wu-chu. Wu-chu is clearly to be taken as the seventh patriarch. The remainder consists of Wu-chu's sayings and dialogues. The emphasis is on Wu-chu's *wu-nien* ("no thought") and his avoidance of virtually all Buddhist practices.

14. For each of these texts I will give very brief descriptions of contents based mainly on Kimura, "Tonkō chibettogo zen bunken mokuroku shokō."

No. 1 (Stein Tib. 468), which presents the teaching of the Chinese Ch'an master Mo-ho-yen of the Council of Tibet, says: "The one who dwells in a quiet place, alone, straightens his body correctly in cross-legged posture. He practices without lying down day and night. When he enters into dhyana itself, if he gazes at his own mind [*bdag gi sems la bltas na*], there is no mind and no thought at all. When the mind of examining moves, it creates awareness. If you ask how awareness is created, whatever mind it is that moves, that very thing does not examine [*myi-brtag*] any movement or nonmovement."

No. 2 (Stein Tib. 709 [10]) presents the teaching of the unknown Ch'an master 'Gal-na-ya. Though the gates of Mahayana dhyana are numerous, the correct one within them is all-at-once entrance into the Madhyamaka meaning.

No. 3 (Pelliot Tib. 116 [7]) begins with Bodhidharmatāra's entrance by principle from the *Two Entrances*. Next Wu-chu gives his three phrases from the *Li-tai fa-pao chi*: "No mind [*myi sems pa*] is morality; no thought [*mi dran pa*] is samadhi; nonproduction of the illusion mind is insight." Among the numerous sayings that follow, identified masters are Hsiang-mo Tsang (parallels the *Leng-chia shih-tzu chi*); Wo-lun (parallels the *Wo-lun ch'an-shih k'an-hsin fa*); Mo-ho-yen; Wu-chu (again parallels the *Li-tai fa-pao chi*); Priest Kim; and Shen-hui (parallels a passage in his *T'an-yü*).

No. 4 (Pelliot Tib. 117 [1]) discusses the *spyod cig bsam brtan* (the *i-hsing san-mei*, or "one-practice samadhi").

No. 5 (Pelliot Tib. 121 [4]) interprets each of Wu-chu's three phrases from the *Li-tai fa-pao chi* in terms of *ma g'yos* (*pu-tung* or "immobility").

No. 6 (Pelliot Tib. 635 [2]) discusses such themes as: All is a construct of mind; is and is-not arise from one's own false thought; if false thought is quieted, who is there to think of is and is-not?; if one has neither grasper nor grasped, it is eternal quiescence.

No. 7 (Pelliot Tib. 811 [1]) discusses the ten good qualities of leaving home.

No. 8 (Pelliot Tib. 823 [1]) corresponds to the old-question section of the *Tun-wu ta-ch'eng cheng-li chüeh*.

No. 9 (Stein Tib. 710 [2]) is missing Ching-chüeh's preface and runs only from the Guṇabhadra entry to the middle of the Tao-hsin entry.

No. 10 (Pelliot Tib. 116 [8]) renders *k'an wu so-ch'u* ("gaze at the locus of 'no'") as *myed pa'i gnas la bltas; k'an* ("gazing") as *lta ba;* and *chien* ("seeing") as *mthong ba.* This text is perhaps 30 percent longer than the text that can be assembled from the Chinese manuscripts.

No. 11 (Pelliot Tib. 623) has only the prologue and first chapter of the Chinese apocryphal sutra, which is often quoted in Ch'an texts.

15. For each of these texts I will give a very brief description of contents. For more information, see Tanaka, "Tonkō zenshū shiryō bunrui mokoroku shokō," and Shinohara and Tanaka, *Tonkō butten to zen.*

No. 1, another of the Bodhidharma genre, discusses the seven types of *kuan-men* ("gates of examining"). At the end it states that the recitation of the Buddha's name (*nien-fo*) in the great voice brings one ten types of merit, the last of which is rebirth in the Pure Land (of Amitābha Buddha).

No. 2, also a work of the Bodhidharma genre, discusses *k'an-shou hsin* ("gazing at and guarding mind").

No. 3, another of the Bodhidharma genre, is a dialogue on no mind by two fictional characters, a disciple and the master. The format and topic are similar to the *Chüeh-kuan lun.* The master at one point says: "In the midst of all events just be aware of no mind; that is practice. There is no practice beyond this." The disciple thereupon suddenly has a great awakening.

No. 4 consists of mostly four-character lines. It opens with: "No thought [*wu-nien*] is the thesis; no doing is the basis."

No. 5 is a dialogue based on four sutras and one treatise.

No. 6 is in verse format and emphasizes *pu-ch'i hsin* ("nonarising mind").

No. 7 is a dialogue between two fictional masters, K'ung (Sunyata) and Tzu (Self). It emphasizes *k'an-hsin* ("gazing at mind") and *wu-hsin* ("no mind").

No. 8 declares that is not necessary to draw in, check, or suppress sense objects. It discusses *shu-k'an* ("ripening your gazing") and *kuan-chao* ("examining and illuminating").

No. 9 is the same text as the *Cheng-tao ko*, a song generally in seven-character lines that is traditionally attributed to a disciple of Hui-neng, and this title may be the original title.

No. 10 consists of twelve poems chanted at the hours of the day.

No. 11 consists of three verses that mention rebirth in the Pure Land.

No. 12 consists of verses on Ch'an and tantric meditation and uses medicinal imagery.

No. 13 is a transmission record that builds upon the *Pao-lin chuan*, a transmission record of the Hung-chou school dating to 801.

16. That Vajrayana was a strong influence at the Tun-huang oasis during the

late period is shown by both literary evidence (the Vajrayana-related texts present in the late stratum) and evidence from art history (the evolution of wall paintings in the caves). See Nakamura Hajime, ed., *Shirukurōdo no shūkyō*, Ajia bukkyōshi: Chūgoku-hen 5 (Tokyo: Kōsei shuppansha, 1975), 195.

Appendix B

1. Komozawa daigaku nai zengaku daijiten hensanjo, *Zengaku daijiten* (Tokyo: Daishūkan shoten, 1979), bekkan:3–50.

2. Maraldo, "Historical Consciousness," 160–66, speaks of the need for a literary history of Ch'an: "But no one to my knowledge has written a systematic history of Ch'an in which the main characters are literary forms and not reconstructed personae, events, and doctrines.... A literary history of Ch'an would be concerned with change and development through time, but in its ideal form it would bracket the question of the factual or fictional character of the accounts. It would focus on the evolution of literary forms but avoid claims about their internal representation or misrepresentation of historical reality.... A genre history would not be unpeopled, but its leading characters would figure more as literary than historical personages. Likewise, it would not be without doctrinal interpretation, but the analysis of teachings and sayings would remain closer to the question of how style affects content."

3. T 14:550c.

4. Our only copy is found in Pelliot Ch. 3559, an early-stratum manuscript. For information see Tanaka, "Tonkō zenshū shiryō bunrui mokuroku shokō: II Zempō, shūdōron (2)," 33–34; and Kawasaki Michiko, "Tsuzoku shirui zatsushi bunrui," in *Tonkō butten to zen*, Tonkō kōza 8, ed. Shinohara Hisao and Tanaka Ryōshō (Tokyo: Daitō shuppansha, 1980), 327–28. Yanagida, "*Dembōhōki* to sono sakusha," 55, has a transcription. For a photograph, see Yanagida, *Shoki zenshū shisho no kenkyū*, pl. 15B. Someone has entered a triangular mark at the right side of each of the twelve names. Aśvaghoṣa appears before Pārśva, but notations to the right of their names indicate they are to be reversed. The title echoes the *k'ou-shuo hsüan-li* ("spoke of the dark principle") slogan of the Fa-ch'ung entry in HKSC (T 50:666b17).

5. *Fu-fa tsang yin-yüan chuan*, T 50:314c. Because of his past karma he stayed in his mother's womb for sixty years and was born with white hair and beard. He attained the fruit of arhat. The creator of this list of twelve was certainly familiar with the *Fu-fa tsang yin-yüan chuan*'s account of a transmission from Śākyamuni Buddha to Monk Siṃha, with whom the line was cut off. There are twenty-three patriarchs following the Buddha, Pārśva being the ninth and Aśvaghoṣa the eleventh. This work was important in determining the Indian patriarchal trans-

mission in Ch'an sources. For a discussion, see TZBK, 61–105. In the *Ching-te ch'uan-teng lu* (T 51:209a and c), Pārśva is the tenth and Aśvaghoṣa the twelfth.

6. T 32:576b: "'Enlightenment' means that the mind substance is free of thoughts. Being free of thought characteristics, it is equal to the realm of space. There is nowhere it does not pervade."

7. T 48:942a28–b1. The transcriptions of Buddha's name vary.

8. The sayings for Guṇabhadra begin with "the Great Dharma Master says" and run as follows: "The *Laṅkā Sūtra* line 'How does one purify these thoughts?' refers to banishing false thoughts, not allowing defiled thoughts, exerting the utmost effort in Buddha-mindfulness, being continuously collected moment after moment without break, being quiescent in no thought, and realizing original voidness and purity. Also: Having once received the teaching and being in a state of nonretrogression and constant quiescence is what the Buddha meant when he asked in the sutra: 'How does one increase it?' Also: Even if you train under a master, awakening does not depend upon a master. In general, in teaching people insight he never lectured on Dharma but made inquiries about things [*chiu-shih erh cheng*], such as pointing to the leaf of a tree and asking: 'What is this?' Also: Can you enter a jug or a pillar, and can you enter a fiery furnace? Can a mountain staff lecture on the Dharma? Also: Does your body enter or does your mind enter? Also: Inside the house there is a jug. Is there also a jug outside of the house? Is there water within the jug? Within the water is there a jug? Down to: Within each and every body of water in the world is there a jug? Also: What is this water? Also: The leaves on the trees can lecture on Dharma. A jug can lecture on Dharma. A pillar can lecture on Dharma. Houses can lecture on Dharma. Earth, water, fire, and wind can all lecture on Dharma. Soil, wood, tiles, and stones can also lecture on Dharma. How is this?"

The sayings for Bodhidharma are: "The Great Master also pointed to things and asked their meaning [*chih-shih wen-i*]. He simply pointed to something and asked: 'What do you call this?' He asked about many things, changed the names of the things around, and asked again. Also: Does this body exist? What body is this body? Also: Cloudy mists in the sky can never defile the sky. However, they can screen off the sky so that it cannot be bright and pure. The *Nirvāṇa Sūtra* says: 'There are no six internal sense organs; there are no six external objects. Because internal and external are fused, it is called the middle path.'" T 85:1284c and 1285b; Yanagida, *Shoki no zenshi I*, 122 and 140–41. The only colloquial element is the negative *pu* at the end of sentences indicating a question.

Hui-k'o's sayings are ten lines of verse from his entry in HKSC, his words about cutting off an arm and standing in the nocturnal snow in order to prove his sincerity to Bodhidharma, and a long sutra quotation. The Seng-ts'an portion is an anecdote about dying in standing posture rather than in the usual sitting posture. For Tao-hsin we have quotations from the Taoist classics and a few Buddhist texts.

The hypothesis that the sayings were at some point independent of the *Lengchia shih-tzu chi* is supported by the fact that the Tibetan translation, the *Ling ka'i mkhan pho dang slob ma'i mdo*, which ends near the beginning of the Tao-hsin entry (T 85:1287a14), is missing most of the Guṇabhadra sayings and all of the Bodhidharma sayings: Stein Tib. 710(2), fols. 25b.1 and 33b.1; Okimoto Katsumi, "*Ryōgashijiki* no kenkyū: Zōkan tekisuto no kōtei oyobi zōbun wayaku (1)," *Hanazono daigaku kenkyū kiyō* 9 (March 1978): 66 and 70.

9. T 85:1289c–1290a; Yanagida, *Shoki no zenshi I*, 287–88. Colloquial usages are: *ni* ("you"); *a-shei* ("who"); the negative *pu* at the end of sentences indicating a question; and *jo-ko* ("which").

10. T 85:1290b–c; Yanagida, *Shoki no zenshi I*, 312–13. Colloquial usages are: *pu* at the end of sentences; *t'ou* as a suffix as in *shu-chih-t'ou*, "tree branch"; and the auxiliary verb *ch'ü*.

11. T 48:293c; Hirata, *Mumonkan*, 33. Colloquial usages are *jen-mo* ("thus," "like that") and *tso-mo-sheng* ("how"). I am not suggesting that these sayings are proto-*kōan*, simply that they share with the case literature types of themes and language patterns.

12. T 51:193b; Yanagida, *Shoki no zenshi II*, 273–75. The only colloquial element is *shih* ("it is so"). In general the *Li-tai fa-pao chi* has few colloquial usages.

13. Yanagida, *Shoki no zenshi II*, 275, remarks that there are many tea-scene dialogues in later Ch'an records but none in Northern and Shen-hui texts, which antedate this work.

14. Liu Hsü et al., comps., *Chiu T'ang-shu* (Beijing: Chung-hua shu-chü, 1975), 7:4594.

15. T 48:379c; Iriya Yoshitaka, trans., *Denshin hōyō Enryōroku*, Zen no goroku 8 (Tokyo: Chikuma shobō, 1969), 3.

16. Iriya, *Denshin hōyō Enryōroku*, 173–75.

17. Daizōkyō gakujutsu yōgo kenkyūkai, *Taishō shinshū daizōkyō sakuin*, 27:15.

18. Iriya, *Denshin hōyō Enryōroku*, 181–83.

19. Hōjō Akitoki (1248–1301).

20. T 48:384a; Iriya, *Denshin hōyō Enryōroku*, 90. Colloquial forms are: *te* indicating potential; *cho* after the verb with a sense of completion; *yü-mo* ("thus," "like that"); *pei* in a passive construction; *ko* after a number as a numerary adjunct (*san-ko wu-ko*); and *tsai* at the end of a sentence indicating a strong conclusion.

21. T 48:384a and 386a; Iriya, *Denshin hōyō Enryōroku*, 93 and 132. Colloquial forms are: *te* ("OK" or "all right," not "get" or "can"); *ji-pien-shih* or *pien-shih* ("immediately"); *shen-mo* ("what"); and *ch'ieh-ju* ("for example").

22. ZZ 2, 24, 5–2, 32, 5.

23. For a translation, see chapter 4 at note 23.

24. T 47:609b. The story is drawn from an expanded version of the *Wan-ling lu*, which contains much material not found in the Sung edition mentioned below. This expanded *Wan-ling lu* can be found in the compendium entitled *Szu-chia yü-lu*, of which little is known except that it is a work of the early Sung. For the text, see Yanagida Seizan, ed., *Shike goroku Goke goroku*, Zengaku sōsho 3 (Kyoto: Chūbun shuppansha, 1974), 45.

25. T 47:598b–c. "House style" (*chia-feng*) is an allusion to the *Lin-chi lu* (T 47:496b17–18).

26. Yanagida, "Goroku no rekishi," 585–86.

27. This edition, printed at K'ai-yüan Monastery in Fu-chou, includes the *Ch'uan-hsin fa yao* and *Wan-ling lu* within the *T'ien-sheng kuang-teng lu*, a successor transmission record to the *Ching-te ch'uan-teng lu*. The text can be found at a number of sites in Japan, including Chion-in, Tō-ji, and Daigo-ji in Kyoto.

Glossary of Chinese Logographs

Terms in the *Bodhidharma Anthology*

ch'eng-fa hsing 稱法行
ch'iao-wei 巧偽
ch'un-p'u 淳朴
chen-hsing 真性
chieh shih fa chu jen 解時法逐人
chieh-chiao wu-tsung 藉教悟宗
ching-shen 精神
hsing-ching 性淨
hsing-ju 行入
jo yü-ch'ü yuan-i shih 若欲取遠意時
ju-shih an-hsin 如是安心
k'o-ch'en 客塵
keng pu-sui yü wen-chiao 更不隨於文教
li-ju 理入
ning-chu pi-kuan 凝住壁觀
pao-yüan hsing 報怨行
pi-kuan 壁觀
pu-chieh shih jen chu fa 不解時人逐法
shen-ming ts'ai 身命財

sui-yüan hsing 隨緣行
t'i-ch'i 體氣
tuan-chü 端居
tzu-hsin hsien-liang 自心現量
wo ts'ung wang-hsi 我從往昔
wu so-ch'iu hsing 無所求行
wu-chien 無慳

Names in *Record II* and *Record III*

An (Dhyana Master) ?= P'u-an or Tao-an; sec. 71 安 / 普安 / 道安
Chien (Dhyana Master); sec. 78 監
Chih (Dharma Master or Master or Dhyana Master); secs. 52–53, 87 志
Chih (Dhyana Master); sec. 86 知
Chüeh (Dhyana Master) ?= Hsuan-chüeh; sec. 74 覺 / 玄覺
Fan (Dhyana Master); sec. 75 梵
Hsien (Dhyana Master) ?= Ching-chou Fa-hsien; sec. 66 顯 / 荊州法顯

Hsien (Dhyana Master); sec. 70 賢

Hsüan (Dhyana Master); sec. 67 暄

Hui-yao (Master); sec. 85 慧堯

Hung (Dhyana Master); sec. 73 洪

Jen (Dhyana Master) ?= Hung-jen of East Mountain; sec. 81 忍 / 弘忍

K'o (Master or Dhyana Master); secs. 57, 82 可

Lang (Dhyana Master) ?= Dhyana Master Lang of Huang-mei; sec. 91 朗 / 黃梅朗禪師

Leng (Dhyana Master); sec. 64 楞

Liang (Dhyana Master); sec. 83 亮

Lien (Dhyana Master); sec. 72 憐

san-tsang fa-shih (Tripiṭaka Dharma Master = Bodhidharma or Bodhidharmatāra); sec. 80 三藏法師 / 菩提達摩 / 菩提達摩多羅

T'an (Master); sec. 84 曇

Tao-chih (Master) = Master Chih; sec. 76 道志 / 志

Tsang (Dharma Master) ?= Chih-tsang or Shu-chou Fa-tsang; sec. 69 藏 / 智藏 / 舒州法藏

Tzu (Dhyana Master; hypothetical reconstruction from Tibetan); sec. 89 自

Wen (Dhyana Master); sec. 88 汶

Yin (Dhyana Master); sec. 79 因

Yüan (Dharma Master or Master or Dhyana Master); secs. 50, 52–54, 90 緣

Yüan (Dhyana Master) ?= Ching-yüan; sec. 68 淵 / 靜淵

Yüan-chi Ni ?= Ni Tsung-ch'ih (the nun Dharani); sec. 77 圓寂尼 / 尼總持

Colloquialisms in the *Records*

a-ning 阿寧

a-shei 阿誰

ch'u-shih 觸事

ch'u-wu 觸物

feng-wu 逢物

han 漢

hsing-tsai 行在

hui-shih 會是

i-ko 一箇

jo-wei 若為

mou-chia 某甲

na 那

nan-nü 男女

ni 你

ni-chia 你家

pei 被

pi-tzu-t'ou 筆子頭

pu (at the end of sentences) 不

shang-tzu 尚自

sui-chi 雖即

tan-shih 但使

t'ou (as a suffix) 頭

tou 都

tsai (following a verb) 在

tzu-shih 自是

Titles of Works in Appendix A

Ch'an-men ching 禪門經

Ch'an-men pi yao-chüeh 禪門秘要決

Ch'an-men shih-erh shih 禪門十二時

Ch'an-ts'e shih-tao 禪策十道

Ch'ou ch'an-shih I 稠禪師意

Ch'ou ch'an-shih yao-fang liao yu-lou 稠禪師藥方療有漏

Ch'uan fa-pao chi 傳法寶紀

Cheng-tao ko 證道歌

Chin-kang san-mei ching 金剛三昧經

Chüeh-kuan lun 絕觀論

Hsiang-mo Tsang ch'an-shih an-hsin fa 降魔藏禪師安心法

Hsien-te chi yü shuang-feng shan t'a ko t'an hsüan-li 先德集於雙峰山塔各談玄理

Hsing-lu nan 行路難

Hsiu-hsin yao lun 修心要論

Kuan-hsin lun 觀心論

Leng-chia shih-tzu chi 楞伽師資記

Li-tai fa-pao chi 歷代法寶記

Liao-hsing chü 了性句

Nan-tsung ting hsieh-cheng wu-keng chuan 南宗定邪正五更轉

P'u-t'i-ta-mo ch'an-shih kuan-men 菩提達摩禪師觀門

P'u-t'i-ta-mo ch'an-shih lun 菩提達摩禪師論

Sheng-chou chi 聖胄集

T'an-yü 壇語

Ta-ch'eng hsin-hsing lun 大乘心行論

Ta-ch'eng pei-tsung lun 大乘北宗論

Ta-ch'eng wu fang-pien 大乘五方便

Ta-ch'eng yao-kuan 大乘藥關

Ting shih-fei lun 定是非論

Tun-wu chen-tsung lun 頓悟真宗論

Tun-wu chen-tsung yao-chüeh 頓悟真宗要決

Tun-wu ta-ch'eng cheng-li chüeh 頓悟大乘正理決

Tun-wu wu-sheng pan-jo sung 頓悟無生般若頌

Wen-ta tsa-cheng I 問答雜徵義

Wo-lun ch'an-shih an-hsin fa 臥輪禪師安心法

Wo-lun ch'an-shih chi 臥輪禪師偈

Wo-lun ch'an-shih k'an-hsin fa 臥輪禪師看心法

Wu-hsin lun 無心論

Yüan-ming lun 圓明論

Works Cited

Asian-Language Sources

Araki Kengo, trans. *Daie sho*. Zen no goroku 17. Tokyo: Chikuma shobō, 1969.

Ch'en Yüan. *Tun-huang chieh-yü lu*. Peiping: Kuo-li chung-yang yen-chiu yüan li-shih yü-yen yen-chiu so, 1931.

Chin Yung-hua, ed. *Tun-huang su-tzu so-yin*. Taipei: Shih-men t'u-shu kung-szu, 1980.

Dai-Nihon zokuzōkyō. 750 vols. Kyoto: Zōkyō shoin, 1905–12.

Daizōkyō gakujutsu yōgo kenkyūkai. *Taishō shinshū daizōkyō sakuin*. Vol. 27, *Shoshū-bu 3*. Tokyo: Taishō shinshū daizōkyō kankōkai, 1983.

Fujieda Akira. *Tun-huang hsüeh t'ao-lun*. Tientsin: Nan-k'ai ta-hsüeh li-shih hsi, 1981.

Gnubs-chen Saṅs-rgyas-ye-śes. *Rnal 'byor mig gi bsam gtan or Bsam gtan mig sgron*. Smanrtsis shesrig spendzod, vol. 74. Leh, Ladakh: S. W. Tashigangpa, 1974.

Hayashi Taiun. "Bodaidaruma den no kenkyū." *Shūkyō kenkyū* n.s. 9, no. 3 (1932): 62–76.

Hirai Shun'ei. "Shoki zenshū shisō no keisei to sanronshū." *Shūgaku kenkyū* 5 (1963): 75–79.

———. *Chūgoku hannya shisōshi kenkyū: Kichizō to sanron gakuha*. Tokyo: Shun-jūsha, 1976.

Hirata Takashi, trans. *Mumonkan*. Zen no goroku 18. Tokyo: Chikuma shobō, 1969.

Hu Shih. "Leng-chia tsung k'ao." In *Hu Shih wen-ts'un*, vol. 4. Taipei: Yüan-t'ung t'u-shu kung-szu, 1953. Also in *Ko Teki zengakuan*, edited by Yanagida Seizan. Kyoto: Chūbun shuppansha, 1975.

———. "P'u-t'i-ta-mo k'ao." In *Hu Shih wen-ts'un*, vol. 3. Taipei: Yüan-t'ung t'u-shu kung-szu, 1953. Also in *Ko Teki zengakuan*, edited by Yanagida Seizan. Kyoto: Chūbun shuppansha, 1975.

Iriya Yoshitaka, trans. *Denshin hōyō Enryōroku.* Zen no goroku 8. Tokyo: Chikuma shobō, 1969.

———. *Rinzai-roku.* Tokyo: Iwanami shoten, 1989.

Iriya Yoshitaka and Koga Hidehiko, eds. *Zengo jiten.* Kyoto: Shibunkaku shuppan, 1991.

Ishii Shūdō. "Shinpuku-ji bunko shozō no *Hai Kyū shūi mon* no honkoku." *Zengaku kenkyū* 60 (1981): 71–104.

Jan Yün-hua. *Tsung-mi.* Taipei: Tung ta t'u-shu kung-szu yin-hsing, 1988.

Kamata Shigeo. *Shūmitsu kyōgaku no shisōshi-teki kenkyū.* Tokyo: Tōkyō daigaku shuppankai, 1975.

———, trans. *Zengen shosenshū tojo.* Zen no goroku 9. Tokyo: Chikuma shobō, 1971.

Kawajima Jōmyō. "Sōfuki ni tsuite." *Indogaku bukkyōgaku kenkyū* 25, no. 2 (March 1977): 146–47.

Kawasaki Michiko. "Tsuzoku shirui zatsushi bunrui," In *Tonkō butten to zen,* Tonkō kōza 8, edited by Shinohara Hisao and Tanaka Ryōshō. Tokyo: Daitō shuppansha, 1980.

Kimura Ryūtoku. "Tonkō chibettogo zen bunken mokuroku shokō." *Tōkyō daigaku bungakubu bunka kōryū kenkyū shisetsu kenkyū kiyō* 4 (1980): 93–129.

Komozawa daigaku nai zengaku daijiten hensanjo. *Zengaku daijiten.* 3 vols. Tokyo: Daishūkan shoten, 1979.

Liu Hsü, et al., comps. *Chiu T'ang-shu.* 8 vols. Beijing: Chung-hua shu-chü, 1975.

Luo Charngpeir. *T'ang wu-tai hsi-pei fang-yin.* Academica Sinica, National Research Institute of History and Philology Monographs Series A, no. 12. Shanghai: Kuo-li chung-yang yen-chiu yüan li-shih yü-yen yen-chiu so, 1933.

Makita Tairyō, ed. *Tō kōsōden sakuin.* 3 vols. Chūgoku kōsōden sakuin, vols. 2–4. Kyoto: Heiraku-ji shoten, 1973 and 1975.

Nakamura Hajime, ed. *Shirukurōdo no shūkyō.* Ajia bukkyōshi: Chūgoku-hen 5. Tokyo: Kōsei shuppansha, 1975.

Okimoto Katsumi. "Chibettoyaku *Ninyū shigyōron* ni tsuite." *Indogaku bukkyōgaku kenkyū* 24, no. 2 (March 1976): 39–46.

———. "*Ryōgashijiki* no kenkyū: Zōkan tekisuto no kōtei oyobi zōbun wayaku (1)." *Hanazono daigaku kenkyū kiyō* 9 (March 1978): 59–87.

Ono Gemmyō, ed. *Bussho kaisetsu daijiten.* 14 vols. 1933–36. Reprint, Tokyo: Daitō shuppansha, 1964–67.

Ōta Tatsuo. *Chūgokugo rekishi bumpō.* 1958. Reprint, Kyoto: Hōyū shoten, 1978.

Satomichi Tokuyū. "Bodaidaruma to sono shūhen (1): Dōiku to Sōfuku ni tsuite." *Tōyō daigaku tōyōgaku kenkyūjo kiyō* 12 (1978): 117–21

Sekiguchi Shindai. *Daruma daishi no kenkyū.* Tokyo: Shunjūsha, 1969.

Shiina Kōyū. "Shōshitsu rokumon to *Daruma daishi sanron.*" *Komozawa daigaku bukkyō gakubu ronshū* 9 (November 1978): 208–32.

Shinohara Hisao and Tanaka Ryōshō, eds. *Tonkō butten to zen.* Tonkō kōza 8. Tokyo: Daitō shuppansha, 1980.

Suzuki Daisetsu. *Tonkō shutsudo shōshitsu issho.* Kyoto: privately published, 1935.

————. *Kōkan shōshitsu issho oyobi kaisetsu furoku: Daruma no zempō to shisō oyobi sono ta.* 2 vols. Osaka: Ataka bukkyō bunko, 1936.

Taishō shinshū daizōkyō. 85 vols. Tokyo: Taishō issaikyō kankōkai, 1924–33.

Tanaka Ryōshō. "Tonkō zenshū shiryō bunrui mokuroku shokō: I. Dentō shijōron." *Komazawa daigaku bukkyō gakubu kenkyū kiyō* 27 (March 1969): 1–17.

————. "Tonkō zenshū shiryō kōmoku betsu ichiran." *Sōtōshū kenkyūin kenkyūsei kenkyū kiyō* 1 (November 1969): 1–10.

————. "Tonkō zenshū shiryō bunrui mokuroku shokō: II. Zempō shūdōron (1)." *Komazawa daigaku bukkyō gakubu kenkyū kiyō* 29 (March 1971): 1–18.

————. "Bodaidaruma ni kansuru tonkō shahon sanshu ni tsuite." *Komozawa daigaku bukkyō gakubu kenkyū kiyō* 31 (March 1973): 161–79.

————. "Tonkō zenshū shiryō bunrui mokuroku shokō: II. Zempō shūdōron (2)." *Komazawa daigaku bukkyō gakubu kenkyū kiyō* 32 (March 1974): 30–49.

————. "Tonkō zenshū shiryō bunrui mokuroku shokō: II. Zempō·shūdōron (3)." *Komazawa daigaku bukkyō gakubu kenkyū kiyō* 34 (March 1976): 1–24.

————. "Ninyū shigyōron chōkansu (gi) kenkyū oboegaki." *Komozawa daigaku bukkyō gakubu kenkyū kiyō* 38 (March 1980): 51–69.

————. "Tonkō zenseki (kambun) kenkyū gaishi." *Tōkyō daigaku bungakubu bunka kōryū kenkyū shisetsu kenkyū kiyō* 5 (1981): 23–41.

————. *Tonkō zenshū bunken no kenkyū.* Tokyo: Daitō shuppansha, 1983.

Ueyama Daishun. "Tonkō ni okeru zen no shosō." *Ryūkoku daigaku ronshū* 421 (October 1982): 88–121.

————. *Tonkō bukkyō no kenkyū.* Kyoto: Hōzōkan, 1990.

Ui Hakuju. *Zenshūshi kenkyū.* Vol. 1. 1935. Reprint, Tokyo: Iwanami shoten, 1966.

Yanagida Seizan. "Dembōhōki to sono sakusha: Pelliot 3559go bunsho o meguru hokushū zen kenkyū shiryō no satsuki, sono ichi." *Zengaku kenkyū* 53 (July 1963): 45–71.

————. "Bodaidaruma Ninyū shigyōron no shiryō kachi." *Indogaku bukkyōgaku kenkyū* 15, no. 1 (December 1966): 320–23.

————. *Shoki zenshū shisho no kenkyū.* Kyoto: Hōzōkan, 1967.

————. "Zenseki kaidai." In *Zenke goroku II,* Sekai koten bungaku zenshū 36B, edited by Nishitani Keiji and Yanagida Seizan. Tokyo: Chikuma shobō, 1974.

————. "Daruma zen to sono haikei." In *Hokugi bukkyō no kenkyū,* edited by Ōchō Enichi. 2d ed. Kyoto: Heiraku-ji shoten, 1978.

————. "Goroku no rekishi." *Tōhō gakuhō* 57 (March 1985): 211–663.

————, ed. *Kōrai-bon.* Zengaku sōsho 2. Kyoto: Chūbun shuppansha, 1974.

————, ed. *Shike goroku Goke goroku.* Zengaku sōsho 3. Kyoto: Chūbun shuppansha, 1974.

———, ed. *Sodōshū*. Zengaku sōsho 4. Kyoto: Chūbun shuppansha, 1974.

———, ed. *Ko Teki zengakuan*. Kyoto: Chūbun shuppansha, 1975.

———, trans. *Daruma no goroku*. Zen no goroku 1. Tokyo: Chikuma shobō, 1969.

———, trans. *Shoki no zenshi I*. Zen no goroku 2. Tokyo: Chikuma shobō, 1971.

———, trans. *Rinzai-roku*. Butten kōza 30. Tokyo: Daizō shuppan, 1972.

———, trans. *Shoki no zenshi II*. Zen no goroku 3. Tokyo: Chikuma shobō, 1976.

———, trans. *Daruma*. Jinrui no chi-teki isan 16. Tokyo: Kōdansha, 1981.

Yanagida Seizan and Tokiwa Gishin, eds. *Zekkanron*. Kyoto: Zen bunka ken-kyūjo, 1976.

European-Language Sources

App, Urs, ed. *ZenBase CDI*. Kyoto: International Research Institute for Zen Buddhism, 1995.

Boin, Sara, trans. *The Teaching of Vimalakīrti*. London: Pali Text Society, 1976.

de la Vallée Poussin, Louis. *Catalogue of the Tibetan Manuscripts from Tun-huang in the India Office Library*. Oxford: Oxford University Press, 1962.

Edgerton, Franklin. *Buddhist Hybrid Sanskrit Grammar and Dictionary*. Vol. 1. 1953. Reprint, Delhi: Motilal Banarsidass, 1970.

Faure, Bernard. "Bodhidharma as Textual and Religious Paradigm." *History of Religions* 25, no. 3 (1986): 187–98.

———. *Le traité de Bodhidharma: Première anthologie du bouddhisme Chan*. Paris: Le Mail, 1986.

Fujieda, Akira. "The Tunhuang Manuscripts, a General Description (Part I)." *Memoirs of the Research Institute for Humanistic Studies Zinbun* 9 (1966): 1–32.

———. "Une reconstruction de la 'Bibliothèque' de Touen-houang." *Journal Asiatique* 269 (1981): 65–68.

Gernet, Jacques, and Wu Chi-yu. *Catalogue des manuscrits chinois de Touen-houang*. Vol. 1. Paris: Bibliothèque Nationale, 1970.

Giles, Lionel. *Descriptive Catalogue of the Chinese Manuscripts from Tunhuang in the British Museum*. London: Trustees of the British Museum, 1957.

Gregory, Peter N. *Tsung-mi and the Sinification of Buddhism*. Princeton: Princeton University Press, 1991.

Iriya, Yoshitaka, Ruth F. Sasaki, and Burton F. Watson. "On Some Texts of Ancient Spoken Chinese." Kyoto. 1954. Typescript.

Jackson, Roger. "Terms of Sanskrit and Pāli Origin Acceptable as English Words." *Journal of the International Association of Buddhist Studies* 5 (1982): 141–42.

Jan, Yün-hua. "Two Problems concerning Tsung-mi's Compilation of Ch'an-tsang." *Transactions of the International Conference of Orientalists in Japan* 19 (1974): 37–47.

————. "Seng-ch'ou's Method of Dhyana." In *Early Ch'an in China and Tibet*, Berkeley Buddhist Studies Series, no. 5, edited by Whalen Lai and Lewis R. Lancaster. Berkeley: Lancaster Publications, 1983.

Jenner, W. F. J. *Memories of Lo-yang: Yang Hsüan-chih and the Lost Capital (493–534)*. Oxford: Clarendon Press, 1981.

Jorgenson, John Alexander. "The Earliest Text of Ch'an Buddhism: The Long Scroll." Master's thesis, Australian National University, 1979.

Lalou, Marcelle. "Document tibétain sur l'expansion du Dhyāna chinois." *Journal Asiatique* 131 (1939): 505–23.

————. *Inventaire des manuscrits tibétains de Touen-houang conservés à la Bibliothèque Nationale*. 3 vols. Paris: Bibliothèque Nationale, 1939, 1950, and 1961.

Lamotte, Étienne, trans. *L'Enseignement de Vimalakīrti*. Louvain: Publications Universitaires, 1962.

Laufer, Berthold. *Sino-Iranica*. 1919. Reprint, Taipei: Ch'eng Wen Publishing Company, 1978.

Luk, Charles, trans. *The Vimalakīrti Nirdeśa Sūtra*. 1972. Reprint, Boston: Shambhala, 1990.

Maraldo, John C. "Is There Historical Consciousness within Ch'an?" *Japanese Journal of Religious Studies* 12, nos. 2–3 (June–September 1985): 141–72.

Maspero, Henri. "Sur quelques textes anciens de chinois parlé." *Bulletin de l'École Français d'Extrème-Orient* 14, no. 4 (1914): 1–36.

McRae, John R. *The Northern School and the Formation of Early Ch'an Buddhism*. Honolulu: University of Hawaii Press, 1986.

Soymie, Michel, et al. *Catalogue des manuscrits chinois de Touen-houang*. Vol. 3. Paris: Bibliothèque Nationale, 1983.

————. *Catalogue des manuscrits chinois de Touen-houang*. Vol. 4. Paris: Bibliothèque Nationale, 1991.

————. *Catalogue des manuscrits chinois de Touen-houang*. Vol. 5. Paris: Bibliothèque Nationale, 1995.

Suzuki, Daisetz Teitaro. *An Index to the Lankavatara Sutra*. Kyoto: Sanskrit Buddhist Texts Publishing Society, 1934.

Thurman, Robert A. F., trans. *The Holy Teaching of Vimalakīrti*. University Park and London: Pennsylvania State University Press, 1976.

Tucci, Giuseppe. *Minor Buddhist Texts Part II*. Serie Orientale Roma, vol. 9. 1958. Reprint, Kyoto: Rinsen Book Company, 1978.

Ueyama, Daishun. "Etudes des manuscrits tibétains de Dunhuang relatifs au bouddhisme de Dhyāna: Bilan et perspectives." *Journal Asiatique* 269 (1981): 287–95.

————. "A Chronological Stratification of the Tun-huang Ch'an Manuscripts." Paper delivered at the CISHAAN Tun-huang/Turfan Seminar, Kyoto, Japan, 2 September 1983.

————. "The Study of Tibetan Ch'an Manuscripts Recovered from Tun-huang: A Review of the Field and Its Prospects." In *Early Ch'an in China and Tibet*, Berkeley Buddhist Studies Series no. 5, edited by Whalen Lai and Lewis R. Lancaster. Berkeley: Lancaster Publications, 1983.

Wang, Yi-t'ung. *A Record of Buddhist Monasteries in Lo-yang: By Yang Hsüan-chih*. Princeton: Princeton University Press, 1984.

Watson, Burton. *Early Chinese Literature*. New York: Columbia University Press, 1962.

————, trans. *The Vimalakīrti Sūtra*. New York: Columbia University Press, 1997.

Wayman, Alex, and Hideko Wayman, trans. *The Lion's Roar of Queen Śrīmālā*. New York: Columbia University Press, 1974.

Yampolsky, Philip B. *The Platform Sutra of the Sixth Patriarch*. New York: Columbia University Press, 1967.

Index

abilities, sharp vs. dull, 25–26
according with Dharma, 10, 11–12, 69, 74
activity, as Thusness, 46
aggregates, five, 49
Akṣobhya Buddha, 47, 154n7
All-at-Once Awakening to Non-arising Insight Songs (Shen-hui), 103, 159n15
all-at-once gate (Chinese Ch'an), 67, 95
an (quieting), 116–17
Analects (Confucius), 6, 9, 59, 107, 139n13
Ānanda, 47
Ancient School (Rnying-ma-pa), 99, 154n7
An-hsin fa-men (Method for Quieting Mind; Bodhidharma), 78–80, 82–83, 146n9
An-hsin lun (Treatise on Quieting Mind), 146n9
An Lu-shan Rebellion, 99
Annals of the Laṅkā Followers and Their Dharma, 110
apprehension, 45
Ārāḍa, 41
arhats, 35
arising/extinguishing, 33–34, 39, 44, 48, 126n74, 155n11
Armless Lin. See T'an-lin
A-rtan-hver, 154n8
Aśvaghoṣa, 108, 160n5; *Awakening of Faith in the Mahāyāna,* 109
Atiyoga (Rdzogs-chen), 67–68
Avalokiteśvara, 1, 3

Awakening of Faith in the Mahāyāna (Aśvaghoṣa), 109
awakening vs. dreams, 17–18, 47

behavior, as Thusness, 46
Be'u-sing, 154n8
Biography, 4, 8–9, 53–57; age of Bodhidharma, 54–55; Bodhidharma arrives in Lo-yang, 53, 55, 56, 139n8; disciples of Bodhidharma, 56–57; identity of Bodhidharma, 54–55, 138n4, 138n6; knowledge of, 6; lineage of, 105–6, 107; lineage of Bodhidharma, 55–56, 65, 140n17; meditation style of Bodhidharma, 66–68; T'an-lin as compiler of, 53, 137n1; voyage of Bodhidharma, 53, 56; on wall-examining, 66. See also *Continued Biographies of Eminent Monks*
birth-and-death, 29–30, 126n58
Bka' thang sde lnga (Five Classes of Commands), 154n7
Black Mountain, 41
Bodhidharma: death of, 4, 58, 60, 139n14; disciples of/successors to, 4, 65, 70, 132n136 (*see also* Hui-k'o; Tao-fu; Tao-yü); lineage of, 55–56, 65, 90–91, 140n17, 148n25; *Method for Quieting Mind,* 78–80, 82–83, 146n9; name changes of, 2, 119n5; representations of, 1; reputation of, 58; sayings of,

Compositor: Asco Typesetters
Text: Dante
Display: Gill Sans